With Best Wishes
To

Amanda!

Jeno

3-5-07

"Jeno's immense self-made success as one of the nation's great entrepreneurs reminds us how real the American Dream is. And his open-hearted patriotism and generosity inspire all of us who have had the pleasure of knowing him. Get to know him: Read his book!"

—Mario Cuomo
Former Governor of New York

"I've known Jeno for 45 years. He is the classic American success story. No one can shake things up and push an agenda like Jeno, and his life is a testament to working hard and sticking to your ideas. I'm proud to consider him a friend and compatriot."

—Walter F. Mondale
Former Vice President of the United States

"Jeno Paulucci has lived a magical life, the sort of towering success that is the stuff of mythology. Except Jeno's story is real, fascinating and enticing. Read and enjoy!"

—Jack Valenti
Former President of the Motion
Picture Association of America

"Jeno is a great Floridian who has led by example. He generously enriches the lives of those he encounters. I treasure his friendship and admire his leadership, character and enthusiasm."

—Jeb Bush
Governor of Florida

"Jeno Paulucci was almost the first name I heard when I came to America in 1971, and the last name when I stepped down as chief executive of Heinz in 1988–and for good reason. He is unique, and his inventiveness and will to win have added an important dimension to the American frozen food industry."

—Sir Anthony O'Reilly
Former Chairman, President and CEO of
H. J. Heinz Company

"Jeno is clearly the king of entrepreneurs."

—Gary L. Wilson
Chairman of Northwest Airlines

"Jeno is the epitome of the entrepreneur. Leave Jeno alone with a small pile of money and in time he'll have a large number of customers plus a big pile of money."
—Charles (Mike) Harper
Chairman Emeritus of ConAgra Foods

"Jeno is one of those special people in life that once you've met you'll never forget. Jeno combines enthusiasm, determination, caring, kindness and forcefulness into an unbelievable human package. Jeno is a tough man to say 'no' to—hell, he's a tough man to say 'yes' to! I truly admire and respect my friend Jeno Paulucci."
—Steve Sviggum
Speaker of the House of
Representatives, State of Minnesota

"Jeno Paulucci had the rare acumen to foresee the vast potential for prepared frozen foods in the hectic economy of post–World War II and the courage to confront giant corporations moving into the market at the same time. That Jeno has survived—indeed flourished—in building one of the nation's major frozen food marketers, attests to the commitment and capabilities that have characterized his career. Nor has preoccupation with business deterred him from fulfilling what he considers his obligations to the community, as reflected in the numerous charities and benefits he has supported and for which he has been honored by both his native city and state."
—A. H. Rosenfeld
Former Publisher of Frozen Food Age magazine

"Jeno is truly an amazing American success story. Starting from nothing as a young boy living on the Iron Range of Minnesota, he gleaned lumps of coal from nearby railroad tracks for the family to get by. From those humble beginnings he built a food empire. From bean sprouts and egg rolls to pizza and frozen dinners, he has had more good ideas on how to make money than anyone I have ever met and he still has more energy than most men half his age."
—Joseph Hall
Former COO of
Food Lion Supermarkets

"Having represented Jeno for over 15 years and won many millions for him—no, not for him but with him—I know that Jeno has a sixth sense about the future, both in business and in court. He has the uncanny ability to feel the future and the true grit to see a case through to success."

—Attorney David Simmons

"Read this book. It will move you. It will inspire you. You will be transported back in time. You will be motivated by the greatest American 'peddler' of all time. Although only five feet four inches in height, Jeno Paulucci towers above all other 'peddlers' of the 20th Century. His book does too. I just wish I could have tasted an 'Argentine banana' [see Chapter 2]."

—Attorney George G. Eck
Dorsey & Whitney LLP

"Jeno is a true 'Iron Ranger.' He has never forgotten his roots; he has never forgotten his friends. He has a heart as big as a whale, and who else but Jeno could sell bikinis to the Eskimos. He has to be the finest salesman in the world!"

—Tom Dougherty
Classmate, Hibbing High School Class of 1935

"Jeno, the iron man from the iron range. Although Floridians have not yet discovered any iron ore under our state, we appreciate the great contributions your entrepreneurship have and are making to our state. Heathrow has set a standard of community excellence which has influenced the present and future of town planning in our fast growing Florida. You have a lot of wisdom to share—thank you for doing so."

—Bob Graham
United States Senator from Florida

"If you would enjoy reading a book about how a unique man rose from the hardscrabble Northern Minnesota Iron Range to great success—and not just in money—this is a book for you. Read about a man who is tough-minded, imaginative and caring at the same time—a paradoxical genius with a great sense of humor. His wife Lois still finds him charming. So will you. He's challenging, creative, inspiring, honest, and full of common sense. Give this book to your children to read too. Jeno, glad I metcha!"

—John Phillips
Former CEO of R. J. Reynolds Foods

On the other hand . . . Jeno insisted on including these other viewpoints.

"If there were pirates today, Jeno would make Bluebeard blush."

—Elmer L. Andersen
Former Governor of Minnesota

"You don't have to lecture me on the truth. I am not your whipping boy. I deserve an apology from you."

—A mayor in West Virginia after
a plan to build a plant in his town was withdrawn

"Jeno is like a camel. Let his nose in the tent and before long he's in and you're out."

—Former owner of a company that Jeno took over

"You've sued everyone else . . . Now you want to sue Mickey Mouse too?!!!"

—Lois M. Paulucci

Jeno...
The Power of the Peddler

By
Jeno F. Paulucci

With Les Rich
and
James Tills

Contents

Introduction

Jeno F. Paulucci is the Number One Overall Entrepreneur in the world.

He was awarded that title by Ernst & Young, the global accounting and business services organization, at a ceremony in Palm Springs, California, on November 20, 2004.

At the same time, in recognition of his nearly seven decades of civic accomplishment, Jeno Paulucci became the first recipient of the newly created International Lifetime Achievement Award for Activism, Entrepreneurship and Leadership. This was the first such award in Ernst & Young's twenty-year history of honoring entrepreneurs from all parts of the world.

Two years earlier, Paulucci had been selected as Entrepreneur of the Year for the United States.

Commenting on the 2004 award, James S. Turley, Ernst & Young's chairman and chief executive officer, said:

"The son of Italian immigrants, Jeno Paulucci has created, financed or led more than fifty privately held companies, creating more than seventy brands. He has consistently hired the disabled or others deemed unemployable—all unionized.

"He is a world class entrepreneur who has used his success to further humanitarian efforts in the U.S. and abroad. Although we now honor him as the number one entrepreneur in the world, Jeno still calls himself just a peddler from the Iron Range of Minnesota."

Dedication

THIS BOOK IS DEDICATED TO MY WIFE,
LOIS MAE TREPANIER PAULUCCI . . .

For fifty-eight years, Lois, you have been my guiding light and spirit, my supporter and my critic, and even the trimmer of my hair to this day.

When I first met you, Lois, you were the most beautiful girl in the fashionable East End of Duluth, and you're even more beautiful today. I was the alien from the Iron Range who'd been making too much money selling wholesale groceries, but was spending more money than I made by having one good time after another. And I had just relocated to Duluth to grow . . . bean sprouts?

You were the belle of Duluth. I was some foot-loose fellow who watered bean sprouts throughout the night and drank in between . . . who'd been classified 4–F because every time I volunteered for the army I had gone out partying the night before, so the medics thought I was a nervous wreck.

Lois and Jeno Paulucci

I had been thrown out, not of the best places, but the worst places, because of all the fights I'd started.

Then I met you, and tried to stop smoking ten or twelve cigars a day and chewing tobacco in between, and drinking anything that poured.

For some reason that I'll never understand, my darling, you took a liking to me. Maybe because opposites attract, thank the Good Lord. That was the beginning of my life, and our life.

You straightened me out in a heartbeat. And you're still doing a great job of cutting my hair—and cutting me down to size whenever I need it, which is pretty often.

So thank you, Lois Mae Trepanier Paulucci. I love you.

THIS BOOK IS ALSO DEDICATED
TO OUR FAMILY . . .

To our fine son Michael (Mick) Paulucci, our daughters Cindy Paulucci Selton and Gina Paulucci. None of you ever complained when I was away from home, working seven days a week at the office or traveling around the country or the world peddling my products or on some civic or economic crusade.

You always understood, and never gave me hell for not going to a baseball game or school event. For that I shall be forever grateful.

Thank you, also, for bringing into this world our four grandchildren, Tiffany Soderstrom, Brittany Soderstrom DeArcos, my namesake grandson Jeno Michael Paulucci, and our granddaughter Angela Paulucci.

They in turn have brought into this world a great-grandson, Angelo Paulucci, and twin great-grandsons Connor and Parker DeArcos.

All of you, our family, are not the *most* important thing in my life and Lois'. You are the *only* important thing in our lives.

I also would be remiss if I didn't acknowledge and thank the following people. Without their help, none of this would have been possible.

My sister Elizabeth, who went without compensation during the early days of Chun King, until we started rolling along.

Jim Tills, my assistant for public affairs.

Joel Conner, my former son-in-law, who has been invaluable. He's now president of Luigino's and has been a dear friend of mine all these years.

Larry Nelson, President of Paulucci International, the financial company that handles many of our various enterprises.

Cha-Leen Daughtry, my administrative assistant in Florida; Jill Molitor in Duluth; and Gail Bukowski, who are my alter egos and who made it possible for me to travel all over the world yet stay in contact with the office at all times, get my work done, and be involved in many projects.

David Ahlgren, my friend and head of R&D operations for my various companies dating back to Chun King.

David Gaddie, President of Republic Banks.

Success—
What the Hell is it?

"**J**eno," my friends and associates keep asking me, "why don't you write your autobiography?"

"Because I don't like damn autobiographies," I'd snap. "Besides, mine is still going on. I wouldn't know where to stop."

But they persisted—those who know me best—saying things like:

- Here you are in your late eighties, worth more than a few hundred million dollars. You started with less than nothing, built around fifty businesses and sold most of them for big bucks.
- You weighed in on all sorts of community and social activism . . . became a major player in politics nationally and internationally . . . counseled presidents and almost-presidents from the Kennedy's to the Bushes . . . built a new city down in Florida.

- You're always looking around for people to help out . . . Indians in Canada, Eskimos in Alaska, disabled people and convicts in the United States, victims of earthquakes in Italy.
- You've got this great family that you never neglected.
- You're still at it. Only a couple of years ago you were named Ernst & Young's Entrepreneur of the Year.

"Tell me something I don't know."

"Well," they say, "isn't it time to tell people how you did it, and how you keep on doing it?"

TO REPEAT, I'VE ALWAYS HATED the idea of an autobiography. There are already too many of them around. Who needs another book that could be titled *How I Got Rich and Became a Pompous Ass?*

So this isn't an autobiography. Well, maybe *sort* of an autobiography. I can't tell you how I did it without giving a good many details of the challenges I faced and how I tried to overcome them. But mostly it's a collection of stories. I'm writing this for those friends of mine all over the world—but most of all for my family. If others learn something from it to use in their lives, all the better.

This is a book about what it takes to be a success in life and as an entrepreneur in this society we live in, where opportunities are limited only by your imagination, but failures are seldom if ever forgiven.

This country needs more entrepreneurs. You may be one of them.

I'll tell you how I did it, and you can take it from there.

IF I'M WRITING A BOOK ABOUT SUCCESS, it's only fair to ask what I mean by that word. It's not easy to define, but here's what I believe success is—and isn't.

Success in life isn't measured by your title, your station in society, or your job. Success is just doing that which you want to do, but being happy with it—by being yourself.

Success is *not* the accumulation of wealth. Success is not measured by money or net worth alone. That's just one of the ways to keep score.

Success is how you play the game.

Success is not resorting to cheating to win.

Success is a way of living your life; and if it is so blessed, in raising a family in a manner of which you can be proud.

Success is seeing to it that you do some good for your community, your state, your nation, and above all, your fellow man.

Success is being able to "spit in the eye" of those who stand in your way by being honest to the point that you are untouchable when they seek revenge.

Success is leaving a heritage you can be proud of, in family and in deeds, so that there are no regrets when the day comes when they pat you in the face with a shovel and say (in my case), "Goodbye, Jeno."

I've titled the book "Jeno . . . the Power of the Peddler." Egotistical? No, the power I'm talking about is not the power to control lives of other people—I'd never try to do that—but the power that comes when the successful peddler becomes an entrepreneur and has the opportunity not only to build businesses but also to benefit the community, the state and the nation.

The key to it all is providing jobs, the most valuable commodity on earth—a subject I'll return to, more than once, in the pages that follow. If you can create jobs, you'll create the power that you can use— properly, not egotistically—for the good of all.

That's the kind of success that this book is really all about.

My Roots: The Mystique of The Iron Range

When you pick up a book like this and glance over it, you might wonder: Okay, success and all that, but who is this guy? Where's he coming from?

That's easy. I'm coming from a place called the Iron Range. That's where my roots are, and they're deep.

THE IRON RANGE is not a mountain range. It's a region of rolling hills and lakes and forests in northeastern Minnesota, very beautiful and very cold much of the year. It once produced rich iron ore for the whole world, and now there's taconite where the iron has to be set free from a lean, stubborn rock to produce pellets that are about 63 percent iron.

But more important, it still produces some of the toughest, rough-and-tumble people you'll ever meet.

That's the mystique of this area.

The Iron Range knew the hard life well into the early decades of the twentieth century, the better to steel the backbone of men and women of purpose who survive by their wits and hard work.

But why are Iron Rangers today—not all, but a majority—so ultraliberal in their thinking . . . some might say even socialistic?

Well, it probably has something to do with the fact that these people—my people—were oppressed as few Americans have ever been oppressed. They'll never forget what the iron mining industry did to their fathers and grandfathers and great-grandfathers.

There was no Workmen's Compensation in those days. Insurance for injuries? No, not a penny from any mining company. And if any worker talked union, he would be fired on the spot and his name added to the black list circulated among the other mining companies so he couldn't work anywhere.

The work was thirteen hours a day, six days a week. To put in that thirteen hours, my father would get up at four A.M. to get to the job at five A.M. He'd open his lunch pail around noon, then go back to work from twelve-thirty to six-thirty. His 35 cents an hour brought home $4.20 a day.

But out of all that labor and deprivation came strength—and a host of leaders in all fields of endeavor.

I'D LIKE TO NAME, in no special order, some of the notable and not-so-notable people who have come out of that Iron Range crucible. Some of them are world-famous. Others may sound vaguely familiar. And some you probably never heard of—but you should. They're all part of my heritage, and I respect them all.

- **Gus Hall** was head of the Communist Party in the United States for years and a perennial

Communist Party candidate for president. He was from Aurora, my birthplace. Sorry about that.

- **Bob Dylan** still sings your blues for his greenbacks. Short on conversation, long on accomplishment. He's from South Hibbing, right across the street from my family's home and my mother's store. When he was a kid named Bobby Zimmerman, he used to come in and buy candy. Bobby is living proof that acorns do sometimes get blown too far away from the tree. To my knowledge, he never did return to Hibbing, even for a visit.

- **Governor Rudy Perpich,** also from South Hibbing, was the greatest governor Minnesota ever had or ever will have. He governed from 1976 to 1979 and again from 1983 to 1991. Never forgot his roots or his friends. Died too soon; quietly and without fanfare. That was his style.

- **Roger Eugene Maris** wasn't born in Fargo, North Dakota, as most baseball record books say. He was born in Hibbing on September 10, 1934. He changed his name to Roger Morris for a while because the kids in the playground called him "mare-ass." But he took his own name back by the time he got into professional baseball. He hit sixty-one home runs for the New York Yankees in 1961, the first to break Babe Ruth's record, staving off the incredible pressure he got from the media and the fans. The fact that Roger Maris isn't in the Hall of Fame is a disgrace.

- **Bus Andy Anderson** started his nationwide Greyhound Bus Lines from his garages in North and South Hibbing.
- **Roger Enrico** from Chisholm, Hibbing's nearest neighbor, retired after a distinguished career as chairman and chief executive officer of PepsiCo, Inc. The most selfless CEO who ever existed, and the most productive.
- **Judy Garland** was from Grand Rapids, Minnesota. What else can I say, except that we're all still dreaming of going "Over the Rainbow" with this unique legend of American culture. There will never be another Judy Garland.
- **Les Crystal** started his career as editor of the Duluth East High School newspaper and went on to be president of NBC Television News. His father, Iz Crystal, was a great friend of mine.
- **Kevin McHale,** the great Boston Celtics basketball star, later became a manager and revived the then-pitiful Minnesota Timberwolves from rigor mortis. Another product of South Hibbing.
- **Hayden Pickering** from North Hibbing, one of my classmates at Hibbing High, became head honcho for DuPont in Europe.
- **John A. Blatnik,** the U.S. congressman from Chisholm. Not only a great congressman for a quarter-century, but also the astute negotiator with Marshal Tito of Yugoslavia during the Cold War.
- **Judge Gerald Heaney** presides over the Eighth District Circuit Court of Appeals. One of

the greatest jurists who ever sat on a bench and the most dedicated, civic-minded judicial statesman a city, state, or nation could hope for. I'd trade him for anybody on the Supreme Court any time.

- **Claude Schmidt,** my friend and president of our 1935 Hibbing High School class. He was a star basketball player and became an ace pilot in the navy during World War II. He was shot down three times in the Pacific, but survived to down about a dozen Japanese aircraft in dogfights.

- **Tom Dougherty** also came from the Class of '35. He was also a navy fighter pilot, flying off carriers. He was shot down a couple of times but lived to bury others as our leading mortician in Duluth. Maybe the saving grace for both Tom and Claude was the Iron Range moonshine we used to drink.

- **The Mondavi family,** from Eveleth, of the Mondavi-Rothschild wine empire. Entrepreneurs *extraordinaire.*

- **Jessica Lange,** the actress, was a graduate of Cloquet High School. I've enjoyed seeing her in dozens of movies from *King Kong* to *Cape Fear,* and especially her performance in *Losing Isaiah,* for which she won an Academy Award as Best Actress of 1995.

- **Barbara Peyton** was the movie actress in the early 1950s who married Franchot Tone in the home of her late grandfather in Cloquet; a real Hollywood celebrity wedding. What's with this trend from Cloquet to Hollywood? After smelling those paper mill fumes and moving to the smog of L.A., maybe it's the pollution connection.

And what is it about the Iron Range that gave birth to these and so many other strong-willed people? I'm not sure, but I'm honored to be one of them. And I want to tell you my story . . . as a legacy of the mystique of the Iron Range.

Part One

Birth of a Peddler

*They call me an **entrepreneur**, and that's okay with me. But what I really am, at heart, is a **peddler**. Maybe the two words mean the same damn thing.*

When you think about it, we're all peddling something, whether it's goods, services, real estate, our resumes, or deeply felt political or religious convictions. We're all selling something to somebody. We're all peddlers.

But all peddlers are not the same.

Jeno's Credo:
I never did learn to
walk slow . . .
Thank God!

The Paolucci family in Hibbing, Minnesota, in 1918.
Michelina, Elizabeth, Ettore and baby Luigino.

Chapter 1

The Difference Makes All the Difference

*P*eople who are truly successful, in just about any enterprise you can name, have a way of standing out from the crowd. They're risk takers, they're forward thinkers, and they're showmen. They get good ideas, and they romance them. They peddle something different in a different way.

I was lucky in some ways. I was born different—way out of the mainstream in a little three-room house on the edge of a mine pit in Aurora, Minnesota. Disadvantaged? You bet.

My father, Ettore Paolucci, had worked in the sulphur mines of northeastern Italy. When the sulphur ran out, he came to northeastern Minnesota in 1912, recruited by the iron mining companies who sought hard-working miners. The work was in underground mines, some half-mile or more down, where it was deep and dangerous.

My mother Michelina followed a couple of years later and they married in America.

A whole colony came from my parents' hometown of Bellisio Solfare (Beautiful Sulphur) near the Adriatic Sea.

Being a little sentimental, much later I bought (and still own) the little hut in Bellisio Solfare where my mother was raised. She lived there with a sister, two brothers, and her father and mother . . . six occupants in a twenty-by-twenty foot room . . . no running water, no toilet.

In the basement lived a donkey that was brought upstairs on cold winter nights. His body heat helped keep the little room warm. But mostly he stayed in the basement and watched my grandfather, called Nonno, make wine. My mother also watched, from time to time, learning a trade that she put to use later on, in America.

In Minnesota, our family—Ettore and Michelina, my sister Elizabeth and me—wasn't quite that bad off, but close to it. My father worked mostly in the mines, but at one point he got a "good" job ($5 a day) as janitor at the high school. But he lost that job when a new city administration came in and passed the patronage to their own people.

We moved from Aurora to Hibbing, then to other houses when work ran out or the iron company claimed the property to expand the mines. We moved from place to place, each house more cockroach-infested than the last.

Living like that sure didn't seem lucky at the time, but looking back, maybe it wasn't all bad. It started a fire in my gut that's never been extinguished, and that wouldn't be there if I'd been born in some comfortable middle-class household.

Years later, when I started Chun King and became known as the poor Italian-American from the Minnesota melting pot who got rich making Chinese food in the shadow of the iron dumps—that was different. The publicity alone was priceless.

But no kid wants to be a complete outsider. At a very early age, I decided to try to be more like the others—and accidentally came up with my first trademark.

How well I remember that Saturday afternoon when I was seven and my sister Elizabeth was ten. The two of us were fooling around with paper and pencil on the floor. While we spoke Italian at home, we both liked English and were good at spelling. We talked about becoming writers someday.

Liz used phonetics to spell out my name, Luigino, which worked out to be J-E-N-O. I tried writing that out in the bold cursive she taught me, adding a big flourish to the first letter.

Repeating over and over again my new name with its distinctive spelling, I made a vow that "Jeno" would show the world that the Paolucci's were better than the life they were forced to live. "Jeno" would find a way out of this mess.

At the same time, I decided to change the spelling of my last name from Paolucci to Paulucci. I thought that would make it a little more American, make me more accepted and liked by others who looked at my family as "Dirty Dagos."

How wrong I was. It takes more than a change of name to end bias, discrimination, and ridicule, as I found out.

For instance, I liked school and got A's, which meant I should be seated in the front of the class according to the rules. But because I was a Dago, I was put in the back row with the other undesirables. I suppose it was then that I started to develop a social conscience. An activist was stirring in my veins. But all I could do at the time was strike back in small ways.

When a German music teacher was rough on me, I brought sneezing powder to class, got in early, and sprinkled it everywhere. I stood back and laughed as all those snobs had fits. But I did get suspended for several weeks.

BY THE LATE 1920s, our family was beginning to prosper. My father was earning $4.20 a day in the mines ($25.20 a week or a huge $100.80 every four weeks). My mother was catering out her increasingly famous pasta dishes . . . and taking in laundry.

The family rustled up $125 to buy a decent house, then another $125 to move it. But we still needed a foundation. The answer was telephone poles. My mother was friendly with telephone workers who liked to come by and sample her wine. They'd tip her off when they were putting in new poles and taking down the old ones. So at age eleven, well short of a driver's license, I'd drive our old Ford out in the evening and use a rope and chain to drag in abandoned cedar telephone poles—and maybe a few of the new ones that weren't in place—to build the foundation of the Paulucci homestead.

But then the Depression came and Ettore was only working one week out of every six weeks. Our lifestyle changed and changed fast.

Then my mother took over. If there ever was an entrepreneur, it was Michelina Buratti Paolucci. She took a risk, like all entrepreneurs must do. But I can't really recommend this one, because it involved breaking the law. With Prohibition the law of the land, she became a bootlegger.

But not just any bootlegger. Michelina was the best of all. She had learned her art from her father, Nonno, many years ago in a basement in Italy.

She made only red wine. Our family bought zinfandel grapes from John Fena, a local produce dealer. They came from California in wooden crates known as lugs—there were twenty-five pounds of grapes in each lug. We cranked our own machine to grind up the grapes. When a barrel was half full of the pulp, we added water and covered the top with burlap. Every so often we'd open the barrel and compress the mash to keep it active.

After school I'd push down the mash and suck on a rubber hose to transfer the liquid to another barrel—and get half-stoned from the vapors.

Typically, the other Italian bootleggers in town left the combination of crushed grapes and water in a warm basement for several weeks. The natural yeasts in the grapes caused the mixture to turn into wine that could be drained off, put in a clean barrel, and allowed to age. The result was a good wine. Sweet but a little heavy.

My mother did it her own way.

Unlike our fellow bootleggers in the neighborhood, she bought yeast from the bakery (Fleischman's was better than the Star brand). Next, she took sugar and melted it into a syrup on the stove. Then she stirred the yeast into this warm mixture. This slurry was the key.

When she added it to each barrel of fermenting wine, it sped up the entire process. It also extended the life of the leftover mash when the finished wine was drained off. Normally you could only use a mash once. But with my mother's added concoction, the second wine was nearly as good as the first.

Because her wine had more alcohol in it, it was also cheaper to make. You could add water and thereby increase the yield per ton of grapes. In the end hers had more flavor, more kick, and yet was lighter in body.

Nobody could match the taste of Michelina Paolucci's red wine.

Customers eagerly paid a dollar for a quart of wine, which cost about a dime to make. We were selling fifteen to twenty quarts a day at our peak, clearing from $13 to $18—about four times what my father could make in the mines when he worked.

Yet we never got rich.

The federal agents raided us again and again. They'd break up the barrels and we'd have a lake of wine in the basement. After the third visit by the feds to the same address, the house was quarantined. We had to move out, and also pay a fine of $500. It took everything my parents had saved.

Over time, we moved from South Hibbing to Michigan Street to Lincoln Street to Washington Street. Wherever we moved, the process was the same. My father and his Italian friends went to work digging a false basement around the outside of the existing one. When it was finished, the entrance was concealed behind cords of firewood. In the hidden chamber stood new wine barrels, and my mother started making wine all over again.

And eventually the feds would come and create another red lake.

Sometimes we'd hold the feds off with payoffs to vultures like the chief of police and other officials, who came around and demanded not only money but also a few gallons of wine for themselves. They also took along helpings of my mother's pasta dishes from her catering business.

One way or another, we saw that the wine business had to wind down. My mother opened a small grocery store in the front room of our house at 2326 Third Avenue East. And it was time for Jeno to see what he could do to contribute more to the family fortune.

Pointer from the Peddler: When it's time to move on, it's time to move on.

I'D BEEN DOING ODD JOBS from an early age, after school and on weekends. In the summer, I'd unload boxcars of watermelons for John Fena, the produce dealer, earning 50 cents a day. In the winter, I'd use a big four-wheel shovel to unload boxcars of coal into trucks, for 50 cents plus a gunny sack of coal to take home in my wagon.

I also found a job washing cars for Mr. Nickoloff, an insurance agent who came from Russia. Every week I'd show up at his house and take his Packard home to wash it. I'd get 50 cents upon delivery of the sparkling clean car.

But I got in the habit of taking the long way home with his car. Barely able to see over the steering wheel, I'd joyride over to some nearby town before going back to our house to wash the car. Unfortunately, a friend of Mr. Nickoloff saw what appeared to be the insurance agent's car rolling around Chisholm with no one apparently at the wheel, and mentioned it to him.

He didn't fire me, but cut the price to 25 cents and said, "From now on, wash the car here and we'll use my water."

About this time, I took my first steps toward being an *entrepreneur*—though if you'd asked me what that word meant, I'd have had no idea.

Lots of tourists came to see the huge Hull-Rust open pit mine, which looked like the Grand Canyon even though it was man-made by people like my father, shovel by shovel. When the company police weren't looking, I'd go down in the mine and fill glass vials that I'd bought at Woolworth's with layers of different colored ore, then go up to the road and sell them to the tourists for a quarter.

Other kids my age did the same. We had a pretty good business going because the vials of many-colored ore were really beautiful.

Then that stopped. The company gave the rights to sell ore samples to just one person, a friend of the superintendent. And the company police warned us kids not to go near the mine and try to collect samples.

To hell with them. I went to Catterini's grocery and bought spices—cinnamon, nutmeg, black and red pepper—and filled my vials with layers of "iron ore" that looked very authentic, just like the varied colors of real iron ore. I'd stop cars coming to the mines, jump on the running board, and offer them my pseudo but colorful vials.

And to hell with the monopoly of the superintendent's friend.

Devious, yes. But being devious is no sin. Especially not when it's a matter of survival. I still keep a vial of that fake iron ore in my office. Wouldn't be surprised if quite a few one-time tourists also still have a vial of it on a shelf somewhere.

But even as I was getting to be a boyhood businessman, when I reached the advanced age of eleven going on twelve, it was time for me to get a "real" job. I went to work at a grocery store in Hibbing for $3 a week, working after school and all day Saturday until midnight, and half of Sunday.

It was there I learned exactly what *not* to do to survive and succeed.

Chapter 2

Thinking on Your Feet

*I*t was called Daylight Market because it had so many windows on its corner location. It was owned by a very dignified man of Croatian descent, David Persha, but this store and others on the Iron Range were managed by David's brother John.

John was eighty miles away from David's headquarters in Duluth, and he had complete authority as long as he showed a profit—one for David, one for himself. He padded his profit by instructing his twenty or so employees to overcharge or manipulate customers, thus putting money in his pocket that was never recorded on the books.

John Persha, rest his soul, was crooked as a pretzel. But my experience with him sharpened a skill I'd already begun to develop—thinking on my feet.

So here I am, mopping the floors and washing all those windows, inside and out. Also unloading hundred-pound bags of flour and sugar, bushels of potatoes, and truckloads of produce. (I really think I'd be

Jeno and his dog Brownie when Jeno worked at the Daylight Market.

six feet tall—instead of five feet, four inches—if I hadn't carried all those loads on my back and shoulders.)

At first big-hearted John wanted to pay me in fruits and vegetables (beginning to spoil) to take home. I said no, standing my ground. He finally said, "Okay, three dollars a week in cash."

I soon learned that all the employees in the store were instructed to cover our week's wages by getting it back, one way or another, from the customers. They did this in ways such as:

- Throwing a big ham on the scale so the indicator jumped around and the customer couldn't see the settled weight. Then they added two or three pounds over actual weight to the bill.
- Weighing out five pounds of hamburger, then scooping out a half-pound or more when the customer wasn't looking.
- When using a hanging scale for fruit, always having a green banana at the bottom where the customer couldn't see it. They sold that green banana over and over again.
- Putting straw or hay at the bottom of tomato baskets, so the customer would get maybe three-fourths of the full weight.
- When the customer wanted bargain coffee at 19 cents a pound, talking her into taking the best brand at 29 cents. But the coffee was all the same, no matter what the customer paid.
- And when presenting the bill, they would push the "no show" button on the adding machines, adding a quarter or a dollar to the sale.

Customers hardly ever checked the total. If
they did, we'd blame the machine.

That's only a sample. I could go on and on. I was
cheating customers to keep my lousy job.

Despite all that, I still remember the cast of characters at that store with something like affection.

There was Emil Vocinovich, the head butcher and
a fine gentleman. He sometimes would get a little
upset with me because when they were real busy in
the meat department I'd run over and put on an
apron and start cutting roasts. Because I didn't know
my ass from first base, the roast would come out
kind of scraggly.

Emil finally told John he'd appreciate it if he'd
"keep that kid the hell out of the meat department."

There was Joe Bujanovich, another butcher, John
Persha's cousin, a tall, tough-looking Croatian with a
great big scar on his nose. Everybody liked him, but
Joe was a fighter and a drinker. On Saturday night
he'd go over to the Garden Tavern and get really
drunk. Then he'd take out his pecker, bang it on the
bar, and yell, "I'm gonna break the bar with this."
The regulars were used to this; they hardly noticed.

There was Frances Laurich, the efficient cashier,
and her sister Helen, who helped out from time to time.

The man I really looked up to—my "role model,"
you'd say in today's terminology—was Ernie Lekan-
der, who worked behind the counter. Ernie was five
feet, seven inches, wiry, and fast on his feet. He had
a great personality. The women customers loved him
and wanted him to wait on them. Now and then he'd

get one of them to go into the cooler with him for a quickie on the meat block—with one of us standing guard outside.

Yeah, Ernie was quite a guy.

Unfortunately he also drank too much, and one night the Hibbing police put him in the City Hall jail, down in the basement with no insulation, just a cement floor. He got pneumonia and died.

At the other end of the scale was Patty O'Malley, a homeless man in his fifties that John Persha had picked off the street, probably to get cheap labor. He had a cot downstairs. Never, ever, took a bath. John gave him maybe $10 a week for the mopping and cleaning up, and he'd use that to buy moonshine.

We got along all right, mopping the floors together. When he was sober he was okay. But sometimes on Saturday nights when he'd had too much moonshine, around midnight he would haul off and hit the hell out of me, for no reason. Just beat the shit out of me.

I was afraid to say anything to John Persha because I knew that if he had to make a choice it wouldn't be Patty O'Malley who was gone, but Jeno.

Looking back, I wonder if it wasn't Patty O'Malley who caused me to get into all those bar fights in the years to come. When anybody looked at me with the glint of danger in his eyes I'd just hit the son of a bitch. I'd made up my mind that nobody was going to get that first punch in.

WORKING AMONG A GANG OF THIEVES, it was ironic—this guy with the dark glasses I almost bumped into one day when I was delivering some meat from Daylight Market to Cane Lakes Café about a block away. He seemed familiar, and when I got inside the café, I looked back at him and his two cohorts.

My God, I thought, that's John Dillinger, the famous bank robber! I recognized him from newspaper photos and in the news clips they had in the movies. They were standing on the corner, studying the bank there on Howard Street and another one a block away.

I dropped the meat and ran around behind them, then through them on the way back to the store, glancing back once more.

John Dillinger, big as life. I read later that he had come up to Wisconsin and Minnesota to case banks he might want to rob. Hoped he didn't want to rob any grocery stores. Hell, that money was already stolen . . . from the customers.

JOHN PERSHA HAD OTHER TRICKS up his sleeve. Every two weeks or so he'd come to me late in the day and order me to make a special pick-up over at Hibbing Van and Transfer and take it back to the store. It was always the same—ten hundred-pound bags of corn sugar. I'd haul them down to his Chrysler coach with its huge front seat. With two bags in the trunk, one on each fender, and one on the seat beside me, I managed to get it all to the store in two trips.

Then that same evening after dark, a pickup truck showed up behind the store and took delivery of the corn sugar.

It was still Prohibition, and the unseen customers were moonshiners.

Those sales never appeared in the daily receipts. I checked out of curiosity. At double the regular price per bag, John must have pocketed about $100 cash on each transaction.

John stole from his customers, he stole from his brother. And he stole from his employees. Specifically, me.

On Saturdays, Frances Laurich, the cashier, regularly gave me a bag with the cash for the day, and I ran the three or four blocks down the street to the Merchants and Miners State Bank and turned it over to the cashier at the window.

One afternoon when I got back, Frances asked, "Where's the change?"

"What change?" I asked, still out of breath.

It was true she sometimes put in the bag a separate amount she wanted back in small bills and coins, to make change for customers. But this time the bank cashier hadn't given me anything back except the slip.

"You must have made a mistake," I said, "or maybe the bank . . ."

But nobody believed me. Instead, they accused me of stealing. John demanded I pay the money back out of my wages. Or else I'd be fired.

That evening I went home despondent. I had been sucked into John Persha's web of crookedness, thinking I could hold my own. Now he was screwing me too.

But here's where thinking on my feet paid off. The following Monday, instead of going to school, I hitchhiked the eighty miles to Duluth and went to see John's brother, David.

I had seen the rich owner of all those supermarkets many times when he came to Hibbing to inspect the store. He'd arrive in his long black Packard, with a driver and a couple of assistants, looking like the King of England, though he spoke with a Croatian accent. Dark and handsome, with elegant manners. On one of his visits I overheard him asking John about me: "Who is that energetic young man?"

So I hoped he might remember me. And I was convinced he knew nothing about his brother's dishonesty.

To my relief, he recognized me at once when I stepped into his office that Monday morning.

"What are you doing here?" he asked with his heavy accent, meaning why wasn't I at school?

But Itzy Gotkin, one of his managers, broke in: "You mean this kid works for you?"

"For my brother in Hibbing," Persha confirmed.

"How old are you, kid?" Gotkin cross-examined me.

I told him I was fifteen.

"Hell, this kid's underage, David," said Gotkin. "There are child labor laws in this state, you know. Better get rid of him fast."

My God, I thought, after all the trouble I'd gone to, was I going to lose my job anyway?

But instead David Persha listened to everything I had to say.

After checking into the purchases of corn sugar from Hibbing Van and Storage, he fired his brother. The Daylight Market stopped screwing its customers, and I kept my job without paying for the missing $17.

That store eventually closed, but the experience gave me a valuable perspective that I would rely on for life. The Daylight Market taught me that you've got to give value to your customers, whoever they might be.

You might get away with short-changing your customer on one sale, maybe two, but the die is cast. You will lose that customer, and that customer will tell others. Negative word-of-mouth is the worst thing that can happen to you.

Therefore, at all times do everything you can to deliver the highest quality and give the highest value.

Don't cheat the customer, because you're actually cheating yourself. It's a horrible way of doing business—and the shortest route to bankruptcy.

I got another job at another store, then an even better job for the coming summer.

At age sixteen, I left home for the first time and went to work for David Persha, becoming a street barker for fruits and vegetables.

THE CITY OF DULUTH is a port at the head of the Great Lakes built by the millions of tons of iron ore and grain that were shipped every year. Giant carriers hauled that ore down lake to the country's steel mills, then the largest, most powerful industry on earth.

It was the spring of 1934, just before my senior year of high school, and the whole world lay ahead of me.

David Persha owned supermarkets all over northern Minnesota, including seven in Duluth. A man who had arrived from Croatia without a nickel in his pocket, he was now worth a fortune. I was flattered when he singled me out and offered to double my pay—a cool $10 a week—if I came to Duluth as soon as school ended.

Located on First Street between First and Second Avenues, the narrow storefront of Dave's Public Market had a large window—about twenty feet long—that rolled up over the downtown sidewalk. A clerk stood behind a long table and sold directly to passersby.

But this hole-in-the-wall was no ordinary roadside stand. The fresh produce sold there constituted all the fruits and vegetables that all of the Persha stores in Duluth had failed to sell for whatever reason. My job—more a carnival barker than a clerk—was to get rid of the stuff before it became overripe or simply turned rotten.

Much later, David confided how he knew from the start that this job was made for me. "My boy, you were a natural," he chuckled, recalling my first day selling strawberries. "You had fifty cases of them but you'd tell the ladies, 'Yes, ma'am, there's only a few left, but I'll be sure to save some for you!' "

Well, he was right. I loved it from the start.

Every morning I got up at four A.M. at the State Hotel, where I paid $3 a week for my room, in order to have everything in place when I rolled up my window at seven. By then the long table in the front of the store was stocked with the day's unwanted produce.

At once I began hollering at the top of my lungs: "Watermelons, forty-nine cents each! Half-bushel of tomatoes, sixty-nine cents! Bushel of spinach, forty cents!"

I worked right through until seven at night and then closed down and fell into bed.

Just before closing on Saturday night, I'd still be chasing someone down the street trying to sell him a bushel of spinach for 25 cents, knowing that if I didn't, by Monday it would be garbage.

As that first wonderful summer went on, I came up with my own special gimmicks.

"Strawberries . . . fifteen minute sale!" I'd shout, setting an old alarm clock I had next to me. "Strawberries going for fifteen cents a quart until the alarm goes off!"

Yelling to beat the band, I held an empty basket in one hand and a full one in the other. I kept dumping the full one into the empty one. Back and forth, back and forth. At the same time, I had two clerks dancing around on either side of me, pouring strawberries into bags and collecting the money.

Then the alarm rang.

The crowd on the sidewalk froze in their tracks, all eyes staring up at me.

The frantic sale was over. Silence.

"What's the price now?" someone would ask timidly.

Pause.

"Same price!" I'd cry.

Hearty laughter from all sides, my own loudest of all.

Then maybe an hour later I'd announce another "fifteen-minute sale" and do the same thing all over, until we were sold out of strawberries or tomatoes or cantaloupes.

And so it went, from seven in the morning to midnight sometimes, depending on what I had to sell.

Always the same overriding worry—tomorrow will be too late. Sell now, now, now.

Every Saturday night, I hitchhiked back to Hibbing to run around the Iron Range with my buddies until the sun came up. On Sunday I watched my mother's home grocery store so she and my sister could go to the movie matinees. Sunday nights I caught a ride with the driver of a Zinsmaster Bakery truck making its run back to Duluth.

I did so well with my shouting and sales pitches that pretty soon the grocery store across the street hired its own street barker. For a while the two of us went at it from dawn to dusk, trying to out-yell each other. I must have more than held my own, because the other store asked me to come to work for them for $12 a week, $2 more than I was making.

After some negotiations with David, I stuck with him for the same $10, but an extra $6 in cash, out of his own pocket.

ONE INCIDENT THAT SUMMER stands out above all the rest.

Opening the store one morning, I was staggered by a horrible smell. Clouds of ammonia billowed from the doorway.

I got hold of Persha from the pay phone nearby. He rushed down and called the fire department. They quickly determined that the refrigeration units had broken down, but except for the leak that caused the ammonia fumes to erupt, no damage seemed to have been done.

By seven o'clock, the store was back to normal, and I began to open my fruit and vegetable counter. The special of the day was a shipment of ripe bananas that had come in the night before. In those days, bananas came in straw in round baskets about five feet tall. They were still on stalks cut directly from the tree. I'd use a stool to yank the stalks out of the baskets, careful to watch out for the frog-size black tarantulas that sometimes came along for the ride from Central America. Evidently they liked bananas too.

When I pulled out the first stalk, I noticed these bananas were different from any I'd ever seen. Instead of a nice glowing yellow color, they had a skin that belonged on the back of a leopard—light tan with little brown spots.

It had to be the several hours' bath in the ammonia fumes that had caused them to look different.

I tried one. It had a distinctive taste, all right. But it wasn't bad at all.

About that time, Persha returned to assess the damage to the store and found me among the forest of banana baskets.

"Taste this," I said, tossing him a sample with its strangely specked peel. "There's plenty more just like it."

He refused with a scowl, saying he didn't like bananas. I figured that's just what our customers were likely to say, once they got a look at them.

"Gee whiz, Jeno," he cried, stomping around and shaking his head. "What are we going to do with all this funny fruit? Just dump it?"

The thought of a total loss was unthinkable for both of us. But by then half an hour or so had passed since I'd eaten the banana, and so far so good.

"I don't know," I said. "They taste fine. Different, but pretty good!"

"Well, okay," he decided. "Do whatever it takes to unload them."

Ordinarily we sold bananas at three pounds for 19 cents. David suggested reducing the price to three pounds for a dime. But if I did that, people were going to ask what was wrong, and I'd have no choice but to tell the truth, that these bananas had basked for hours in ammonia fumes.

Then it came to me. On the spot, I ordered my two assistants to clear the entire window table and put out all the bananas right away. While they were still cutting them off the stalks, I launched my pitch for the day: "Argentine bananas," I yelled. "First time in the city! *Argentine bananas!*"

"How much?" my first customer asked.

I didn't hesitate. "Three pounds for only 29 cents! Supply limited."

Instead of lowering the price, I had raised it a dime.

When passersby stopped, I shoved a banana into their hand and raved, "Try this! Great taste, huh? How many pounds can we give you?"

No one asked about the spots or the unusual taste. Hell, they wanted to be the first ones to buy and consume these rare Argentine bananas.

We sold them all out in a matter of three or four hours. Days later, people would come back and ask

when we were going to get more bananas from Ar-
gentina. My answer disappointed them: "Never again."

That banana episode taught me that everything
has its value.

> *Pointer from the Peddler: Never sell your product or
> service short. People want to buy something different
> from a different peddler.*

Romance the item with a name or slogan, but
don't lie. I didn't say the bananas were from Ar-
gentina, just that they were Argen*tine.* And since I'd
already eaten one, I knew I was giving full value.

Again, I was being more than a little devious
with the bananas. Same with the fifteen-minute
sales of strawberries. But I sure wasn't cheating anybody. And the customers were having just as much
fun as I was.

But my fun was almost over. The chief of police,
Ralph Fiskett, stopped by to see me at the window
one day. Said they were getting complaints about all
the noise.

"What noise?" I asked innocently.

"Your voice!"

The doctors and dentists and lawyers all around
were up in arms, he told me. My yelling for twelve
hours a day or more, six days a week, was driving
them nuts.

"Can't you holler a little quieter?" the chief
pleaded.

I tried for about ten minutes. But I didn't see how I could do my job and not shout. The chief came back and warned me three or four times. Finally Persha himself talked to me.

"Jeno, you've got to turn down the volume. Just sell."

Just sell? I thought that's what I was doing.

Anyhow, by the third week in August, the professional and business tenants on First Street had had enough. They signed a petition and that caused Persha to give up on street barkers. After all, these neighbors were his customers, too.

So I lost my $16 a week summer job.

I returned to Hibbing and went back to work at the Daylight Market, now reopened under new ownership as Minnesota Markets, then another store called Sunnyside Market, working morning and evening while attending high school as a senior. Soon I'd be graduating, and thoughts came to mind of going on to junior college and taking a pre-law course.

But I wasn't destined to be a lawyer. Having learned to think on my feet as few could, I was destined to be the prince of peddlers—an entrepreneur, by God, though I still didn't know that word.

Chapter 3

Fifty-Two Bucks

*W*hen my mother opened her front-room grocery store in 1932, I was still toiling for Daylight Market. Our original order for stocking the store cost the large sum of $53 from the Rust Parker Wholesale Grocery Company of Duluth.

We had a meat counter, a candy counter, an ice cream freezer loaned to us by Island Dairy Creamery (who sold us the ice cream), plus grocery shelves for canned goods, sugar, coffee, and some cereals—along with my mother's own spaghetti sauce and pasta dishes. And after Prohibition ended in 1933, for old times' sake, a few bottles of homemade wine.

All told, it cost us about $350 in cash and we were in business. Our hours were seven A.M. to eleven P.M., or until midnight if someone was going to spend a nickle or more. Open seven days a week.

For more than twenty years, our family made a go of it. We eventually sold the store so my mother could retire in Miami, Florida.

Michelina in the doorway of the Paulucci Grocery, the front room of their home.

The couple who bought the store went broke in six months by keeping shorter hours and running the store to suit themselves . . . not the customers. By that time I was prosperous enough to buy it back. I will never sell that $500 house. It was home, and our family's first real business—and my starting point for all that was to come.

IN SEPTEMBER 1935, I began my pre-law studies at Hibbing Junior College.

I had to keep working, of course, now at the re-opened Minnesota Markets, at $10 a week mornings, evenings, and Saturdays. I'd hustle groceries from six in the morning until nearly eight in the evening, and in between rush off to college, only to listen to my so-called professors drone on and on.

We had the most monotonous professors you could ever imagine. I consistently fell asleep in class.

Finally I began asking myself if I really wanted to go through all the crap necessary to become a lawyer. Come to think of it, attorneys had a lot of competition, right? They were also limited in their earnings. (That was before the vultures started class action lawsuits, where they get a large part of the settlement . . . in fact, most of it. That's why I call some of them vultures.)

What if I could do something where there was no limit to how much I could make in a week, and be my own boss besides?

Back at the old Daylight Market, I had heard stories about a terrific salesman of the early Depression.

A man named Harry Bachman who would blow into town with a chauffeur-driven car—a big Buick, they said. Harry sat in the back seat until his driver jumped out—limo cap and all—and opened the door for his boss. Mr. Harry Bachman—black homburg hat, spats on his shoes—then strolled into the store of his choice. His driver followed in his wake with armloads of samples. Harry piped his tune, and the grocer danced, buying truckloads of food and staples, a cornucopia of canned fruit, salmon, bulk coffee and sugar, soaps and cleansers, salad oil—well, you get the picture.

Harry, I was told, made close to $1,000 a week on straight commission, representing a well-known St. Paul wholesale grocer called Hancock Nelson Mercantile. But that good life came to an end one day when his driver tried to outrun a train at a railroad crossing. The driver was killed, and so was Harry.

At work I had heard of a new wholesale grocery outfit that was opening up, the C. A. Pearson Company, that didn't have any salesmen yet on the Iron Range. On my own, I had even gone to Duluth to talk to their regional manager, Mr. Arvid Erickson. But nothing came of it.

One day the new owner of the store where I worked, Mr. Larson, and his assistant Carl Nelson confronted me.

"Jeno," they cried, "we hear you're interested in selling for C. A. Pearson."

I admitted I had been thinking about it.

"Do you realize what a risk you'd be taking? You wouldn't get a salary, you know, and you'd have to pay all your own expenses. That job is *strictly on commission.*"

But what did I have to lose? Hell, I was already broke most of the time going to school. All I would be gambling was my time and maybe the tires on our family's 1929 Ford to get around my territory. I was confident I had the makings of an aggressive, go-for-broke salesman. Above all, I wanted a chance to make an unlimited amount of money, depending on how good I was, how hard I worked, and the ideas I had generated to sell whatever it was I was going to sell.

"I like my chances," I told them.

Their response took me by surprise.

"Why don't you give it a try then?"

SO I QUIT MY LAW STUDIES. I quit working at the Minnesota Market.

My boss had a word with Mr. Arvid Erickson, the Pearson manager in Duluth, whom I called on before. The next time I went to see him, I became a traveling salesman on straight commission, splitting the profits fifty-fifty but no salary or draw against commission, and I had to pay my own travel expenses.

I made up my mind that I was going to top the legendary Harry Bachman, but without the spats, without the homburg, without the chauffeur . . . just me and some samples in my '29 Ford. And no trying to outrun trains.

At age seventeen, then, I took the gamble and became a wholesale grocery salesman on straight commission . . . a traveling salesman.

I called on retail grocers on the Iron Range, in Duluth, and in Superior, Wisconsin—the Twin Ports separated by St. Louis Bay off Lake Superior. During the winter when ice in the bay froze from shore to shore, I—like others in those Depression days— would drive across the bay to save the 10–cent toll charge on that damn toll bridge between the cities.

I'd take the chance of my 1929 Ford sinking into the bay, if the ice was too thin, just to save a dime.

My best customer, as you might expect, was my former boss David Persha with his City and Public Markets, about ten stores then as I remember it. He wouldn't give me an order on weekdays, so every Sunday I'd get up at five A.M. in our little $500 house with the grocery store out front and drive to Duluth to call on David and his buyer, Max Cherson. Max was sharp as hell but a real good guy who became my dear friend for some sixty years after that.

Then I'd go back to Hibbing to tend the store so my mother and her friends could spend 10 cents each for the Sunday movie matinee.

Soon I was on my way to my first payday with C. A. Pearson. As I added up my total receipts for my first six weeks on the job, I smiled—not only because the numbers checked, but also because I was pleased with how far I had come in such a short time. In my first week, I had sold $57 worth of groceries. Not so hot. But at the end of my sixth week, I had increased my weekly average to $1,000. I figured I had coming to me, at 5 percent commission, in the neighborhood of $200 for that six-week period.

The weeks of sleeping in the car, shaving in gas stations, and living off lunches of tinned salmon and peaches scrounged from samples in the back seat were about to pay off.

I arranged to see Mr. Arvid Erickson on Sunday morning (not on Saturday; that was too good a day to catch my customers in their stores).

For a while it appeared that Mr. Erickson, who was hunched over his desk at work, had no intention of paying me at all. He didn't acknowledge my existence.

Finally, I cleared my throat and told him why I was there.

"Oh yes," he said absent-mindely. "I have your check right here."

He pulled it out of a drawer and handed it over, not even glancing up from his papers. I looked at it, blinked, and stared again. And still, I couldn't believe it.

Fifty-two bucks, I said to myself.

Then, not so slowly, and not to myself, I said, "What the hell is this fifty-two bucks!" I went on to do the arithmetic, showing Mr. Erickson that I was entitled to more than $200.

Once I was done, Mr. Erickson blustered, "Well, you sold only our low-profit items."

"Bullshit!" I cried, no longer able to see straight from the tears in my eyes. "Show me your costs!"

"If that's the way you feel about it, Mr. Paulucci," he huffed, "then you're all done here."

Mr. Paulucci! Here was a guy who had just screwed a seventeen-year-old kid out of almost all of six weeks of hard-earned wages, and when the kid had the nerve to complain, he was fired. All I could think of was I had to show this guy up right here and now.

I grabbed the telephone off his desk and got hold of the information operator (no charge in those days).

"Give me the number of Hancock Nelson Mercantile in St. Paul," I said, thinking of my idol Harry Bachman. I then went to a pay phone and asked the operator to ring the number.

The phone rang and rang, before somebody finally picked it up.

"Hello," a voice croaked on the other end.

"I'd like to speak to the president of the company," I demanded, going for broke.

"Well, that won't be so easy to do," the voice chuckled. "I've never seen Mr. Clay in here on a Sunday. This is the night watchman."

"What did you say his name was?" I asked, calming down a bit.

"Mr. H. E. Clay."

"Do you know where he could be reached at this hour? This is kind of an emergency."

"Well, I suppose you could call him at home," the watchman conceded, and gave me the number.

I'm sure I got Mr. H. E. Clay out of bed that Sunday morning. But I was convinced I had an offer he couldn't afford to turn down. I would start selling for his company—strictly on commission. My territory would start off where Harry Bachman's left off on the Iron Range. After all, Harry got killed, and I knew Hancock Nelson wasn't doing any business up there at all. I had already seen that myself.

Anything I brought in would be pure gravy, I pointed out. I offered to drive down to St. Paul that very afternoon and get started.

Mr. Clay said that it was, after all, Sunday. Could I come down the next day? I showed up as promised and got the job . . . as agreed, on commission, fifty-fifty profit split, no salary or expenses. All they gave me were some canned goods samples to use in selling.

They were all heart. But full of optimism, I loaded the samples in the back of the Ford and headed north again.

I had no idea what lay ahead of me.

All I knew for sure was that I had become a competitor of C. A. Pearson, and I was going to show this Mr. Erickson and his bunch of crooks that I would take my sales somewhere else, and leave them in the dust.

Fifty-two lousy bucks!

Chapter 4

How to Stay a Step Ahead

*A*nybody who sets out to sell on straight commission without salary or expenses, as I did, knows what it's like to be an entrepreneur. I sure as hell did, though that word still hadn't entered my vocabulary.

If you don't sell, you don't eat. And you sure can't help your family. What I was—and am—was a peddler. And I was good at it from the start. I made a lot of money—more than $2,000 a month (minus expenses), and my gross kept increasing for the next seven years. I started out selling on the Iron Range— the towns of Hibbing, Keewatin, Nashwauk, Bovey, Coleraine, Grand Rapids, and Deer River to the west; and Chisholm, Buhl, Mountain Iron, Virginia, Eveleth, Gilbert, Aurora, and Biwabik to the east. Then I expanded my territory from Minnesota to Wisconsin and North Dakota.

Those were great days. It's true that, in my newfound prosperity, I had a little too much fun, drinking

Jeno decides to become a traveling salesman.

and carousing from port to port like a carefree, drunken sailor.

But my head was always on straight when I was working. And I had obstacles to overcome.

The retail grocers in those small towns had been doing business with established wholesalers for years. Nobody was going to hand over any business to a newcomer just because he walked in the door. Many of the stores, in fact, were in heavy debt to Kleffman Mercantile in Hibbing, which was carrying them from month to month.

I needed some techniques to get a step ahead, get a jump on the competition in some innovative way. So I dreamed up several.

The first time was almost an accident.

One day the main office at Hancock Nelson in St. Paul sent me a telegram: "Cover your customers on salmon. Poor harvest this year. Prices will be higher." The purpose of the memo was clear. If we told our customers of the impending price hike, two things would happen, both of them good. We'd look like heroes, by giving customers a chance to buy before prices went up. And if they were smart—or they were being served by a pushy salesman like Jeno F. Paulucci—they'd buy more than usual to take advantage of the lower price.

By mistake I happened to show the telegram to a buyer and was amazed to discover the weight this piece of "official paper" carried.

I left with a huge order from a man who'd never bought salmon from me before.

I then showed the same telegram to other customers. Sure enough, it worked again, and suddenly I had several new orders.

Then it came to me. Why wait for Hancock Nelson to send me another telegram?

Why not send one to myself?

I went to Western Union in Hibbing and filled out a blank form. My message to me? "Cover all customers on canned peas. Recent freeze means a short crop. Prices higher."

I handed my message to the operator.

"I can't send this," he protested.

"Why not?"

"Well, you're sending this to yourself."

"No I'm not."

"Sure you are. You're Jeno Paulucci. I know you."

This called for some fast talking. I handed him my business card.

"Look, I represent Hancock Nelson. You know they've been sending me telegrams, right?"

He nodded.

"Well, I'm sending this to Jeno Paulucci all right. But I'm sending it as a representative of Hancock Nelson. So it's just like the other telegrams I've been getting, see?"

I showed him the one I had gotten about the salmon. He nodded again, looking a bit confused.

"Now will you send it?"

"Yeah, in that case, I guess I have to."

From then on I got no argument. Whenever I heard at sales meetings about a short crop or a good buy coming, or whatever, I used a telegram to myself to generate orders from grocers who normally wouldn't take my word on the weather outside.

I developed variations of this gimmick. For instance, if I had a solid line of peaches and pears from Libby's or Del Monte that wasn't moving as they should, I showed customers an official Western Union dispatch: "National Canned Fruit Week coming up in April. Alert customers to displays."

At the same time, I unfurled a specially printed sign promoting the event, and confided, "Hey, I don't know if the other wholesalers have contacted you, but don't be left out in the cold on this one. It's worth a nice, juicy in-store display."

(Okay, so there wasn't any National Canned Fruit Week except in the local areas where I had declared it myself.)

More often than not, grocers liked the idea. My quality line of pineapples, peaches, and pears or whatever sold well, and everybody was happy in the end.

I did other things to stay a step ahead of the established outfits.

The manufacturers paid the freight costs on their products to the wholesaler's dock. But my deal forced me to pay the freight cost from that point to the stores I was supplying. The warehouses of major competitors were in Hibbing and Duluth. My wholesaler, Hancock Nelson, was way down in St. Paul. With such a built-in disadvantage, there was no way I should have been able to compete on certain products—canned peas, corn, or tomatoes—where the cost of shipping on small orders was more than the product itself.

But I didn't want to give the business away, so I went around in advance of the packing season for these crops and made a special offer. "Okay, I've got a whole railroad carload of peas coming in," I'd tell my customers. "How many *cases* can I put you down for?"

With the larger volume, I could offer an attractive price, and the customer ordered from me. When my carload arrived in Hibbing or Virginia, I rented a truck and, with a couple friends, made the deliveries in person.

I did a little fast-talking in dropping them off, as well.

If the grocer had ordered fifty cases, for example, I'd say to my helpers, my old friends Claude Schmidt and Bogan Radich, "Let's bring in seventy-five." And I'd say to the grocer, "Where do you want your order of peas?"

"Down in the basement," he'd say.

Down in the basement went those seventy-five cases.

"Okay, will you sign for these, please?"

"Hey, wait a minute. I didn't order seventy-five cases. I wanted fifty."

"Oops, did we make a mistake? You mean we have to haul twenty-five cases back out to the truck? These peas are a really good deal, you know . . ."

More often than not the customer would shrug it off and say, "What's the difference? I'll take 'em."

I had just increased my sale by 50 percent.

Hey, they were really good peas, too!

Only once did I drop off too much of a good thing. A Fairway store in International Falls had ordered 150 cases of corn from me.

"Where do you want them?"

"The back room."

We piled not 150, but 250 cases in that tiny storeroom. The busy manager hastily signed for them all. But the next day I got a call from him. He was mad as hell. The wooden floor had caved in, and the entire shipment at forty pounds per case—about five tons—was not in the back room, but the basement.

I had covered him in peas, all right. Covered his entire basement.

(That was one customer I never called on again. If I had gone back there, he would have killed me. Maybe I was a little too devious that time.)

Eventually, I even got the drop on Kleffman Mercantile, the local wholesaler in Hibbing.

The popular salad oil in those days was a corn oil called 77. It came in all sizes—gallons, half-gallons, quarts, pints. Practically every store sold a carload of the stuff every year. Larger supermarkets moved maybe four times that amount.

This was just a ton of business, too much to turn my back on. Yet Kleffman had a natural 10 cents a case advantage over the Duluth wholesalers and a whopping 40 cents advantage over me, with my shipments coming from St. Paul.

Did I bow out gracefully?

Hell, no! I went in and took *all t*he business.

In fact, Kleffman got so frustrated they complained to the 77 company that I must be cheating somehow. So the manufacturers sent a representative to Hibbing to find out what was going on. Their man, who happened to be Italian himself, didn't pass up the opportunity to live high on the hog for several days at my mother's house, feasting on her ravioli and spaghetti and helping himself gratis to her cigars from the store.

But once he understood what I was up to—and once my mother made it clear that the freeloading had to end at some point—he went back to his people and told them, "Leave the crazy dago alone. He's doing a good job for us up here. We're selling more 77 oil than we ever did, and it's all legit."

Here's what I had done.

I noticed that grocers only paid attention to the price of the big-ticket item, the gallon size of the salad oil. A case of six gallon containers sold for about 70 cents a gallon or $4.20. If you offered them $4.10 a case, you didn't get their business. But if you offered $3.90, you did. And you got all of it.

After doing some calculations, I realized that the gallons only accounted for around 40 percent of the grocers' sales volume. They actually sold more of the half-gallons, quarts, and pints. And when it came to those sizes, the grocers either didn't know what the heck they were paying, or didn't seem to care.

The solution to gaining market share was simple. I undercut Kleffman's case price on gallons by 30 cents—getting all their business—but raised it high enough on the other 60 percent to offset the losses on the gallon size. I made my full profit, and none of my customers caught on.

Or if they did, they had short memories.

Here are a couple more ways I stayed ahead of the competition.

If a customer didn't buy a certain item, I'd come back a month later with a new angle. In the end it was not taking no for an answer that paid off for me.

For example, when a good client of mine, Hjalmer Lindgren in Bovey, Minnesota, wasn't in his store one day when I came to call, I tracked him down at a hospital in Grand Rapids, ten miles away. His wife was due to give birth any second, but I wasn't coming back that way for another four weeks, and I couldn't afford to miss his order.

He was upset.

"She's the one in labor, Hjalmer, not you," I said, trying to calm him. "Let's talk a little business."

"Well, what have you got, kid?" he finally said, hoping to get rid of me.

I pulled out my list and left after contracting for my usual twenty-foot truckload delivery. The only thing Hjalmer didn't buy was my suggestion to name his new baby boy Jeno.

After extending my territory into Wisconsin, I began pestering the fellow who ran the People's Market in Superior. He had a good business, and I wanted him to carry my canned salmon. He was also a butcher, and one day when I called on him he was working behind the counter.

"I've got pink salmon on special," I greeted him from the doorway. "Can I put you down for ten cases?"

"Don't want it, don't want it," he kept repeating louder and louder from the moment I stepped inside.

Finally, he bolted around that meat counter, seized me by the arm, and escorted me straight out the front door into the street. I was grateful he'd put down the butcher knife first.

"Now do you understand I don't want your cock-eyed salmon?"

So I went around the block, found my way into the rear entrance and popped my head back in the store.

"Well, if you don't want ten cases, how about five?" I proposed genially.

This time he smiled in spite of himself.

"I've never seen anyone so damn persistent," he said, beginning to laugh. "Okay, send me the ten cases, not five."

About this time I also developed a phone order system, so buyers didn't have to wait for my monthly visits. That way I could cover even more ground.

And that was how I built my business.

Since it was going so well, I decided it was time to increase my commisson. My arrangement with Hancock Nelson was 50 percent of the profit on everything I sold, while paying all my own expenses. But as I figured it, I was selling about one-third of Hancock's total volume, so I negotiated 60 percent of the profit for myself, instead of 50 percent.

Then one day I woke up from the good time I was having.

OVER THE YEARS MY SALES had risen to at least a million dollars a year, which would translate to $35,000 to $40,000 in income. But my monthly checks had stalled out at around $2,500.

Something was wrong.

During my next trip to St. Paul, I stopped in to see an acquaintance who worked at the main office, and I suggested we have a few drinks together. Determined to keep my wits about me that night, I took an unusual precaution: I swallowed eight ounces of olive oil ahead of time. The idea was to keep my stomach coated and the alcohol from entering my system too fast.

This old Italian remedy seemed to do the trick. I was still all ears when my friend finally spilled the beans.

"Hey, Paulucci," he crowed sometime after midnight, when he was well-oiled himself, but not with olive oil. "You think you're so smart!"

"I do?"

"Yeah," he sneered. "Don't you have any idea how the company's been screwing you the past two or three years?"

"Screwing me? You're kidding."

"Don't you know you should be making more money than old Griffin himself?"

He was referring to Mr. Griffin, the president of the company. H. E. Clay was long gone by this time.

"How could that be?"

"Take my word for it."

(Did I forget to mention that my drinking companion was also the company's bookkeeper?)

I was shocked. "Then how come I'm not seeing it?" I asked, leaning over the bar table. "Griffin's certainly not living on twenty-five hundred a month like I am."

"No, of course not," he confided, his chin close to mine. "That's because I've been instructed that the more you sell of a product, the higher I raise the cost of it on the books."

"Run that by me again," I barely whispered.

"I mean that as your sales go up, your rate of commission goes down."

"So . . . that's why my checks stay the same."

"You got it, pal. Old Griffin isn't about to be shown up by some punk tuna salesman."

I never was more sober in my life, and it had nothing to do with olive oil.

The next morning, I drove back up to Duluth to see a lawyer named Dick Galoub who had helped me out before. When I told him I had at least $10,000 coming—the amount I calculated my employer had short-changed me over the past three years or more—he became anxious.

I didn't have any real proof of my charges, he argued. The only hope was to push for a quick settlement. Meanwhile the company came up with a tough city lawyer named Smith.

In the end my guy settled. For a lousy $500.

After that, things on the job were never the same. Because I had uncovered their bookkeeping scam, they had to start paying me what I was worth. This greatly disturbed their newest president, a fellow named Oscar Kincaid. Soon Oscar called me in and gave me an ultimatum: Either I go on a salary-

and-bonus arrangement like everybody else, or we part company.

"After all, Jeno," he reminded me, "right now you're making more money than I am."

"Ask for a raise," I suggested.

I told him I'd think it over, stalled him for a while, then told him to "stick it" and walked out.

Inside of a year they lost 75 percent of the business I was doing and later Hancock Nelson Mercantile—alma mater of the legendary Harry Bachman—closed their doors forever.

Pointer from the Peddler: The old saying is, "Pigs get fat and hogs get slaughtered."

I guess it applied to both of us in this instance. I should have been happy with 50 percent commission, and Oscar Kinkaid really should have asked for a raise. That way we might have continued to make money, which would have been fair to both parties.

But it was time for me to move on anyway . . . time to be in business for myself, time to peddle in my own name.

ONE EVENING WHEN I WAS STILL RIDING HIGH with Hancock Nelson, a man showed up at my door in Hibbing. I looked at him closely. Could it be? Yes, it was my first boss at C. A. Pearson. They had evidently closed up, and Mr. Arvid Erickson himself was looking for a job.

After applying at St. Paul, he'd been told the northern half of the state "belonged to Jeno." If there was anything available, he'd have to get it directly from me.

I had to tell him there was no room at the inn. And I told him to get the hell out.

I'm sorry, God, but I still couldn't forgive that man for that miserable fifty-two bucks.

Chapter 5

The Odor of Opportunity

While negotiating my future or lack of it with Hancock Nelson, I stumbled on an opportunity that seemed just what I was waiting for—the chance, in fact, of a lifetime. It all began at a tiny grocery store off the highway near a town called Backus, in Minnesota's lake and resort country.

I always got a friendly welcome there, and a good order. One day, as I stopped in for my sales call, I happened to notice a new item for sale at the checkout counter—a cellophane packet attached to a small card. Each packet contained a powdered seasoning: "Pure granulated garlic." Hmm.

Garlic was used mostly by Italians to enhance the flavor of cooked foods and salads. My mother always preached that garlic is good for you. Doctors confirm today that garlic is therapeutic; it can lower high blood pressure and cholesterol, help you get over a cold. It has all kinds of therapeutic powers.

Jeno ponders "the chance of a lifetime" peddling dehydrated garlic.

The plain vanilla housewives of those days knew nothing about that. They wouldn't peel a clove of garlic if their lives depended on it. Couldn't stand the smell.

But dehydrated, granulated garlic with no smell—that could be something else. Hell, it might become as common in the kitchen as salt and pepper. I sniffed the packet again. No smell at all.

Where did this come from? I wondered, squinting at the card. "It says here: 'Basic Vegetable Company, Indio, California.' "

"Naw," the store-owner scoffed. "That may be what it says, but it was packed right here by an older gentleman and his wife at their cabin, over by the lake. Guy named Clark Johnston. Had a heart attack some time back, I guess, and come up here to retire."

I kept staring at those dozen little packets of garlic that sold for 10 cents apiece. I hadn't seen anything like it before. "I'd like to meet this Johnston."

"Okay. I'll get my wife to watch the store and we'll drive over."

A few minutes later, I was standing out back of a rundown shack that seemed to be half tent and half boards. I introduced myself to Clark Johnston, a shabby old guy, balding and unshaven, but active for someone who had a heart condition. I told him about my interest in his product, and he amiably lifted a piece of canvas off a contraption about the size of a small pinball machine.

"Takes a while to set up for a run," he said, "otherwise I'd start it up and show you how it works."

"Maybe you can talk me through it," I suggested.

I listened in growing fascination as he explained how his prized machine worked—pointing to the garlic hopper, the circular pockets for each packet, the sealing rollers, and finally a stapler that attached the individual packets to the card.

"I'll tell you the real secret of this machine, mister," he declared at last, whacking the side of it like a church pulpit.

"Garlic is very *hydroscopic.* If air gets to the dehydrated garlic while it's being packaged, you're dead, see?" he said, pointing a finger at me. "The garlic turns hard and brown. Useless. You'd never sell it."

He thumped his pulpit again. "My machine doesn't let that happen."

With that, he placed the piece of ragged canvas back over it. When I left that afternoon, I had a $60 case (120 cards) of Clark Johnston's garlic cards in the trunk of my car.

The next time I visited Duluth, I called on a truck jobber named Ed Lee, who wholesaled and delivered small items like potato chips and mayonnaise to retail stores.

"Do you think you can sell this?" I asked, handing him one of the cards.

"What's it cost?"

We tossed numbers back and forth. If the full display of 12 packets retailed for a dime a packet or $1.20, he figured the grocer would buy it for 90 cents, to make 30 cents profit. But Ed Lee had to make a profit, too, so . . .

"Okay, how about seventy-five cents a card? You put these around your outlets and we'll see what happens."

"Why not?" he shrugged.

I left feeling pretty good. If nothing else, I had just made $30 on the case of garlic cards that had been bouncing around in the back of my car.

Ed called me back a little while later.

"Sold all those garlic cards without a problem. Got any more?"

I tried to reach Clark Johnston, but he didn't have a telephone. I finally got the friendly grocer in Backus to hotfoot messages back and forth to the Johnston lake shanty. His first report: Johnston had 5,000 cards on hand.

"What price can I get if I buy them all?" was my next question to be relayed to Johnston. Forty cents a card, Johnston proposed to my messenger.

Back and forth we went, until he agreed to dispose of them all at 25 cents each—if I sent my check up front for the full $1,250 for 5,000 cards. Accepting his promise to ship the cases of cards as I needed them, I sent off the money.

Just like that I committed myself to a silent partner I barely knew.

I had big plans for hydroscopic garlic. But one truck jobber wasn't going to make me a living.

My next stop was the Edgewater Beach Hotel in Chicago, where I had taken time off selling for Hancock Nelson to attend the National Wagon Jobbers Convention. I took a booth for $100 and set up behind a homemade sign: *Dehydraveg, Duluth, Minnesota.*

The truckers, who turned out in droves, picked up my sample cards and asked the price.

"Seventy-five cents a card," I offered. "Ninety dollars a case."

In three days I took orders for all 5,000 cards.

In addition, I made up a list of truck jobbers all over the country—Cleveland, New York, St. Louis, San Francisco. Suddenly, I had nationwide distribution of a hot product out of Backus, Minnesota.

I've got something going here, I said to myself as I drove all night from Chicago to get back home.

However, before quitting Hancock Nelson for good, I made an unscheduled trip to Backus. My grocer-messenger had told me that Clark Johnston said we had an obstacle to overcome before we went any further with our joint venture, and I wanted to find out what it was.

This time Johnston pointed to a couple of fifty-gallon drums that stood among the junk behind his ramshackle residence.

"That's it," he informed me gruffly. "Maybe another four thousand to five thousand cards I might be able to scrape together." Those two drums were the last of his supply of "dehydrated garlic." The outfit in California had discontinued the item.

"And nobody else processes it?"

He looked at me keenly.

"You go to all the stores, young fella. Have you ever seen any granulated dehydrated garlic for sale?"

I had to admit I hadn't. A feeling of hopelessness came over me.

"There is one thing we can do," Johnston spoke up hesitantly, rubbing his unshaven jaw.

"What's that?" I asked unhappily.

"Build our own garlic dehydrating plant."

I laughed out loud. "Sure, just call me Henry Ford."

Johnston smiled, but he didn't laugh.

"Oh, I don't think it would be all that hard. After all, I know the whole process myself."

I stared at this strange old man closely. After all, I thought, his garlic machine had turned out to be the real McCoy.

"What would it cost?" I asked coolly.

"I think we could do it for five thousand bucks."

"That much?"

"Maybe four thousand."

With the money I'd saved from my years selling on the road, and after having the time of my life, I could probably just about cover that amount, with enough left over to get by until the business was established.

On the spot I agreed to provide the front money Johnston needed to start up our own garlic processing operation. We shook hands.

I was twenty-four years old and eager as sin to be on my own at last.

SAYING GOODBYE ONCE AND FOR ALL to Hancock Nelson, I moved to Duluth, where I'd kept up my friendship with David Persha and his wife Mary. I spent most of the time, however, riding trains back and forth across the country, peddling five cases of garlic here and ten there.

I sent the orders on to Johnston, back there with our $4,000 garlic dehydrating machine, and the checks came directly to me. I turned around and invested all my profits in our new dehydrating operation.

With an unlimited supply, I daydreamed, there was no telling what the market might turn into.

I had my own business, and I was going for broke with it.

Then something happened to temper my excitement.

The orders were rolling in, but I had noticed a funny trend. There didn't seem to be any repeat orders. Why? It had taken longer than expected to get the processing operation started, but according to my grocer-messenger, we were now in full production. So the problem couldn't have been back orders.

Time to make another unannounced visit to Backus.

At Johnston's place on the lake, no one answered my knock. I went around to the back, and there stood a young man about my age taking stapled cards out of that magic garlic machine.

We shook hands, and he introduced himself as Clark Johnston's "right hand man." I had to admire how smoothly that invention of Johnston's worked, and watched entranced as it spit out its sealed packets of "hydroscopic" powder.

"Is Johnston around by any chance?" I finally asked.

"He and his wife went to Brainerd for the day," he answered, "to see a doctor."

"Is he all right?" I asked anxiously.

"Just a checkup, I think."

I glanced around. The place didn't look much different than it had before. I didn't see anything that looked liked a garlic dehydrating plant, just Johnston's same old pinball-sized "pulpit."

"Where's the rest of the crew?" I inquired, suddenly suspicious. Johnston had complained over and over about all the help he had to hire.

The young man gave me a strange look.

"What do you mean, crew?" he said laughing. "I'm it."

"Who dehydrates the garlic?" I demanded, pointing at the fifty-gallon drums standing nearby.

"Nobody," he shrugged as if I'd asked him who was buried in Grant's tomb. "We order it from a company in California."

"Not Basic Vegetable, in Indio, by any chance?

"That's it."

So there was no $4,000 garlic dehydrating plant replicating the process of Basic Vegetable, the company Johnston had told me had gone out of business. He was buying the dehydrated garlic from them as he always had, and pocketing all the money I was sending him, instead of getting our own plant up and running.

Having discovered one huge problem, I went on to address another—the fact that we didn't seem able to get any repeat business. I figured I'd start by eliminating the most obvious explanation.

"Have you been able to fill all my orders?" I asked, my mind racing wildly.

"Well, we had a few back orders, but there was nothing that got us behind, and so . . ."

"Could we take a look at those orders?" I interrupted, desperate to get to the bottom of the situation.

They weren't there, he told me. Johnston and his wife were in the middle of moving to a new home, and all the paperwork had been boxed up and taken away.

Where?

"They bought an old gas station on the edge of town and plan to live in back," he said, wiping his hands on a rag and covering up the garlic machine again. "We could go over there, I suppose, but I haven't got a key."

I must have looked pretty upset, because on his own this young fellow opened up to me.

"Look, Mr. Paulucci . . ."

"Call me Jeno." At the moment I was calling myself a lot worse.

"Okay. Jeno, I wouldn't trust that guy too far if I were you. I'm looking to get another job myself."

"What do you mean?" I asked. He apparently had no notion of the scam concerning the dehydrating plant. He was talking about something else.

"Well, sending out the orders is part of my job. Johnston's really pretty lazy . . . leaves it all up to me. So it wasn't hard to see what he's been doing."

His face looked guilty and sorry at the same time.

Instead of filling the orders in my name, this kid confessed he'd been using the name and address belonging to a friend of Johnston, a fellow named Hill, down in Minneapolis. This guy turned around and billed the jobber, receiving the payment himself, which he passed on to Johnston.

That was why I hadn't seen any repeat orders. They were coming in all right, but the money was going to Johnston.

"Why does he want to cut me out?" I wondered aloud.

The young man shrugged sympathetically.

"I don't know exactly. How much are you paying for each card?"

"Forty cents."

"There's your answer, I guess. This fellow Hill is paying *sixty cents* a card."

I had the truth at last.

Johnston had been screwing the hell out of me.

If that son of a bitch had showed up that day, I might have killed him.

AFTER DRIVING AROUND BACKUS and stewing for a while, my head cleared and I developed a plan. Thinking like a lawyer, I realized I needed evidence to prove he was stealing from me. All I had on him so far was the word of his part-time employee, and my own suspicions.

I went back to the place at the lake to ask the part-timer one more question. He was still there, wiping his hands on his pants and cleaning up.

"You mentioned this guy Hill, the jobber Johnston was using. You wouldn't happen to have an address or phone number, by any chance?"

The young man grinned in spite of himself.

"Couldn't forget that if I wanted to. I've printed dozens of those labels lately. You sure can sell that crazy garlic, I'll say that much. My wife'll barely let me in the house at night."

I tried to smile as I dug out a pen.

IT WAS STILL DAYLIGHT when I reached Minneapolis city limits. After stopping at a couple of gas stations for directions, I located the house where this Hill lived. I stood on the front porch and pounded on the door. No one at home. Just to make sure, I found a pay phone and dialed his number. I let it ring off the hook. No answer.

So far, as you've noticed, I was just doing the logical thing—just your average lawyer-detective. But then I took my first wrong step.

I can't go back empty-handed, I justified in my own mind. So I looked up the number of a locksmith.

"Look, I've got this little emergency," I told the man who answered. "I've locked myself out of my house. How about coming over and letting me in?"

Well, he was alone and couldn't leave the shop. But I kept pleading with him, and finally he agreed to loan me his set of passkeys. I went over and picked them up, and before I knew it, I was back at Hill's darkened house. Sure enough, one of the keys opened the front door.

I went quickly through the rooms, switching lights on and off. Nothing promising upstairs. In the basement I turned on the lamp over a desk.

It was all right there—the orders I had taken . . . correspondence between Johnston and Hill about filling the orders . . . canceled checks to Johnston at the higher rate of sixty cents a card.

Everything the kid at Johnston's place had confessed to me had been true. I scooped up the papers and let myself out.

The next day I visited a prominent attorney in Duluth named James Courtney.

I told my new counselor how I'd been deceived and backed it up by showing him all the papers I had taken from Hill's desk. The only thing I didn't tell him was how I got my hands on the papers.

After shuffling through the evidence, Courtney smiled hopefully. "What assets does Mr. Johnston have?"

I must have looked puzzled.

"If we want to file suit and force him to stop what he's doing immediately," he said without waiting for an answer, "the best way is to get him to deal with us. You tell me you've invested a substantial amount of money . . ."

"More than four grand, plus the profits he owes me on the repeat orders . . ."

"Right," he nodded. "And because it does appear wrongdoing has taken place, I recommend a writ of seizure to ensure Mr. Johnston's undivided attention to this matter."

"Okay, what do we seize?"

"You tell me," he answered, looking up over his spectacles.

I thought about this for a long moment. "How about a garlic machine."

My white-haired attorney filed the papers, and the sheriff from Walker, Minnesota, went out with the writ of seizure to obtain the garlic machine from Johnston until matters could be settled between us.

No luck.

The sheriff reported the machine was no longer on the premises.

All this due process stuff was taking time, and I could feel my garlic business slipping away forever.

After all, I couldn't ship any new orders until I got this resolved. And my attorney was right. Without that machine in our possession, Johnston wasn't paying any attention whatsoever to our lawsuit.

Then came my next big mistake. I took matters into my own hands.

I talked my old friend David Persha into driving over to Backus with me in his great big Packard. With no trouble at all, we found the gas station where the Johnstons were living in the rear quarters. I knocked on the door. No one answered. I looked through a window and there it was, Clark Johnston's "pulpit," just sitting there.

I went out of my mind.

To this day I don't know how I did it. But I kicked the door in, charged inside, picked up the machine all by myself—it must have weighed 250 pounds—and carried it straight out to Persha's car.

I was so angry I never felt a thing.

Poor David, whom I once thought looked like royalty with his Packard, stood there in his fancy overcoat and didn't know what to make of what he was seeing. But he helped me load the machine into his trunk.

"Let's get out of here!" I yelled.

"Um . . . where to?"

To hell with the sheriff in Walker, I thought.

"The police station . . . in Brainerd."

Well, Johnston must have showed up right after we left. He had also acquired a telephone since I last saw him. When I entered the Brainerd police station thirty miles away and announced I had something in the car to deliver into their possession, the police officers just stared at one another.

"Are you Jeno Paulucci, by any chance?"

"Yes sir, I am."

"Well, we just happen to have a warrant for your arrest."

"Arrest? What for?"

"Breaking and entering and grand larceny."

David and I both spent the night in the Brainerd jail.

Nothing new about that for me. As a teenager, I had seen the inside of plenty of beat-up Iron Range jails because of my drinking and fighting. But it was all new to David. As a respected and successful family man, he was inconsolable.

"This will be in all the newspapers!" he cried over and over.

I felt terrible and tried to apologize. On top of everything else, I was nearly broke and had no one left to turn to.

The next morning, David's wife Mary had to sell some stocks so we could both post bail at $5,000 each.

Our trial date was set for a month later, in Walker.

Both of us were ready to plead not guilty and fight the charges . . . until our attorneys had a talk with the prosecution and sat us down privately.

"We can't win this," they told us.

"Why not?" I demanded in outrage.

"You broke in and stole the machine. It's an open and shut case."

"So what do we do?"

"We settle."

Simply put, I waived all claims against Clark Johnston for cleaning me out of more than $10,000, in both lost profits and my investment in a totally fictional garlic dehydrating plant. In return, Johnston waived any claims of his own, and the sheriff agreed to drop all criminal charges against David and me.

This time I had really screwed myself.

Pointer from the Peddler: Never, ever, take the law into your own hands . . . whether you're Bill Gates or a budding entrepreneur selling garlic out of the Iron Range.

But the thought of Clark Johnston getting off scot-free remained unbearable. I approached my attorney, James Courtney, one more time.

"Isn't there anything we can do to get back at him?" I pleaded.

"Well, you've given up all your rights to recover any money from him, of course," he concluded. "But it does look like you might get him convicted of fraud."

"Let's go for it," I said without blinking.

The fraud charge was filed in Duluth.

Both Johnston and Hill, the jobber, were served with papers. Forced to come out of hiding at last and hire his own lawyer, the great con artist, for the one and only time, made his own mistake. He showed up drunk at the house where I was staying. We traded insults, and he turned into a wild man, threatening to kill me.

Finally, he had to be restrained and hauled off to jail. It was a wonder he didn't drop dead on my doorstep. Maybe his heart troubles had been a scam as well.

His lawyer's first legal act was to post bail for his new client. It was also his last.

Just before the trial date Courtney called me in.

"I've been looking over the evidence again," he said, beaming across the desk at me. "There shouldn't be any problem. All we need for a conviction is right here, as far as I'm concerned."

He tapped the folder in front of him, containing all the papers I'd taken from Hill's place.

As I stood up to leave, he stopped me, saying, "By the way, how did you get all this good stuff anyway?"

I decided to come clean at last.

"From Mr. Hill's house," I answered, my head down.

"You mean he *gave* the papers to you?"

"No."

"How did they come into your possession, then?"

I took a deep breath, told my story, and watched my white-haired attorney's face—and our case—collapse. My first instance of breaking and entering was just as wrong, and illegal, as my second. If it all came out in court, I'd probably go to jail again. On top of that, because I had obtained the evidence illegally, it was not admissable in court.

In short, we had to drop the suit.

I had doubly screwed myself.

Completely broke by now, I still wanted desperately to salvage my garlic business . . . I couldn't let go of my dream. I somehow managed to talk poor David Persha into putting up the money and becoming my partner.

I had a new approach. Well, actually it was the one I thought Johnston was going to use. We would make our own garlic machine, our own pulpit, and process the garlic ourselves, dehydrated or not. I just knew an engineer somewhere could duplicate it.

Well, we bought ourselves a machine. Set it up in the back of David's store on First Street in Duluth, along with hoppers of garlic. Tinkered with it, adjusted it lovingly. But it never worked. The garlic turned hard and brown.

Throwing more good money after bad, I found a company in New Jersey that packed pharmaceuticals in a hydroscopic manner, and they agreed to try packaging the garlic for us.

It turned hard and brown.

We never could figure out how to keep air from getting in during the manufacturing process. Johnston took the secret to his grave.

I was out of the garlic business. Broke. My prospects had never looked more bleak.

But at least one person was glad to see the end of it. Mary Persha breathed a sigh of relief when all that garlic was finally cleaned out of the back room of their store.

Chapter 6

Opportunity Knocks—Again

David Persha had fallen on hard times. He'd been watching over his empire of supermarkets about as carefully as he watched over the Daylight Market, where his brother John had cheated him blind. One by one the stores had fallen away, and the only thing left was his "No Points" Store on First Street in Duluth. "No Points" meant they sold only essential items you could buy without World War II rationing tokens.

Ten years after coming to work as a street barker for the older man I had idolized, our fortunes were no longer that far apart. I was broke and he was close to it.

But he was like a father to me.

And like a father, he offered to let me work in his store during the day, to keep me going. I also got a job as a timekeeper at Butler Shipyards in Superior, across the bridge. My shift was nine P.M. to five A.M. I'd work so fast checking workers in and out and figuring the time cards (no computers at that time) that

Writing from his YMCA room, Jeno asks for help to launch the business that would become Chun King. The bean sprout growers are Ben Furata (left) and Jeno's partner and mentor, David Persha.

I was able to sleep four or five hours a night in a bed in the adjoining Red Cross room. Unless someone got injured, which was very seldom.

It was a great way to do my bit in the war effort, being I'd volunteered for the armed services but had been rejected twice.

It must have been early 1944 when I stopped at a supermarket in downtown Minneapolis. It was a fancy place called Witt's Food Emporium, a combination grocery store, meat market, and delicatessen located on Hennepin Avenue, a fashionable address at the time (but not now).

Out of curiosity, and force of habit, I lingered to check out the slick produce displays. As I was wandering up and down the aisles, I came upon a vegetable I'd never seen before. Tiny, white, root-like. I had to ask the clerk what it was.

He gave me a couple to taste and said, "They're called bean sprouts." He handed me a leaflet from an outfit called Modern Foods.

"Bean sprouts," the leaflet said, "are a crisp, delectable vegetable used primarily in Oriental cooking. Excellent and heathful in salads of any kind."

"Sell much of this stuff?" I asked the clerk.

"It's starting to catch on."

"How long do they last?"

"Oh, they're delicate all right. Two, three days. After that, they turn brown and we have to throw them out."

When I left, I had the leaflet in my hand. There was a local address on it. Well, I had some time on my hands.

Modern Foods turned out to be a small, shabby building in a rundown neighborhood.

"How can I help you?" asked a Japanese gentleman inside. He gave his name as Ben Furata.

"Well, I wondered where you got hold of these bean sprouts," I replied, pointing to the leaflet. I had visions of some nice little Oriental farm somewhere.

He smiled and gestured for me to follow. In a small back room a half-dozen Nisei (American born) Japanese were hovering around galvanized metal tubs covered with burlap. Furata pointed to the tubs.

"We grow the sprouts ourselves," he declared proudly.

Indoors? I couldn't believe my eyes.

He patiently explained the entire process. It all started with a green pea-sized bean—a mung bean— from the soy bean family. You could buy them for about 5 cents a pound, then in each tub soak about 10 pounds of the beans overnight in warm water.

The tubs were about twenty-four inches deep, eighteen inches wide, and twenty-four inches long. Put a drain hole in the bottom of the tub; cover it with a mesh screen. After soaking the beans, you put them in the bottom of the tub, covered them with a clean burlap bag (a gunnysack), and then watered them every four hours for four days.

No dirt. No sunlight. Just water. The beans turned into bean sprouts. You got a crop every week. Hydroponic gardening it was called.

You ended up with eighty pounds of bean sprouts per tub, on average. That was less than one cent a pound plus the cost of water and labor. Hell, if I were running the operation, it would cost me about 3 cents a pound total and I'd sell them for 25 cents a pound or more. An operation so incredibly simple it looked to me like a license to print money.

Furata laughed at my reaction. On the way out I thanked him for his time and, for the heck of it, bought a bushel of the amazing white sprouts. I drove back to Duluth, not quite sure what to do with my purchase.

I stored the basket in David's cooler at the store, but left it too close to the freezer coils. The sprouts froze up. Instead of just throwing the garbage out and forgetting the whole thing, I made one of my impetuous decisions.

Why not grow my own?

So I persuaded David to join me as my fifty-fifty partner. I started the business with $2,500 borrowed from a friend. I wrote Antonio Papa a letter at his home in Hurley, Wisconsin: "Will you loan me $2,500 so I can go into business?"

Antonio sent me a check. No note to sign. No questions asked. I didn't ask David to put in any money. His brain equity more than contributed to his half of the business.

We opened our hydroponic farm in the rear of David's No Points Store, the garlic fumes having disappeared by that time.

Furata had been kind enough to show me all the steps.

I got hold of burlap and a metal tub, punched a few holes in the bottom, and added the mesh screen. Finally, I purchased some soybeans and began watering. Pretty soon I had sprouts growing, all right. I also had a terrible smell—something close to rotting potatoes. There was no way I could sell that odor.

David's wife Mary begged me to go back to garlic.

Swallowing my pride, I called Ben Furata and asked him to send two more bushels of sprouts by Railway Express, at 10 cents a pound.

"By the way, Ben," I asked before hanging up, "you did say you use soybeans to grow the sprouts?"

"Soy *family*," he corrected me. "*Mung beans.*"

Mung beans! You live and learn.

This time I packed the genuine article, which I'd obtained from Furata, into half-pound cellophane bags and made a label to stick inside: "Fresh bean sprouts. Great for salads or Chinese meals." I scratched my head before adding: "Distributed by the Bean Sprout Growers Association of America."

I carried my half-pound bags of sprouts around to grocery stores in Duluth and talked the managers into taking them on consignment. If any sold, they could pay me. Otherwise I would take the bags back.

Or throw them out.

Which is what I had to do when the sprouts turned rotten. The heat build-up in those airtight bags killed them overnight. Once more I called Ben Furata and ordered two more bushels by Railway Express. (He must have thought Duluth was going nuts for Oriental salads.)

This time, I simply put the fresh sprouts around the stores in bulk quantities. My price of 25 cents a pound was a little high, but I hoped it added to the special aura of this new vegetable (like Argentine bananas). They sold well enough on trial, so I sat Persha down to talk.

"David," I began with all the conviction I could muster, "I think I could go on the road and sell these darn bean sprouts like I did garlic."

David, to his credit, didn't laugh and hand me the broom.

"How do we package them?" he asked as soon as I had outlined my newest scheme.

"Ten-pound boxes," I declared. "We ship them by Railway Express to the produce wholesalers."

"Okay, but how can we afford to do that if we're paying ten cents a pound for the sprouts themselves?"

I had no answer for that. But after thinking for a couple of minutes, David did.

"Didn't you tell me it cost this Furata only about two cents a pound for the beans in the first place? If we're giving him ten cents, there's got to be some slop in there."

"So?"

"We ask Furata to close up shop in Minneapolis, move to Duluth, and grow bean sprouts for us on a cost-plus basis. Those Japanese who work for him will get more work than they've ever had in their lives, and we can afford to pack and ship their sprouts all over the country. Give me his number. I'll call him.

"We'll be back in business. If things go wrong, hell, it couldn't be any worse than the garlic business, could it?"

We both broke up laughing.

I took off on the train to test the market for bean sprouts around the country. When I got back to Duluth, I stopped first at the No Points Store. I was amazed by what I found in the back room. There were Ben Furata and six other Japanese-Americans, their galvanized metal tubs and burlap all set up, chattering among themselves in their language and already growing crops of beautiful bean sprouts.

I was never sure how David talked them into it.

The deal called for us to provide rent-free space, pay the added water and power bills, and pay for the mung beans that Furata was getting from suppliers in Texas and Mexico. For their labor, Furata and his people received three cents for every pound of sprouts they produced. We also guaranteed a production level of so many thousand pounds every month. Jesus, could I sell that much? I'd try.

With our total cost for bean sprouts down to about six cents a pound, we could afford—at least in principle—to go into business.

And we got lucky. Did we get lucky!

Because of continued wartime food shortages, grocers needed something to put on their empty shelves. Instead of being turned away at the door by the big chains like A&P and Kroger, I found buyers who were eager to see me. I got large orders from them, as well as from produce wholesalers.

Back in Duluth, our "money machine" kept cranking out crop after crop of bean sprouts inside the transformed No Points Store. Out front on busy First Street, we were causing all kinds of havoc in the neighborhood. Boxes and bushel baskets crowded people off the sidewalk. Semis waiting to be loaded for the trip to Railway Express tied up traffic and drew complaints from other retailers on the block.

In fact, our bean sprout location was just a block away from the old store where I had been a barker not that many years ago. Another nuisance in the neighborhood.

Pretty soon David and I had to get our own offices—two rooms across the street above Crystal's Delicatessen.

We were shipping fresh sprouts all over the country in boxes. We were also shipping them in bushel baskets for Chinese food processors—Ben Gee out of Chicago and Meadowmere in New York, to name two examples—who then sold the sprouts in glass jars.

Suddenly, we were a going concern.

THEN, OUT OF NOWHERE, came the plague.

Whatever containers we used, boxes or bushel baskets, Railway Express was our only hope of getting the contents there fresh. And their erratic delivery schedule was killing us.

All of our customers were complaining that the sprouts often arrived brown or in a deteriorated condition. We thought they were probably selling or canning them anyway, but we couldn't prove it, and they went on deducting huge claims from our invoices.

Facing disaster, David and I put our heads together in hopes of finding a solution. For a while neither of us spoke.

"Maybe we could dehydrate the sprouts," I muttered, "sort of like the garlic."

David slapped the table and stood up. "I know an outfit in town that could do that!"

I visited a man named Lennie Underdahl at Midwest Food Dehydrators in Duluth. They had a wartime contract to dehydrate potatoes for the government. I told him what I wanted to do and his response was straight-forward: "We can try."

I brought him a supply of fresh sprouts. They de-hydrated just fine, and looked great. There was only one problem. We couldn't *re*hydrate to save our lives. They remained tough, stringy, and inedible.

David and I put our heads together once again.

"Maybe we should freeze the damn things," I said.

"What do we know about freezing anything?" Dave asked.

"Nothing," I had to agree. But then we located someone who did. David and I traveled down to the Fairmont Canning Company in southern Minnesota to consult an expert in food processing, one Dr. Eickelberg.

"The first thing you have to do is blanch them," said the good doctor.

"What the hell is blanching?"

And that was how we started.

Before we knew it, we owned a square metal con-tainer the size of a huge breadbox. You filled the tray inside with fresh bean sprouts, closed the lid, and gave them a thirty-second steam bath—the blanching—that deactivated the enzymes in the sprouts and pre-pared them for freezing.

This blancher became the core of our first food-processing line. Making room in the First Street building, we added a few water sprays and a Klik Lok packaging machine, and a used pickup truck to rush the blanched sprouts to the nearby Northern Cold Storage Company. There the same freezing operation they used on Lake Superior herring produced fresh-frozen bean sprouts.

All we needed now was a brand name to put on the boxes of sprouts.

Our knowledge of Chinese was confined to high-school geography.

Somebody suggested "Shantung," the province where Confucius was born.

Fine.

We priced a case of twelve of our new eight-ounce Shantung packages at $4.40 each. That gave us a healthy return of about 50 cents a pound.

We were back in business.

What about shipping? It was still Railway Express or nothing. By opening the latched roof covers of a special boxcar, we could have an ice company blow in a mixture of salt and ice to fill the bottom and both ends of the car. In the middle were packed 2,000 cases of frozen bean sprouts worth $8,800. Taking nothing for granted, I made sure I supervised the icing operation myself. We couldn't afford to have a single package become defrosted en route.

There remained the problem of the samples I took with me on selling trips. To keep them frozen, I developed a system of shipping them ahead in boxes of dry ice. When I arrived in a new town, I picked up my box at Railway Express and hustled off to my sales calls. I liked working fast, but this was ridiculous. I lived in constant fear that my samples were going to turn to mush on me.

It all seemed to work. And it was still wartime, and no one else had Shangtung or any other kind of bean sprouts to offer.

And then we hit the jackpot.

I happened to be in Boston at the Copley Plaza hotel, when the phone rang in the broom closet they called my room. It was Bert Wallschlegar from Milwaukee who, with his partner, was setting up a network of wholesale brokers for us across the country.

"You're a hard man to keep up with, Jeno," he greeted me, having made several calls to track me down.

"I like to think so, Bert. What's up?"

He sounded excited and out of breath. "Well, I just met with the buyer for General Foods—they handle Birdseye frozen, you know."

"What did they take?"

"A carload."

"A what?"

"A carload. The buyer said to give him an entire boxcar."

Ordinarily, a good order was 500 cases. All of a sudden, we were talking four times that in one delivery. "C'mon up to Boston, Bert," I invited. "We've got to celebrate."

When Bert arrived at my door, I had a surprise of my own waiting for him.

He looked around at my luxurious quarters. "What happened to you?" he said as he stepped inside. "God, I've traveled with you, Paulucci. You were the guy they invented the original buck-a-day room for."

"Those days are over," I said quietly.

And they were.

After Bert's phone call, I made a decision. No more sleazy dollar-a-night flophouses, or $5 a week

YMCAs. No more telling myself I would spend big once I made it big. From now on I was going first class. The first step in my new lifestyle was to go down to the front desk and demand the finest two-bedroom suite in the house.

Pointer from the Peddler: When you make the decision to go first class, it's an incentive to work even harder to pay for it. It worked for me.

"Did you bring the order from General Foods?" I asked as soon as Bert had his coat off.

He dug it out of his briefcase, and I confirmed with my own eyes the sale of a lifetime. "One refrigerated carload of Shantung frozen bean sprouts at $4.40 a case."

While Bert was there, I phoned my partner back in Duluth.

"David, can you call those wizards at Railway Express right away, and find out what's the biggest reefer [refrigerated boxcar] they have?"

He rang back in a few minutes.

"They have one huge one. Trouble is, it's somewhere on the West Coast right now, and we can't get it for three weeks. Why do we need it, anyway?"

"Just line it up. I'll explain when I get back."

I asked Bert if he could get in touch with the General Foods buyer one more time. He took the receiver.

"Tell him we're back-ordered on the Shantung and ask if we can make delivery in three weeks."

Bert hung up from his call and smiled. "No problem, he says, as long as he gets his carload."

And what a carload it was.

When that reefer showed up in Duluth three weeks later, it was a monster. It was the biggest railroad car I had ever seen in my life. It easily held twice the normal amount of cargo. By the time it shipped, it contained 4,200 cases of frozen bean sprouts covered with enough ice and salt to send it across the Equator, let alone to New York, which was its destination.

On that single order we received a check for $18,480. At a profit of $3 a case, we cleared an astronomical $12,600. How many nights was that at the Copley in a $25 two-bedroom suite? Some 504 to be exact, or about a year and a half's worth. That's how much that order was worth.

TO EXPLAIN WHAT HAPPENED NEXT, let me relate an old grocery salesman's joke.

A customer walks into the supermarket and sees a huge display of salt. Nothing but salt, all over. Tons of it.

"Gee whiz," he mutters in amazement to the clerk who happens to be working the display. "You guys must sell a lot of salt."

The clerk stares at him and says, "As a matter of fact, we don't."

The customer is confused. "I don't understand," he says, staring at the huge display.

The clerk glances unhappily at the pile of salt.

"*We* don't sell a lot of salt. Now, the fellow who sold us this, *he* sells a lot of salt."

Well, that was the problem we created for General Foods with that huge order. We got to keep our check, but we never got another one from them. They couldn't sell our frozen bean sprouts.

And what happened at General Foods happened all over the country with our orders, big and small.

What went wrong?

The sprouts looked appetizing when they were frozen, whether in a refrigerated boxcar or in the dry ice I used for my samples. But a dramatic change took place in the cooking process. The cell structure just collapsed and they came out of the pan looking like a strand of human hair. And they were just about as tasty.

Believe it or not, we had been in such a hurry to put our Shantung brand on the market, we had never taken the time to defrost them, then cook and taste them.

What was the name of that movie a few years ago? David and I were "Dumb and Dumber."

I'd thought I was an entrepreneur (I knew that word by then). But I'd failed the first test of any entrepreneur, in any industry. Or any peddler, for that matter. I didn't have a quality product.

Yet there must be some way out of this.

Chapter 7

A Can Called
Chun King

*D*avid and I were trying to hang on to our business by supplying the fresh bushels to Ben Gee and Meadowmere and the other big-city Chinese processors who continued to gouge us because of the spoilage. We sure as hell needed another way to package the sprouts.

"What if we canned them?" I suggested.

"How do you do that?"

I had no idea.

Then I remembered a brand of canned peas called *Poplar* from my days of selling for Hancock Nelson. Those Poplar peas were packed about twenty-five miles away in a small Wisconsin town of the same name. I dialed up Poplar Canning Company and got the owner on the phone, a man by the name of Norman LaPole.

"Would you be willing to can bean sprouts?" I asked.

"Who for?"

Canning Chicken Chow Mein put Chun King on a label.

"We're the Bean Sprout Growers Association of America, in Duluth," I replied, not mentioning that the Association consisted of one Italian and one Croatian. I explained briefly the kind of product we had and its acceptance in the market. "I mean during the off-season, when you're not packing peas."

"Sure," LaPole said agreeably. "But you've got one problem."

"What's that?"

"I don't have any cans."

"No cans?"

"Yeah, it's wartime. Haven't you heard?"

Funny guy, this LaPole. But he was right.

With all the shortages of materials, especially steel, the government had put a long list of canned goods on hold for the duration. Unless it was a vital part of dinner, no canned goods could be sold. And in 1944, no one was going to argue that chop suey was essential to the American diet.

"You see any way around this problem?"

Long pause. "Tell you what," LaPole said at last. "I'll get back to you."

I thought he was giving me the brush-off. But two days later he called back. "Talked to Continental Can," LaPole informed me. "We might be able to get reject cans from them."

"Reject? What's that mean? The cans leak or something?"

"No, no," he laughed. "The cans will be fine. It's just that the metal is scratched or marred slightly. They can't use it for their regular customers. They call it 'reject plate.' "

"How much of this stuff do they have?"

"Enough to make up 500,000 cans."

"And Continental Can will sell us this reject plate which you can turn into cans we can use? Is that what you're telling me?"

"Sure, once you get government approval."

"How do I get that?"

"You need to get approval from the War Production Board in Washington."

I thanked him. A week later I made my first visit to the nation's capital. I took a cab past all those glorious monuments, walked up the stairs of an impressive government building—saluting the flags—and found myself across the desk from the director of the War Production Board, a down-to-earth gentleman named Glenn Knaub. He listened patiently as I made my case for our new canning operation. Leaving no sob story untold, I talked about all the people—especially the women supporting their families during the war effort—who would be out of work if we didn't get those cans.

I didn't say exactly how many people that was, of course. It wasn't my fault that he might have confused the Bean Sprout Growers Association of America–David and me in an office with a telephone—with a somewhat larger group such as, say, the Cranberry Growers Association of America.

I came to the point.

"Continental Can has all these reject cans that aren't doing anybody any good. Do you think we can lay our hands on them and save all these jobs?"

"Why don't I write them a letter and see?"

Well, maybe I should have settled for that and not pressed my luck. But I knew I wouldn't enjoy my trip back to Duluth wondering when this guy might get around to dictating a letter that could get us back in business.

"Look, Mr. Knaub," I said, pulling a paper out of my suit coat. "This is kind of urgent. Maybe we could call this fellow right now."

I had brought along the name and number of the regional manager for Continental Can, a Mr. Alpanalp. Knaub's secretary managed to get him on the line in Minneapolis, and we confirmed they did, indeed, have reject plate available for us.

Knaub hung up and smiled.

"Everything seems to be in order. Why don't you go home and write up your request formally? I'll approve it."

"Fine," I said. But there was no way I was going to wait that long. "See you in an hour."

I hustled back to my hotel, found a typist, and returned to Knaub's office, letter in hand, with plenty of time to spare before my self-imposed deadline of one hour. And before I had finished breathing down his neck, I talked Knaub into calling Continental Can a second time to tell them a letter was on the way authorizing the immediate release of 500,000 of those cans to the now-prestigious Bean Sprout Growers Association of America.

That was just enough for about 20,000 cases of bean sprouts, with twenty-four cans in each case. Hell, Dave and I sold those 20,000 cases in about a month.

So I called Director Glenn Knaub on the phone this time. I told him our association would go out of business without more scratched cans.

"Mr. Paulucci," he replied, "you can tell your members that I'll take care of it."

Sure enough, Director Knaub called Continental Can Company's head man in Chicago, a fellow by the name of Clay Nichols, and told him that he really should find some more scratched reject cans. Got to keep the association going.

Believe it or not, we got some five million cans before the scratching ended, and then we started getting good non-scratched cans after rationing was over.

> *Pointer from the Peddler: Image is everything. If you don't have enough clout on your own, be an association. That's one way to cut through the bureaucracy.*

Once David and I had our precious cans, I asked LaPole how much he would charge to pack our sprouts if we trucked them over to his cannery in Wisconsin. He came back with a question of his own: "What do you figure on selling a case for?"

I'd already done my homework. There were two dozen cans in a case. "I think I can get $3.60 for a case of twenty-four of those twenty-ounce cans."

"I want fifty cents a case," he said bluntly. "That'll cover my labor and overhead. You pay for the cans and all delivery charges."

Well, I wanted desperately to say we had a deal.

But what I said instead was, "I'll get back to you."

In order to survive, we needed to make, before taxes, a dollar on every case sold. Our costs, in addition to the 50 cents a case for LaPole, were about 2 cents for each can, or another 50 cents a case. Brokerage and shipping deducted yet another 60 cents. A total of $1.60 so far. That left the cost of the sprouts themselves.

And that was the monkey wrench in the works.

The workers in the back room had got the idea into their heads that we were making a killing on their bean sprouts. Pretty quickly three cents a pound had not been enough for their labor. When business was looking up, we agreed to pay six cents. When David and I got into frozen sprouts, they thought if we could afford to expand like that, we should pay even more. They bargained up to eight cents.

Two months later, they were grousing again.

By that time, we were paying about ten cents, when you figure in the mung beans and overhead, for every pound. (Just about what I had paid for my first innocent bushel in Minneapolis—so much for the savings of moving Modern Foods to Duluth lock, stock, and metal tubs.)

With about twenty pounds in a case, this meant an additional expense of $2. In all, a case was going to cost us $3.60—exactly what I thought we could sell it for.

What happened to the dollar in profit we needed to make?

It wasn't there.

For us to can the sprouts profitably, we needed to somehow cut the cost of growing them in half. Yet here were the growers asking for still more money.

It looked hopeless.

Then a funny thing happened.

In the latest round of labor negotiations, we discovered by accident the cost figures our supplier/worker/tenants had been giving us weren't entirely kosher. While charging us $10 for every hundred pounds of mung beans, they actually paid only $7. Instead of a five-pound yield for each pound of beans, their harvest was closer to seven pounds. In short, we realized we could cut our sprout costs in half and start canning them after all.

There was only one catch. We had to get rid of Ben Furata and his bunch, and grow the bean sprouts ourselves.

Now let me say right here that I believe in fair treatment of the people who work for you. I also believe in unions. A few years later, when we were running our own cannery, I not only welcomed unions, I insisted on them coming in—for reasons I'll outline later on. In all my businesses, most of the operations have been unionized—and to this day we've had not one hour of work stoppage.

But in the back room of the store on First Street, this was an example of unfair treatment of the employer by the employees. And something had to be done about it.

I started spending my evenings in the First Street building learning the finer points of the five-day growing process. Meanwhile, we ordered our own supply of 300 metal vats from a local sheet metal company and stored them in a nearby warehouse.

We were ready for a final labor showdown.

How did we know one was coming? A telegram had arrived addressed only to the Edison Building.

When our secretary opened it, we discovered quite by accident that Ben Furata had a cousin in Denver, George Oyama, who was feeding him negotiation instructions: "Tell them you must have twelve cents a pound or else threaten to quit. Be willing to settle for eleven cents, but bluff them first!"

That was "sayonara" as far as I was concerned.

Furata delivered his ultimatum: As soon as the current crop of bean sprouts were harvested (in five days), his crew was leaving unless they were granted their demand of 12 cents a pound.

"Five days, huh?" I confirmed, showing the ultimatum to David.

"That is right," Furata assured me.

"We'll get back to you," I said.

Before he was out the door, I was dictating to my secretary my own letter to Furata: "We are sorry, but we can't comply with your request. We accept your resignation and expect you to be out of the building in five days."

The reaction was total shock. They had been bluffing, of course. Now they had given themselves no choice.

Their crops were staggered so that a partial harvest occurred every day. As soon as their tubs were empty for one day, we moved ours in. On the third day they tried selling us their remaining tubs.

"No thank you. We have our own. Take them with you."

By the fifth day, all of our vats were in place. Ben Furata and his troops were gone, and I was supervising our new workers—hired at the then legal minimum wage of 50 cents an hour, believe it or not—on how to water the next wave of crops. We never missed a harvest.

With our costs in line, we began our bean sprout canning operation with Norman LaPole.

CHUN KING WAS MY FIRST LASTING BRAND NAME, except, of course, for Jeno.

I'm proud to say it's still a major brand in supermarkets all over, though it's been a long time since I've owned it.

As you might imagine, it took a great deal of thought and research to come up with that name. Here's how it happened.

Dave and I had been using the name Shantung for our bean sprouts. Horrible name. I wanted a new one.

"Dave, let's change it to Chungking," I suggested. "Has a nice sound, Oriental and impressive."

When we called the Stewart-Taylor Printing Company, they sent a salesperson—a man by the name of Marvin—who came over to our two-bit office where we were growing the sprouts.

I said to him, "Please change the labels to Chungking."

"You can't register that name," Marvin replied. "It's the name of a city in China."

"I know that. So make it two words, Chung King."

"That won't work either," he warned.

"Look, I'm busy. Drop the g and make it Chun King . . . and get the hell out of here, please."

That was the end of the research. In two minutes the matter had been settled.

And not a moment too soon.

With the war marching on, Chun King canned bean sprouts took off faster than Shuntung frozen ever had. And we were getting a steady stream of re-orders, because by this time we had figured out how to prepare the bean sprouts so that they tasted good after you cooked them. They were a huge hit.

Here's an example of how huge. On a selling trip to Boston, I stopped in to see a broker named Dan Mordecai. Dan and I called on First National Stores and the Stop & Shop chain. Spending three minutes at each place, we sold two carloads of bean sprouts.

"Dan, this is too easy," I declared after the second stop.

"What do you mean? Nothing's easy in this business."

"Naw, we're giving these sprouts away," I in-sisted. "Let's go back to your office before we do any more damage."

I called my partner in Duluth. "David, tell our sec-retary to send out a notice to all our brokers that as of *today,* the price of canned bean sprouts goes up to four dollars and forty cents."

That was the same figure we had been using for the Shantung frozen sprouts that we couldn't move with a bulldozer.

"Jeno, don't you think that might be a little high?" Dan shuddered.

"No, Dan, it ain't going to be too high. Wait and see."

My instincts were right.

And the fact that no one balked at the higher price confirmed something that I hadn't really focused on. We had the market to ourselves. There were no other suppliers of canned bean sprouts, anywhere.

I toured New England with Dan's people, and we sold more than forty carloads of canned bean sprouts at $4.40 a case. Figuring 1,000 cases to a boxcar, that trip alone netted orders for more than 40,000 cases, or about *one million* of those number-two reject cans.

As long as we delivered good value, I knew that buyers would be willing to pay the higher price. The huge orders were the proof.

We needed more cans. Clay Nichols, in charge of Continental Can's operations in the whole western half of the country, was able to come up with a steady stream of "reject plate" that lasted until long after the war was over.

By now, I was thinking of broadening the product line. I already had plans to start canning chop suey vegetables—a combination of celery, a little pimiento, a few other ingredients, and our basic bean sprouts. To meet demand, I would need a second source of sprouts, someone who might even take over the entire growing operation one day.

I stopped over to see Lennie Underdahl, whose firm, Midwest Food Dehydrators, had attempted to dehydrate bean sprouts for us. Lennie was actually the front man for a group of investors from Madison, Wisconsin. They had invested in a 400,000–square-foot building at 525 Lake Avenue South in Duluth, and their government contract for potatoes was running out.

We quickly struck a deal. David and I would supply the mung beans, and Midwest Food would grow the sprouts on a cost plus five cents a pound basis. But in order for them to get a crack at our "money machine," they also had to take off our hands what was left of the dying Shantung brand. That included the processing and our leftover inventory. Lennie's people also agreed to pack any further orders for the frozen sprouts at cost plus 50 cents a case.

Shantung was off our hands. The booming Chun King brand was rapidly becoming nationally known and accepted.

What could *possibly* go wrong?

Well . . .

Chapter 8

When Things Go Wrong

*I*n my experience as a lifelong peddler, one thing I've learned is that just when things are all going right, they're about to all go wrong.

That's when the real test comes. Do you have the fortitude, the gumption, the street smarts, to turn misfortune into fortune? All of us have to find that out about ourselves.

In the spring of 1945, Norman LaPole called me with devastating news: "I can't pack for you any more."

"What the hell are you talking about?" I'd just received a commitment for five million more cans, enough for more than 200,000 cases of 24-pack. At a profit of nearly $2 a case, I suddenly saw a lot of money going the wrong way out the door.

"I've got to pack my peas," LaPole said.

"Can't you do both?"

"No way."

"So you're going to put us out of business just like that?"

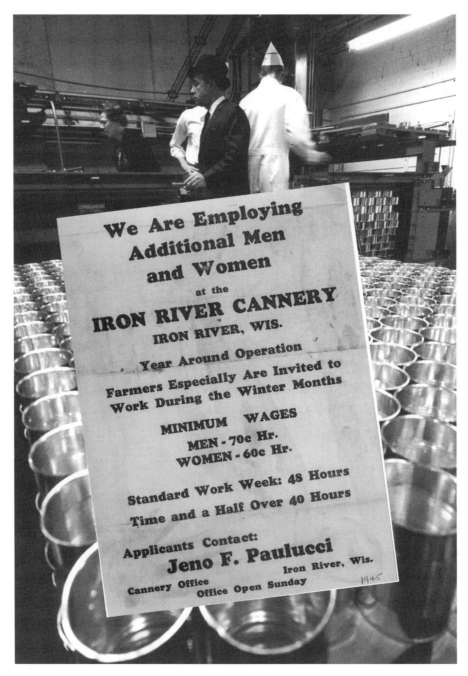

Hard-to-get cans and a new cannery were hurdles to overcome.

There was a long pause and then he said, "There's an abandoned cannery over at Iron River, about fifteen miles from here. The boiler and other things need fixing, but you could buy it for next to nothing and fix it up."

"And?"

"And I'll supply the labor to run it," he said. "Same deal—fifty cents a case."

Well, it wasn't the same deal. LaPole was improving his position considerably. We would be buying the canning plant and picking up the overhead and all the headaches that went with it. But I didn't see any other way to keep going. So for a total investment of about $100,000, we set up our own cannery operation at Iron River.

THE END OF WORLD WAR II finally came. Suddenly cans were available to everybody, including Chinese food packers, and for the first time the grandly named Bean Sprout Growers Association of America faced competition.

We soon found ourselves selling against perhaps a dozen companies across the country, most of them Oriental operations. Labels included China Beauty, Ben Gee, Min Sun, all in Chicago; Fuji out of Ohio; Jan-U-Wine on the west coast; and, of course, LaChoy owned by Beatrice Foods in Ohio, where Amish people provided the workforce. By itself, this wouldn't have been so bad, because we had a pretty good head start—if we had known what we were doing in the first place.

But it turned out we didn't, and they did.

All at once we started receiving calls from our customers, who only weeks before had been clamoring for more bean sprouts—and who were now saying, "Take them back."

"Take them back?" I exploded. "What do you mean? You bought them."

"They've turned brown. Take them back."

After some frantic phone calls of my own, I found out what I should have learned when I first talked to Norman LaPole many months before. The reject plate we were using from day one had been enamel coated. This lining was fine for some purposes but anyone in the business, I was now told, knew that for something like bean sprouts it was absolutely necessary to use a hot-dip or plain-lined (unenameled) can to which you added a citric acid tablet. The tablet reacted with the metal of the can and bleached the bean sprouts.

This was what all the other guys were doing now that regular plate was available.

And that's why their bean sprouts were staying nice and white and ours were turning brown.

Back when there was no competition, nobody cared about the color. Taste and making a buck were all that mattered, and our brown sprouts tasted just fine.

But given a choice, it was no contest. Our brown bean sprouts were just taking up space on the grocers' once-more-crowded shelves.

I got hold of LaPole and asked him how this could have happened to us.

"You must have known," I chewed him out. "Why didn't you say something?"

"What difference would it have made?" he dismissed me airily. "Scratched enamel plate was all we could get. It was that or nothing."

"So what do we do now?"

"Close up shop," he said with total lack of concern. "Forget the whole thing. You got your dough."

Then he tossed another bombshell.

"By the way," he added. "Part of that money belongs to me."

"Just what money are we talking about here?"

"Well, for starters I got inventory over here that I already packed."

More enamel-lined cans that I couldn't sell. I should have told him to screw himself.

"Okay, we'll figure something out on that. Anything else?"

"Yeah. I found out you've been using a case price of four-forty" he accused, as though he had caught me in bed with his wife.

"That's right. So?"

"Our deal was based on a case price of three-sixty. If you're making eighty cents more, I think I'm entitled to half of it. I figure you owe me forty cents on every case you sold at four-forty."

Then I did tell him to screw himself.

After all, he was just a business subcontractor who had agreed to provide a service at a fixed price. Whatever information he based that price on wasn't my responsibility. Maybe if he'd come back to me early on and said, "Hey, I'm taking a beating on this deal, can you help me out?" we might have worked something out.

But not only had this guy sweetened the pot for himself along the way, but, from where I sat, he had negligently withheld information that could have saved us from the disaster that now threatened to wipe us out. To top it all off, instead of feeling maybe a twinge of guilt and offering his help, here he was swooping in to pick our bones clean—like a vulture.

The following week the vulture showed up at our office with his faulty arithmetic to settle matters. The two of us argued back and forth all day long. I stood firm: We would pay him his 50 cents a case for the inventory left on hand. Not a penny more.

When he headed back to Wisconsin that afternoon, he had in hand a check for $25,000 as full settlement.

Good riddance, I thought.

Well, the vulture couldn't even hold up his end of the bargain long enough to drive home. Before I left for the day, the phone rang.

"I changed my mind," he announced. "The deal's off."

"What do you mean?"

"I marked your check 'null and void.' I'm mailing it back to you."

"And?"

"If you don't give me the extra forty cents a case you owe me, I'm going to sue."

"Go to hell," I said this time. And then I hung up on him.

Well, he didn't go to hell, just then. Instead, he went to court.

David and I had to hire two attorneys—the one we used in Minnesota and another certified to appear in Wisconsin, where LaPole had filed suit—were convinced we had an open and shut case, one that would never go to trial.

Well, it did go to trial, and it lasted six weeks.

Our legal wizards from Minnesota and Wisconsin were both demanding cash at the end of each week, or they wouldn't show up the following Monday. Because they were still telling us we couldn't lose, David Persha and I were foolish enough to keep paying them.

When the jury brought in its verdict, David and I were floored. Instead of upholding our claim that La-Pole, the vulture, was entitled to no more than the agreed upon $25,000, they declared a verdict against us for $64,000.

On the way out of the courtroom, I asked our lawyers what had happened. Having already pocketed $18,000 in legal fees, they shrugged their shoulders and sang a different tune from when they were telling us we couldn't lose.

"Sorry fellows," they said to David and me. "We never had a chance. This was strictly a kangaroo court."

It turned out LaPole was on the board of commissioners in the county where the suit was heard. He was also a personal friend of the judge, as well as most of the jury, as we found out later.

Things were going seriously wrong. Our financial troubles began to snowball. In addition to the $82,000 the lawsuit had cost us overall, we had to issue emergency credit memos of more than $100,000 to answer the complaints of customers who were returning our brown bean sprouts.

With nothing approaching that in cash or net worth, our only hope was to stay in business somehow until we could satisfy our creditors with future products.

I needed something to change my luck. Then it happened: I got married.

Chapter 9

One Partner for Life

*F*inancial problems are the last thing you want to have on your mind when you get married. But those kinds of problems were all too much on my mind when I finally tied the knot on February 8, 1947 with my lovely young bride, Lois Mae Trepanier.

We'd had a long and up-and-down courtship. Somehow she'd looked the other way when I'd taken her out and lit up a big cigar. But once we were together, I had a feeling that somehow things were going to work out.

It didn't *seem* that way at first. But I knew in my bones that my luck had changed. Marrying Lois was the best thing I'd ever done in my life. Was it ever!

But there were a lot of loose ends to tie up.

Having found my partner for life, it was about time to part company with my partner for business— my father figure, David Persha.

One windy afternoon, less than a month and a half after I had gotten married, our cannery in Iron River burned to the ground. The only fire truck sat in

Lois and Jeno, partners for life.

its barn twenty-five miles away with a flat tire. The inventory of canned bean sprouts, I was told, exploded like Fourth of July rockets. But this was no celebration; it was a disaster. The factory and its contents had been badly underinsured.

By this time, the stress on our partnership had taken a terrible toll.

The fire seemed to be the last straw.

We sat down together and I summed up where we stood.

"Okay, the fire has put us out of business for the time being," I stated the obvious. "We've got some insurance money coming, but we still owe the vulture. Maybe it's time to call it quits."

"You mean split up?" David asked.

"That's what I'm thinking."

David sat there and thought. But he didn't argue with me. It was an unhappy moment for both of us, but clearly one he had already considered.

"Okay, Jeno," he said when he spoke at last. "Being the older man, and the one who got you started in the first place, I think you'll agree it's only fair if I make the choice."

"What choice is that?"

"Who keeps the business, me or you?"

Undeniably, he was twenty years my senior. On top of that, I owed him a great deal in many ways.

"Okay," I said, "what do you want to do?"

"I'll buy you out."

"What's the price?"

"Well, the only money that's going to be available is the insurance proceeds from the fire. I'll pay you fifty thousand out of my share."

I nodded gloomily.

"You'll be able to pay off your fifty percent share of the sixty-four thousand we owe LaPole," he added, apparently seeing this as further incentive for me to accept the deal.

He paused and then said, "There's one thing more."

"What's that?"

"I want to keep you as part of this somehow. I want you to sell for me."

Salesman? He wanted me to go back and be a salesman?

"Sure. I'll pay you three percent on everything you sell." My face must have told him that I wasn't too keen on the idea.

"Don't you think you owe me that much, Jeno?" he pressed.

I thought about it some more and said, "Let's try it. One thing though . . ."

It was my turn to look backward and forward at the same time.

"I want the bank to guarantee that the first fifty thousand that comes from the insurance company all goes into my account."

"I see no problem with that."

"Then I'll draw up an agreement for all of us to sign. If we're all settled here, I'm going next door and get another haircut."

But before I could walk out the door, I was presented with another problem.

"Oh, I meant to tell you," David began, "I got another call from Lennie Underdahl today. He said if we don't pay him, they are going to sue."

Lost in all the other problems we were having was the fact that our relationship with Midwest Food Dehydrators had gone sour. Although I hated to admit it, this problem was my own doing. They had finally realized that I had stung them pretty good by palming off our line of Shantung frozen packages on them.

"Our contract does say that if the packaging becomes obsolete, we have to buy it back," David said, repeating back what I was sure Lennie had told him. (David never read contracts.)

"Did he say how much of the packaging they have," I asked.

"Twenty-eight thousand dollars worth."

I blew up.

"Who says the packaging is obsolete? Nobody has officially retired the product. Maybe we can come up with a different technology so the sprouts don't become tough and stringy anymore. Maybe we could . . ."

Okay, now I was completely making it up as I went along. But I didn't have any money to pay a claim. David looked worried again, the satisfaction of taking over the business already beginning to pale.

"No more lawsuits," he decreed. "We better pay him."

"No way," I said, knowing there really would be no way to pay Lennie.

"What the hell are we going to do?" David asked, throwing up his hands.

"I don't know about you, but I'm going to get that haircut."

And with that I strolled out the door.

My trip to the barber's chair turned out to be profitable.

I calmed down and during the haircut I came up with a business proposition to offer Midwest Foods. I recalled, for one thing, that when I'd first struck the deal with Lennie, it had occurred to me to include a non-compete clause in our agreement. Midwest Foods could not go into the Chinese food business themselves for five years.

After running my idea by David, we arranged for a meeting at the Hotel Duluth with Lennie Underdahl and three of his key investors from Madison, Wisconsin.

Mark Goldberg, one of those investors, spoke up first.

"We understand that you wish to settle our little disagreement, Mr. Paulucci."

I nodded, a little red-faced.

"Well, we have come a long way, and we are all ears."

I offered up my new pitch.

"I understand that you gentlemen are interested in entering the Chinese food business. Lennie, of course, has shown me the fine facility you have on Lake Avenue—all that unused capacity, as well as the know-how you picked up from us. Am I right?"

They looked at one another, hopefully, suggesting there may be some truth in my assumption that they wanted to go into Chinese food. (I had heard rumors to that effect, of course. In the barbershop.)

"But what about our non-compete agreement?" asked Glenn Roberts, a shrewd lawyer who seemed to be in charge of the investor group.

"Yes, that would seem to tie our hands fairly tightly," Goldberg agreed dryly.

"Gentlemen, I am coming to that," I said, nodding to David. "My partner and I are prepared to sell that right to compete back to you. You can go into Chinese foods yourself, tomorrow."

Interest clearly shone in their faces this time.

"How much?" Roberts asked, after the investors huddled for a minute.

"We need fifty thousand dollars cash, and a two percent royalty on sales," I declared flatly.

The third investor, Lou Paley, a man who had made his fortune as a junk dealer, spoke up. "Does this mean you'll buy the unusable Shantung stuff back from us, perhaps by deducting twenty-eight thousand from the cash payment?"

"Not exactly," I hedged.

"What do you propose, then?" Goldberg asked.

"You can keep it. If I can sell it, I'll buy it back from you at a discount." I looked right at Paley, the junk dealer, when I added, "Twenty-five cents on the dollar."

He shrugged grudging approval. After all, junk was junk.

"You mean that we'd get seven thousand dollars if you sold it all?" asked Goldberg, double-checking to see that he understood what I was offering.

"That's the deal."

They took it.

Back in our office, David and I agreed to split the $50,000 down the middle. But his congratulations on turning a potential lawsuit into a $25,000 profit for each of us only went so far. He remained skeptical about my offer to try to sell the leftover inventory.

"Who the hell would want it?" he howled. "For one thing, it only works in a Klik Lok machine, and for another, it's got the Shantung label all over it. Not exactly a household delight, as we both know."

Our patience with each other had grown a little thin, which was understandable. After all, this was another shot in the dark. Maybe our last one together. But it was also an opportunity to test one of the credos I'd begun to develop and keep in my head.

Pointer from the Peddler: The credo goes like this: "It pays to be ignorant, because when you are smart, you already know it can't be done . . . without even trying."

I put an ad in a trade magazine devoted to frozen food processing. Our secretary also typed the names and addresses of individual processors on envelopes in her spare time, and we sent copies of the ad directly to dozens of them as well. Along with the ad, we included one Shantung package, and the message: "Have x-zillion of these (the brand is yours for the taking). If interested, contact the Bean Sprout Growers Association of America."

And one day, someone did.

The call was long-distance from a fellow in Oregon who was packing frozen strawberries.

"How fast can you send me those packages?" he asked anxiously. His strawberry crop was in, and he had run out of packaging.

"You got a Klik Lok machine to run them on?" I asked, just to be sure.

"Yeah, yeah, no problem."

"What about the label?" I quizzed him. "That bother you?"

"Hell, no. I'll overwap them later. Most of my sales are institutional anyhow. I've got to get these berries out of the field. Just tell me what you want for those packages."

He sent me a sight draft for the full $28,000, payable as soon as our boxcar arrived in Oregon. We made sure it got there in a hurry, and he picked up the freight charges as well. After giving Midwest their 25 cents on the dollar, or $7,000, David and I divided up the rest.

It was the last pleasant moment of our partnership.

NOW IT WAS TIME for me to hit the road as the sales force for Chun King Sales, Inc. But I wondered how David was going to resume canning in what was now his company, after the fire.

"Don't worry about that," he assured me. "I've got Joe Bujanovich and some other people lined up. I'll be all right. You just take care of the selling."

In spite of the fire, he still had inventories of canned bean sprouts and our new chop suey vegetables in warehouses across the country. This gave him time to set up new canning lines at a building he had acquired earlier on Michigan Street. Meanwhile, he would continue to raise sprouts at the First Street location, and also introduce a third item, chow mein noodles.

This was as close to a game plan as David had for salvaging the business.

Less than three months later, I asked him to sit down with me again. By this time, he was desperately short of money. Not only had he gone through his share of the insurance money and the Shantung packaging inventory I had recovered, but also all the money one of his personal friends, the president of City National Bank, could afford to lend him.

Whose fault was this latest calamity?

Well, David, God rest his soul, had spread the word that it was Jeno's fault. He was telling everyone who would listen that I had taken all of his "working capital." He was referring, of course, to the $50,000 insurance money I had made sure I received off the top, as payment for my share of the business. In doing so, I had pulled a fast one on him, he said, and left him broke. It was agonizing to hear these public accusations after all we had been through together.

But it was also my chance.

"Look, you're having trouble making a go of it," I said frankly. "How about if I buy *you* out this time?"

He smirked at this. Still, he asked, "How much can you pay?"

"I'll give you the same fifty thousand dollars you gave me . . ." I proposed. Except that I wasn't going to make his mistake. " . . . only I won't pay it up front."

"What do you mean?"

"I'll pay you for the business as I sell off the inventory. I will give you seventy-five percent of the selling price for each item as I get rid of it."

David shook his head, and smiled in spite of himself.

"Sometimes, Jeno, I think I taught you too well."

The old dog wanted to show me he still knew a trick or two.

"Tell you what," he countered. "In addition to the seventy-five percent of the selling price, give me a one percent royalty on sales—just like Midwest Dehydrators agreed to pay us. Then we've got a deal."

"They're paying two percent," I reminded him, making sure we had our numbers straight.

"For you, old friend, one percent," he laughed.

And because he had been my partner through thick and mostly thin—without him, I reminded myself, I would never have gotten into bean sprouts in the first place—I went along with the 1 percent.

"Okay," I agreed. "If I make it, you collect. If I go under, you don't."

And on that basis, we signed the necessary papers and I then formed the Chun King Corporation.

In that May of 1949, I became my own boss forever.

And damn near gave away half the company, almost at the start.

LIKE DAVID BEFORE ME, I was continually short of working capital. I needed a loan, and went to an attorney named Herschel Fryberger at one of the town's largest law firms. I told him I was willing to sell a half-interest in my company for $25,000.

"What kind of business did you say you were in?" he asked, clearing his throat noisily when I had finished. "Some kind of Japanese food?"

"Chinese."

He stared out his window—an impressive view that took in the entire harbor. His voice rang out bold and confident. "A little free advice, son. This is timber and iron ore country. Shipping country. That Japanese crap doesn't belong here. No money in it. None at all."

With that, Herschel Fryberger turned down the chance to own half of Chun King Corporation. And while sinking back into his overstuffed chair, he lost the opportunity for a lousy $25,000 to take home half of the $63 million in cash I sold it for less than twenty years later.

His arrogance woke me up, at least. I decided then and there I wasn't going to take on another partner ever again.

I'd have to get my $25,000 some other way.

It didn't seem that way at the time, but without a doubt, being turned down on my offer to sell half the business was another stroke of that good luck that every entrepreneur must have. I did scare up the twenty-five grand I needed. And I did know, in my heart, that I was going to be successful.

Part Two

Building a Business—
And Selling It

To be a successful entrepreneur, you have to start with a quality product (and not enough people do). Then you have to give good value for what you charge (and not enough people do that either). And after that—work hard, and then work even harder. If you enjoy what you do, and you're committed to it, you won't mind the hard work. You'll love it.

But that's not enough. Sweat is no substitute for brains. You also have to find a way of standing out, running your business differently from everyone else. Zigging where others zag. Eventually you'll build the business of your dreams—which is time to think about selling it and going on to something else.

Jeno's Credo:
I'm not suited to be
involved in big
businesses . . . even
when I own 'em.

*Michelina advised Jeno to "season up" his products,
and Chun King prospered.*

Chapter 10

A New Home for a New Business

*I*n the late 1940s, I found a business home—for then and for now.

I had always admired that sturdy four-story brick building at 525 Lake Avenue South in Duluth. It sits right on the canal that connects Duluth Harbor with the western tip of Lake Superior. Lake Avenue itself crosses the canal onto Minnesota Point by means of an aerial-lift bridge that rises into the air every time an iron ore or grain cargo ship passes through. The harbormaster stops traffic in both directions and the bridge soars into the air until the boat has passed. Then it's lowered back into place.

This first time I saw this place was many years earlier, as a toddler, when I was taken on a trip from the Iron Range down the steep slopes of Duluth. I'd looked around at the busy harbor and leaned too far over the wall. An iron ore carrier was coming through and blasted its horn, scaring me so much I almost jumped into the water twenty feet below. I had to be yanked back to keep from drowning.

Now it seemed to me that 525 Lake Avenue South was the perfect place to set up shop for the Chun King Corporation, which was also in some danger of drowning at the time.

In Duluth-Superior's heyday as a distribution center, the 400,000–square-foot building had been the home of the world's largest wholesale grocer, Stone Ordean Wells. In 1947, after being picked up for a bargain $25,000, it was the headquarters for Lenny's Foods, formerly known as Midwest Food Dehydrators.

Thanks to my bright idea of selling back the right to compete with Chun King, the premises were once again humming day and night.

Lennie Underdahl's backers in Madison, Wisconsin, had invested hundreds of thousands of dollars in canning lines and huge kettles, special bakery equipment for the noodles, bottling facilities for the soy sauce and even tank cars that carried soy sauce up to the railroad siding in back. They had their own quality line of Chinese ingredients up to and including their own mushrooms, which they raised in soil fertilized with horse manure, in the dark up on the top floor.

And all this was taking place right before my eyes. I had rented space inside my archrival's building. My office was a tiny cubicle in a back corner. At 75 cents a sheet from the local Superwood Company, I'd put up walls made of reject wallboard. The entire office set me back $25, nails included.

Unlike my landlords, I had only a single item to peddle: chicken chow mein. And my shoestring processing operation was perhaps even more low rent.

I had come upon a beat-up quonset hut eighty miles away in the Minnesota lumbering town of Grand Rapids. The building housed equipment left over from a failed attempt to can rutabagas. Its chief advantage was that we could fire the steam boilers six, sometimes seven days a week, without paying for fuel. For 50 cents an hour around the clock a Welshman and his son shoveled the free wood chips from a neighboring paper mill.

All I packed each day were 15-ounce cans of chicken chow mein. Jim Bingham and my friend and brother-in-law Kelly Cardiff ran the plant, Chuck Vojacek ran the line, and I'd go out selling. We packed what I could sell, which averaged about 300 to 500 cases of 24 15-ounce cans a day. I was making about a dollar a case profit, which wasn't too bad, considering labor was still 50 cents an hour.

Each night the pack of 300 to 500 cases would be trucked to Duluth. I'd drive sometimes; other times Kelly would drive down those hills of Duluth, always praying that the brakes would hold. I still have the truck—a cab-over-engine Dodge—and it still runs great after sixty years.

That's how Chun King started. It was a struggle every day. Oftentimes I'd think back to the days of Hancock and the money I was making—carefree as hell and drunker yet.

But now I was married to that wonderful woman, Lois, and I had responsibilities. What a change! She sure straightened me out. Thanks all over again, Lois!

As always, my first concern was a quality product, with a difference. Earlier, during the war, I'd experimented in our Iron River, Wisconsin, plant with a formula for packing a beef-style and chicken-style chow mein. If everything was in proportion, the chow mein poured right out of the can. If not, it slid out of the can and stood on end like jellied cranberry sauce. We had to dump so much product that we abandoned the line altogether.

Now I faced the same problem with Chun King chicken chow mein.

So I turned to the best chef I knew—my mother.

"Jeno," she said, after tasting some recipes that came out of whatever cookbook I could find, "remember when we used to have people over for dinner who were not Italian? For them, I would always season *down*. But for this Chinese food, we have to season *up*. Give it some flavor."

Michelina's advice to add spices and seasonings—and lots of chicken broth and garlic, of course—became the strength of the formula for our chow mein. Later on, she did the same thing for chow mein noodles, using fresh whole eggs and a special leavening in the dough that had made her Italian pastry so special at home.

Now all I had to do was make sure that the formula didn't change on the processing line.

And, of course, it did.

I'd come back to Grand Rapids every other week, once my selling trips were done, only to find that somebody thought he or she could improve on the *Mona Lisa* by adding more chicken, or could save me money by using less. I guess people can't help but try to tinker with success, but every time they did, the product did not come out to my standards of Quality First, Cost Second.

I tried reasoning with people, explaining that the formula worked, so there was no need to change it. But still they kept altering it.

Finally, I took to yelling.

"Don't do me any favors!" I ranted and raved. "Stick to the formula!"

When I was there, I began to taste the product that came off the line every few hours. When my mother was there, she did the same thing. It was a daily ritual. In that way, we controlled the quality.

At the same time, I kept a close watch on my costs.

One method—a trick from my old partner David Persha—was to tip over the garbage can first thing in the morning to see how many fresh ingredients we were throwing away.

And I kept records. Did I keep records!

Every Thursday I'd disappear in the afternoon—sometimes the evening—and spend three hours or more analyzing cost sheets that covered everything. No computers needed. Basic arithmetic would tell me how much it cost to produce each case or can. My key number was gross profit margin. If something was eating into our margins, I took care of it at once.

As a result, I turned a profit at Grand Rapids from day one. And that's how, slowly but steadily, I began to pay off my bills.

Pointer from the Peddler: The devil is in the details. Nowadays they call it micromanagement. Call it what you will, until your company is large enough, you yourself must keep track of everything—quality control, costs, everything. And after you're a big, successful enterprise, keep tipping that "garbage can" over now and then. You never know what it's going to tell you.

MEANWHILE, FROM MY PLYWOOD OFFICE at 525 Lake Avenue South, I watched the fortunes of Lenny's Foods.

They had damn near filled that 400,000 square feet with canned Chinese foods under the Yu Sing label. Incidentally, Yu Sing in Chinese means Bright Success. It wasn't a bright success for the seven investors from Madison, who owned the company and the building, but it was for me (and Yu Sing is a brand name I use to this day).

Their trouble was that although they knew how to can Chinese foods—vegetables, chow mein noodles, and a chicken chow mein that wasn't as good as mine, but was okay to sell—they didn't have a clue as to how to sell them. Selling was my long suit, so to speak. I was the peddler who packed only what I could sell.

They had more than 250,000 cases of 15-ounce cans packed and stored in that building; an investment of more than $500,000 plus all the canning equipment they owned (not leased, like I did).

Pretty soon, they asked me to buy them out lock, stock, and barrel. They gave up. I ended up paying them 25 cents on the dollar or 50 cents a case, and I paid them for the product as I sold it—not before—picking up more than $500,000 worth of inventory with no up front investment whatsoever.

All I did was run their cans with the Yu Sing label on them through the labeling machine and put a Chun King label right over theirs, and then sell and ship it all over the country. I was really in business. I also leased their canning equipment and space on Lake Avenue South, started packing my Chun King products, and left the Grand Rapids quonset hut.

So I could take comfort in having become a real Chinese food packer with my own brand and my own full product line. But I was forced to think constantly about money I didn't have.

Out selling or at the office at four A.M., I rationed my time. When salesmen would come to call, I refused to gab with them, refused to spend thirty minutes bringing each other up to date about the family and so forth. Many salesmen think that way; I don't. Business is business. I didn't go to lunch with salesmen or customers then and I don't do it now. I won't spend two hours with someone to do ten minutes of business.

In fact, I'd keep my hat on in the office to let people know I was in a hurry, maybe just getting ready to go out. And I even put up a sign in my office that was one of my earliest Credos: I'm busy, you're busy—let's make it quick.

And there was one regular visitor I had no time for at all.

Norman LaPole. Remember Norman—the canner who had won a judgment from David Persha and me for $64,000? This tall, angly fellow, who looked like a caricature, a vulture-version of Abraham Lincoln, would show up at my office once a week to collect.

I was paying him $500 a week, plus interest, for as long as it took to retire my half of the debt (David, with assets of his own, had already covered his $32,000 share).

I went through hell to scrape up the money for those payments. The Duluth bankers continued to treat me as though I had the plague. My business remained so hand-to-mouth that I got to know exactly how long it took for a check to go from Duluth to Kokomo or wherever and back, so I could squeeze the last nickel out of my account.

If I was caught short, I would dream up sales and borrow against the face value of the invoices. I'd call up the broker, or an established customer, and beg, "Will you please take this order? If you change your mind and want to cancel tomorrow, that will be fine." In the interim, I would borrow against the supposed order.

"Well, if it helps you any," they'd oftentimes agree, and also would take the shipment.

But still it wasn't enough.

Before long I had to hock everything my wife and I owned. Every stick of furniture in our apartment. Everything except her wedding ring. (She volunteered it on many occasions, but there was no way I was going to let her do that.)

I went to City National Bank on Superior Street. There I met a banker in charge by the name of Herman Matzke, and a Mr. William Gray.

Bill was a nice guy, but Herman Matzke was a tough, short-sighted asshole, in my opinion . . . my apologies to his heirs.

I had to ask Messrs. Matzke and Gray for a $5,000 loan.

Yes, a lousy $5,000!

You'd think I had asked for the bank charter, the way Matzke took off.

He got real personal.

"You want a five thousand dollar loan from us? What do you know about business? Nothing! You come from the iron mines. Why don't you go back to the mines?"

That son of a bitch really degraded me, and my family as well.

Of course, he was one of the elite of Duluth—called the Kitchi Gammi Club—who thought anyone with a vowel ending his name was either a crook, an idiot, or useless.

A digression: Today I personally own eight banks in the Duluth area. My president, David Gaddie, who's a great financial man, follows my policy of taking care of the little guy or woman. One day not long ago I was asked to do a TV commercial for my banks.

"Sure," I said. "Here's what I'd like to say:

> *"Hello, I'm Jeno.*
> *"Folks, you know me. To tell you the truth, I never liked bankers. But now I am one, so why don't you do business with Republic Banks? We will treat you right, not like those other jerks."*

My president declined my offer, diplomatically. "Thanks anyway, Jeno. That might be a little too drastic." So I didn't do any commercials, but that distaste for Matzke-type bankers lives with me to this day.

I told Mr. Matzke to go to hell and I got the $5,000 loan from Oscar Schultz, who was president of a small state bank in Duluth. I've never forgotten his name. Oscar had come from Moose Lake, Minnesota, where loans are made to farmers for cows and farm supplies. He had no compunction about loaning me the $5,000, especially when David Persha's dear friend and later mine, Judge Royal Bouschor, endorsed my note.

Sometimes, when LaPole stopped by, I couldn't pay the full $500. I had to ask him to settle instead for $250 or $200 and then watch his lanky form stomp out of my plywood quarters, grumbling to himself about the nerve of some people.

One day I'd had enough and hollered after him, "You know, you weren't entitled to that sixty-four thousand dollars in the first place. Hell, you should be paying us for all those 'rejected' cans of bean sprouts."

The vulture turned and laughed in my face.

"So what?" he smirked, waving my check. "Make sure you keep up, or I'll take this Chun King business, too."

Even though I still owed him more than $25,000, I said to him, loud and clear, "Okay, you crooked son of a bitch. I'll get the money and pay you off as agreed, if not sooner, so you don't get all that interest you're charging me.

"But you know what? I'm going to make this promise: I'm going to break you. In a few years you'll be bankrupt. Belly up. How I'm going to do it, I don't know yet.

"But believe me, it will come to pass in a few years." *And it did, in spades!*

He let out another belly laugh, and went on his way.

But LaPole wasn't the only fox still feeding in the hen house.

After buying back the business from David Persha, I stopped by his Michigan Street building to remove the canning equipment, which was included in the buyout. Each piece seemed to be individually numbered with fresh paint, and I asked Joe Bujanovich, who turned everything over to me, what the numbers meant.

"Nothing," he grumbled, looking a little sheepish.

"What do you mean 'nothing'?"

"Well, it shows where each piece goes," he admitted.

"You mean there's a blueprint that goes with this stuff? Maybe I ought to have it to help me set up."

"There's not exactly a blueprint," Joe said, getting vague again. "I mean it wouldn't help you."

"Why not?"

"Because it shows where everything goes in *this* building."

"Oh. Who asked you to do that?"

"Mr. Persha."

Now why go to all that trouble, I wondered. Unless he expected to get it all back someday. It didn't look like my old friend was rooting very hard for me.

Other signs bothered me as well.

I heard that a Wisconsin fire marshal was investigating the Iron River cannery fire. The rumor had me suspected of arson. Nothing came of it, of course, but who cared enough to stir up that old pot?

Next Les Carlson, my accountant, called to say he had just been contacted by the fraud division of the Internal Revenue Service. "They want to examine the books."

"Fraud division?" I exploded. "What are they after me for?"

"Somebody must have filed a complaint," he said. "Otherwise these special guys wouldn't be called in."

"Did they mention who might have called them?" I asked, my suspicions growing.

"Well, they never revealed a source." Les fell silent before adding, "But obviously it would have to be someone who knows your affairs pretty well."

The tax investigation turned out to be an ordeal all by itself.

Just before the big showdown with the IRS agents, I stopped for a cup of coffee at the Zelda Inn and figured out on a single napkin all the taxes I would owe during the current year. It was something like $13,000. But the money wasn't due yet.

The meeting took place in the office of a special tax accountant Les had brought in to look out for my interests. The three IRS people, including a man-and-woman team from this special division I had never known existed, were hard as nails. Their questions took up the rest of the day and most of the next. All the time I kept waving my white napkin that said $13,000 and not a penny more.

Well, I was wrong.

When I finally received my tax bill for the year, it was for $13,000 *and one hundred dollars.*

Having received the tip, the IRS had little choice but to make the investigation. I had no quarrel with them. It didn't help, though, to receive another bill for $13,000 from the special tax accountants.

Before I knew it, another government agent visited me.

"I'm here to enforce the Walsh-Healy Act," he announced.

"Fine. What the hell is that?"

It turned out to be an obscure federal regulation requiring any workers involved in a government contract during the war to be paid time-and-a-half for anything beyond forty hours a week. Had nothing to do with me, I thought. I had a union contract for forty-eight hours at straight time, and I wasn't a government contractor.

"But didn't you also utilize the services of Midwest Food Dehydrators, who were, at the time, government contractors?"

He had to be referring to our last-minute deal with Lennie Underdahl to raise bean sprouts for us.

"Who told you that?" I demanded, my suspicions rising to the boiling point.

"I'm not at liberty to say."

Another few weeks of expensive accounting maneuvers followed. In a result I never understood, I ended up owing my so-called ex-employees $15,000.

Another bill on the pile.

Soon I didn't have to wonder any longer who had it in for my struggling Chun King business.

My brokers, who knew David Persha as well as they knew me, began to receive calls from him. He was giving them orders as if he were still in charge, telling them not to release the warehouse inventory to my customers and other such nonsense. After hearing one thing from me and another from Persha, the poor brokers didn't know which way to turn.

Finally, I got a call from a wholesaler in St. Louis who had been with us from the beginning.

"Hell, I don't need two loony people like you and David," he told me flat out. "We're dropping your account."

I hung up, and was out of my chair like a shot. This guy was right. Even in the old days the two of us had both acted nuts at times, but never like this. I caught up with Persha at his office on Michigan Street, where he was probably waiting to get his canning equipment back.

"You son of a bitch!" I cried, yanking him out of his chair by the throat. "I'm going to kill you if this crap doesn't stop!"

David turned white.

"No, dying would be too good for you," I said, letting him go.

He was so scared he couldn't talk.

"And I'm not going to jail for murder on top of everything else I've been through."

Before I stormed out, however, I did threaten to break him in two if his crazy vendetta didn't stop.

By the time I got back to my office, I had calmed down enough to call up his attorney, Thorwald Hansen. I was thoroughly ashamed at how badly things had gone between David and me. I said I wanted to settle this thing once and for all. My terms to get David off my back were straightforward: "I'll pay an additional fifty thousand over five years—ten thousand dollars a year with no interest. But he's got to waive his one percent royalty. That's it. He's out of it."

Hansen's counter offer was $75,000 and 0.5 percent royalty.

Well, the three of us finally sat down together. (I kept my hands to myself this time.)

Looking across at David, I could see he still thought of himself as a deal maker.

"What do you want the royalty for?" I demanded. "Don't you think I'm going to go broke? Isn't that what you wanted?"

He still couldn't talk to me.

"Take the seventy-five thousand dollars," I insisted. "But no royalty."

David Persha took the money.

In fact he and his wife Mary packed up and moved to Houston, Texas. Like the banker Herschel Fryberger, David—my old friend and partner—just walked away from a substantial future annuity.

Good riddance, I thought. Yet I still loved the guy as my mentor and, years later, my friend again.

SO THE BILLS DID GET PAID, and the business became prosperous. Not all that long afterward, I was able to buy that 400,000–square-foot prime location as my new home, 525 Lake Avenue South, for $125,000. I said goodbye to the quonset hut in Grand Rapids.

One of my two main offices today is in that same building. I'm sitting there as I write this. My office is a bit more comfortable than the plywood cubicle, but it's not really plush because I don't believe in plush.

Also, I don't believe in needless expense. It's not enough to have a quality product. You also need to watch your costs at all times, so that you can be the low-cost producer in whatever industry you're in, and still produce a better quality product than your competitors, *with value.* That's what business is all about.

Coming up are a couple of examples of how that was done.

Pointer from the Peddler: There are going to be times when the walls seem to be crashing around you. But if you've got a business you believe in, hang in there. Do whatever you have to do to survive. But don't hock your wife's wedding ring; that's bad luck.

Chapter 11

Slicing Costs Off Celery Stalks

While I was building the business, I decided that costs were made to be cut. You've got to have high quality; that's always number one. But if you use your imagination—and you're willing to take a risk— you can find a way to maintain *high* quality at *low* cost. Here's an example involving that humble vegetable, the celery, staple of all Oriental foods (the chicken wings and cheese dip came later).

The story starts with water chestnuts. In the days of the Bean Sprout Growers Association of America, I was contacted by a fellow by the name of James Banks, in Winter Park, Florida. He said he could grow water chestnuts there in Winter Park (on land that today is filled with multimillion-dollar homes).

I thought water chestnuts fresh from Florida would go great with our sales of fresh bean sprouts. So I came to Florida in 1944 for the first time and met Jim Banks at an Orlando airport, Herndon it was called, much smaller than the present Orlando

Harvesting an advantage in "the celery capital of the world," Sanford, Florida.

International Airport. I was disturbed by the *Whites Only* signs on some of the toilet doors; *Colored Only* on others. I looked for a sign on another restroom that said *Dirty Dagos.*

What the hell. Jim Banks seemed to have a going operation. We made a deal.

But after a while, the labor to cut off the hard shells was getting out of hand.

ON ANOTHER TRIP TO FLORIDA, I told Jim Banks that I didn't think our arrangement was going to work out. Being he was a helluva nice guy, he said, "Jeno, as long as you're here, have you ever been to a celery packing plant?"

I said no, but I'd sure like to visit one, being I was beginning to use a lot of fresh celery from California for the Chun King canned Chinese foods. In fact, it was my most expensive ingredient—using about twelve pounds for an average case of twenty-four cans of chow mein or chop suey vegetables.

At that time, celery from California came fifty pounds fresh to the crate at an average cost of $5 per crate or 10 cents a pound. But after we had the leaves and butt end trimmed off, we ended up with about thirty pounds or a net cost of about 17 cents per pound and $2 per case of twenty-four-pack.

So sure, I was interested in a celery packing plant in Florida. Was it far away from Winter Park?

"Hell no," he answered. "It's about ten miles away in Sanford, which is the celery capital of the world."

Today Sanford is the home of Paulucci International, my other executive headquarters (the first one is at 525 Lake Avenue South in Duluth), and near the new city my family built at Heathrow. It's wonderful country, full of lakes and rolling hills and trees—a kind of southern version of northern Minnesota.

But the only celery you'll find in Sanford is at the produce counter in the supermarkets. The growing is done to the south, in the Belle Glade area around Lake Okeechobee.

In those days, Florida grew a Pascal celery, which is a light green color. California grew a Golden celery which was more accepted by consumers. Now it's just the opposite; but back in the middle to late 1940s, Pascal celery was second best.

All my competitors in the canned Chinese food business were using California Golden celery, same as I was doing, at a cost trimmed to yield of about 15 to 17 cents a pound.

If I could save even a penny a pound, it meant 12 cents a case of every twenty-four cans of my products. So I was very interested in seeing this plant.

Jim Banks drove me to the Chase Company plant and we parked in the rear of the building. When we got out of the car, I noticed an open top truck backed up to a rear door of the packing plant. There was a continuous conveyor belt emptying nice large single stalks of celery into the box of the truck.

I climbed up the truck body and looked in. There were beautiful stalks of celery in that truck with more and more coming. I asked Jim Banks if there was by any chance a chop suey packer in the area. He said he didn't know, but that we should ask the foreman, Joe Wolf.

"Mr. Wolf," I said, after we were introduced, "where is all that nice celery going?"

"Oh, that's rejects."

"Rejects, hell!" I said. "That's fresher than fresh."

Joe answered, "Mr. Paulucci, we call them rejects, but actually they're the extra stalks we have to trim off. You see, when the celery comes out of the field, it's in large bundles. Maybe two to three dozen to a fifty-pound crate. But when we get orders for small sizes—four to six dozen to a crate—we just strip off those stalks and feed them to the cattle."

By this time I'm seeing dollars bills—thousands of them—floating by my eyes.

"Joe," I said, "to hell with this Mr. Paulucci and Mr. Wolf stuff." (We later became good friends.) "How do I go about buying these stalks from you? I need them more than the cattle do!"

Joe said, "Why don't you go see Mr. Billy Leffler, the president of the Chase Company. His office is right in downtown Sanford."

So I thanked Joe and asked Jim Banks to please take me to the Chase offices so I could meet Billy Leffler. The offices were just down the street from my present Paulucci International headquarters building. (Little did I realize that at the time. Never was much of a psychic.)

Jim waited for me outside as I went in and introduced myself to a receptionist.

"Hello, I'm Jeno F. Paulucci, from Duluth, Minnesota."

"What do you want?" she asked this strange-looking Yankee.

"I'd like to see Mr. Billy Leffler."

"Do you have any appointment? Mr. Leffler is very busy."

Busy, hell, I thought. That must be him in that glass caged office, looking out the window.

"Look, madam," I said, "I'm from Duluth, Minnesota, and I have to see Mr. Leffler now." I said it loud enough so Billy Leffler could hear me.

Sure enough, he turned from the window, came to the door, and said, "I'm Leffler. What are you looking for?"

"I'm sorry to take up your time unannounced, Mr. Leffler, but I just had to see you. I have good news for you! I'll buy all your celery strippings right at your door and you won't have to haul them to the garbage.

"I'm prepared to pay you ten dollars a ton."

I was thinking quickly to myself. That's half a cent a pound. I can have my people put 50 pounds in a wood crate that I could buy for 25 cents. That totals 50 cents. Shipping 500 cases in a refrigerated truck in those days was 25 cents a mile or $500 for the 2,000 miles to Duluth.

That would come to $1.50 a crate or 3 cents a pound. With a 60 percent yield after trimming leaves, my cost for the celery was going to be 5 cents a pound . . . not 15 cents or 17 cents for celery I was getting from California. In other words, a savings of 10 cents to 12 cents a pound, or $1.20 to $1.44 a case of twenty-four-pack chop suey vegetables.

Billy Leffler looked away, bored, and said, "Not interested." He closed his glass-cage door in my face and went back to his window.

Bullshit, I said to myself. I'll see this guy again.

I went back to Duluth and thought about it. Hell, I thought, I know what to do. I'll have celery cutters, washers, and baggers built on a flatbed thirty-foot trailer. I'll have it all wired so all we have to do is drive the trailer to the celery wash-house and connect to a water hose and electric power. I'll cut the leaves off, dice the celery into half-inch cuts, wash it down, put it in hundred-pound mesh cabbage bags (only 30 cents each), and then put the hundred-pound bags of diced celery in layers on a refrigerated semi and ship them to Duluth for $500 freight.

Then even if I pay Chase double the $10 a ton— $20—my cost for a hundred pounds will be one cent per pound—but 100 percent yield because it will all be cut up at the site.

My mesh bag will be .003 cents per pound and my freight, with a 30,000 pound load of celery all diced, will be .017 cents per pound. So the total delivered Duluth cost would be 3 cents a pound . . . a savings of 12 cents to 14 cents a pound or $1.44 to $1.68 a case for twenty-four cans of Chun King chop suey vegetables.

How could I lose? Only if Billy Leffler said no again. If he did, I could try another nearby grower I'd learned of, called Duda and Sons.

What was my gamble? Maybe $10,000 at most for the trailer, equipment and all.

And my possible gain? At least a dollar a case lower cost than any of my competitors, so I could make a better quality line of Chinese foods and yet possibly make 50 cents a case more profit. If I could pull this off, the real extra profit was going to be in the millions!

Well worth the gamble.

THE PAULUCCI FAMILY WENT TO WORK. My sister Liz and her husband Joe Scinocca drove the truck and trailer to Sanford. I met them, and we took it to Mr. Leffler's office and parked it outside. We had a canvas tarp over all the equipment.

I went into the office and presented myself again to the gracious receptionist. "Do you remember me? I've got to see Mr. Leffler."

She pointed to his door, figuring I'd get it slammed in my face again.

"Hello, Mr. Leffler. I'm Jeno. Remember me? Would you please come outside? I'd like to show you something."

To get rid of me, and to satisfy his curiosity about that big canvas-covered thirty-foot trailer outside the window, he came out.

"Look what I did, Mr. Leffler, to make it easier for you and more profitable."

We pulled back the canvas and I said, "Now all I have to do is back this up to the rear door of your packing plant and plug into your water and power, and I'll take all your strippings and pay you double at twenty bucks a ton. Sound like a good deal for you?"

Billy Leffler looked at me and said, "You mean after I told you I was not interested you went back to Duluth and did all this? You must be either crazy or a genius." And he made a quick decision. "Okay, I'll sell you the strippings but you've got to pay for the power. The water is free."

That's how I started a new corporation called Florida Fresh, Inc.

As our Chun King volume went up to 5 million cases of twenty-four-pack per year, we realized real extra profit of $2.5 million a year and a better product all the time. More water chestnuts, more bamboo shoots, and more chicken in the chicken chow mein, all adding quality and value.

That's how I beat my competitors in the Chinese food game. None of them ever woke up to what my "edge" was. They went broke one after another, except for LaChoy, which, as I mentioned before, was owned by the conglomerate Beatrice Foods in those days.

Florida Fresh eventually was renamed Central Produce & Equipment, Inc. We kept buying celery from Chase Company and also Duda and Sons (today the largest produce grower in Florida), and selling it not only to Chun King but to other food processors as well. After some fifty years, we're buying strippings all over Florida and even from the Buena Vista area of California.

As I've said, you've got to find ways to zig when your competitors continue to zag. Buying Florida celery strippings was my zig. Besides that, Lois and I liked Sanford so much we made it our legal residence and spent most of the year in Florida, returning to Duluth during the summer months. Some people go to Florida to retire. We went there to start a new life.

WHILE WE'RE ON THE SUBJECT OF COST-CUTTING, let me mention a couple of other "zigs" that turned out to be right on the money.

As I was building Chun King, I got more and more visits from salesmen with cans, shipping cases, and labels to sell, plus seasoning, chicken, and other raw materials. They worked for brokerage firms in the Twin Cities, Milwaukee, or Chicago.

I thought to myself: Hey, these guys get paid a salary plus travel expenses, and their broker companies make money on top of all that on what they sell to me.

Besides that, the manufacturers that those commission brokers represent store their products and pay storage and cartage expense before I receive my order at Chun King.

Hell, I thought, I'm going to eliminate all that extra expense—the brokerage commissions, the storage cost, and the freight expense from storage to me.

How?

Easy. In 1947, I set up a firm called United Brokerage Company. I contacted all the manufacturers currently being represented by the brokers and told them, "If you want to sell to me, please appoint United Brokerage Company at 525 Lake Avenue South in Duluth, attention Carl Frederickson [my Chun King accountant], and they will represent you for a 5 percent commission."

I also informed them that there would be no need to store merchandise I bought from them. They could ship direct to me. "I'll store it and charge you the normal storage and freight charges you are presently paying."

Hell, it was a license to print money and I sure was happy with the results! I went merrily along, invoicing manufacturers for brokerage, warehouse, and freight charges. The manufacturers had no choice; they knew I could get others sources for the goods. It was either comply or goodbye.

After about five years, I got tired of the complaining from the cut-out middlemen, the brokerage community, so I gave United Brokerage Company to a friend and former employee, Stanley Laskowski.

Stan made a great success of it, with his fine family involved, and has offices today in Duluth and Minneapolis. He sells mostly to wholesalers and retailers and represents my Michelina's and Yu Sing brands also.

But it was fun while it lasted and a helluva profit center, too!

ANOTHER COST CENTER THAT NEEDED ATTENTION was freight. After all, Duluth is about 500 miles north of Chicago. At the 25 cents a mile it cost to rent a semi and driver (today it's close to $1.50) I was paying $250 more in freight charges round trip than my Chinese food competitors in Illinois and Ohio.

A shipment of 1,000 cases, about a truckload, was costing me 25 cents a case more than it did my competition. If I used a contract common carrier, regulated by the Interstate Commerce Commission, the cost was double or 50 cents more.

When you're shipping five million cases a year, that adds up to real money as a freight disadvantage.

By 1952, I decided the time had come to find a way either to cut my freight costs—both on raw materials to Duluth and shipments out of Duluth—or move out of there.

I didn't want to move out of Duluth. So I started my own fleet of Fruehauf-made semi-trailers and Mack trucks, which ended up costing me 20 cents a mile. But I'd also bring back raw materials for myself and for others. So through this new operation—called the Orient Express Trucking Fleet—I was able to compete and overcome freight disadvantages on shipments all over the United States and into Canada.

The Orient Express grew and grew until I had about fifty of those rigs—thirty to forty foot—when I finally sold the fleet along with Chun King itself.

Pointer from the Peddler: Take in more than you pay out. Do the arithmetic. It's that simple.

Chapter 12

Sometimes You've Gotta Bite the . . . What?

When you're backed into a corner, with no way out, they say you've just got to bite the bullet. In my case, it wasn't a bullet, but a . . . But let's not get ahead of the story.

In the fall of 1948, I was busy trying to be everywhere at once and keep Chun King, my own first company, going. On top of that, my wife Lois was due to give birth at any moment to our first child.

And where was I? Close at hand, like any decent dad-to-be?

No, I was in *Albuquerque, New Mexico.*

I was flying back to Duluth from a sales trip when a snowstorm blew up and they diverted us to Albuquerque. All I could do was call the office and tell them I was stranded.

In return my secretary said she had some bad news.

"Is Lois all right?" I croaked into the phone.

I *knew* I should have called her first.

A product's proof is in the "cutting." Frequent taste tests help maintain competitive quality.

"Oh, she's fine. It's Food Fair. The broker just called. We're out."

I went into shock. Hung up and wandered outside.

The old sense of injustice returned. And the anger. How unfair it all seemed. Food Fair, which ran a chain of supermarkets on the East Coast, was our biggest account. They couldn't get LaChoy products during the war, so they had agreed to take ours instead. I had assumed they would stay with us once the war ended, or at worst let us share shelf space with LaChoy. And up until now, that's just what they'd done.

To lose such a major account was unthinkable! And what the hell was I doing in Albuquerque, anyway? I shouldn't be out selling. I should be home with my wife.

I went back inside, took a deep breath, dug out more change, and rang up the broker representing us in faraway Philadelphia.

"Jeno here. What happened to Food Fair?"

I could hear my young broker taking a deep breath of his own.

"Their buyer returned my call yesterday. He said no use bothering to come in. All they wanted to do was redeem those credit memos for Chun King. He's sorry, but they're going back to LaChoy."

"So you didn't go see this guy or anything?"

"No, he seemed to have his mind made up. I just thought you should know right away."

I fell silent.

"I'm sorry, Mr. Paulucci. Did I do something wrong?"

"No, no," I assured him. "What's this guy's name—the Food Fair buyer, I mean?"

"Harry Pripstein."

"What's he like?"

"Well, he's an older guy."

"How old might that be?"

"Well, he's got to be in his thirties, at least, Mr. Paulucci."

I sighed. An older guy, not much older than me.

"Don't close out that account yet," I said before hanging up. "And stop calling me Mr. Paulucci. I'm *Jeno!*"

I had no choice, I kept telling myself while pacing that terminal in Albuquerque, past the cheerful gift shops and check-in counters. I had to keep Food Fair. Without it, my business was certain to go under.

When the ice and snow let up and I finally got back to Duluth, I rushed to my wife's side. She was still fine, awaiting her first-born. Then I called Harry Pripstein, the "older guy" in his thirties who was the top buyer at Food Fair's Philadelphia headquarters. When I asked for a chance to prove Chun King's worth before he dumped us, he agreed to what we called in the business a *cutting.*

Here's how it works. Right there in the buyer's office, the salesman opens samples at random of both products—yours and the competitor's—and asks the buyer to taste them. On the spot, the buyer judges which has the best quality and value. In my heart I was confident ours would come out on top. I had a strategy in mind. But could I take the time to go to Philadelphia?

"Go get 'em," Lois smiled. "I'm fine."

My young broker met me at the airport.

He was a willing enough kid, but he didn't have enough experience to be much help to me in this crisis. I sent him off to Food Fair to buy all the LaChoy products we would need for the cutting, except for the LaChoy noodles. I'd brought a can of those myself, along with my can opener and samples of our own products.

At ten o'clock sharp Harry Pripstein welcomed us graciously into his office. He was every bit the down-to-earth, approachable gentleman he had sounded like on the phone.

My young broker retired to a corner, out of the line of fire.

I marched right up to Harry's desk and unpacked my canned samples. Already I was telling him how his business meant life or death to my company, and what a bang-up promotional job I could do for him because of my marketing edge over LaChoy.

"Bought their cans fresh off your own shelves this morning," I beamed at him, my future spread out between us.

I took a can opener out of my pocket and perched on the edge of a chair.

"Where do we start, Mr. Pripstein?"

"Your choice," he modestly deferred.

I decided to go for the jugular. First impressions were everything. I opened the can of LaChoy chow mein noodles I'd brought all the way from Duluth and waved it under Harry's nose.

"Rancid, I bet?"

(They'd better be, I thought to myself. I'd kept them in a special heating incubator at the office long enough to turn a mummy to dust. I wasn't exactly cheating, of course. Just accelerating what happened naturally, in my opinion, to all LaChoy's noodles on the grocer's shelf.)

A startled frown came over his face, as he looked at the LaChoy noodles which had, in fact, started to decompose. He mumbled something about the noodles still selling okay, now that they were back on the Food Fair shelves.

"Smell mine," I prodded, taking the LaChoy can out of his hand and replacing it with a can of Chun King noodles.

"Absolutely fresh. Vacuum packed. Nitrogen gas instead of air. Completely odorless. I don't know why LaChoy doesn't do this. Taste them."

He did.

"Good, huh? It's the fresh eggs."

I recited our ingredient list and dismissed theirs.

I kept cranking my can opener.

"Hey, I want to show you our bean sprouts."

I knew I was on solid ground here, after all the late nights I had spent watering those metal tubs on First Street, learning to grow them from scratch. Plus the exclusive additive we had inherited from Lennie's Foods that got rid of stringy roots. These were great bean sprouts.

"Short, plump," I pointed out, as I held one up. "Nothing like those skinny, hairy things of LaChoy's."

And all the time Harry Pripstein was nodding. Here was the man who had been all set to eliminate our business and he was eating out of the palm of my hand.

It was time to clinch the deal.

I opened the cans of Chinese vegetables. First La-Choy's and then Chun King's.

"I want you to take note now, Mr. Pripstein, who has more of those authentic Chinese ingredients, the bamboo shoots, the water chestnuts . . ."

I raised both lids.

My eyes popped. Out of the corner of my eye I saw my young broker's jaw drop.

For there right on top of all those choice vegetables in my can was . . .

One big, dead grasshopper.

Sweat broke out on my forehead. My entire life flashed before my eyes. I took a quick look over at Pripstein. He hadn't noticed the grasshopper yet, because the upturned lid of the can blocked his view.

There was only one thing to do.

"You know, Mr. Pripstein," I said smoothly, "these look so good I've just got to have some myself."

With my fingers I scooped the grasshopper up into my mouth, masking it with vegetables, and swallowed it.

"Geez, they're good," I marveled.

Steady as a rock, I held out the can. "Would you like some, sir?"

He politely waved it away.

"They really do look good though, Jeno."

I breathed a sigh of relief.

Harry Pripstein took a liking to me then and there, being I was young and energetic (only twenty-nine years old) and because I liked my products so much I ate them myself.

"I'm not going to throw LaChoy out," he said, concluding our cutting. "But I'll tell you what—I will keep buying your products, and treat you like one of our regular suppliers [instead of the emergency fill-in we had been during the war]. Let's see how we get along. If you show me you can increase our volume and profit on Chinese food, I will replace them with your line."

What could be more fair?

Eventually Harry gave us the biggest order Chun King had ever seen: $57,000 worth of products going into more than 200 supermarkets. Food Fair remained our most valued customer right up to the day I sold the company. And Harry Pripstein and I were on our way to becoming lifelong friends.

As I walked out of Food Fair's headquarters that morning—my shell-shocked young broker at my side—a great weight lifted from my shoulders. I had saved the account and saved the business.

Chun King was going to make it.

On October 26, 1948, Lois gave birth to our son Michael. No complications. No problems. And a helluva lot more important in our lives than just saving some damn business.

THAT WASN'T THE LAST BIG ACCOUNT I had to save at the last minute. Far from it. In any industry, hanging on to important customers is a continuing process. And usually you've got to take chances.

For instance, there was the situation that arose with A&P—the Great Atlantic and Pacific Tea Company—in 1951 or 1952, I think it was.

A&P had more than 2,500 stores at the time and controlled more than 25 percent of the nation's food business. They had a regional buying office in Milwaukee, whose blessing I had to get before we could sell Chun King to any A&P buyer anywhere.

The head buyer was Tony Vogt. His brother's name was Bernard. No matter what I proposed to them for pricing or promotion of Chun King products, Tony Vogt wanted it different. It was almost as if he, instead of me, were in charge of Chun King.

So I pondered: Jeno, are you going to run your business or let Tony Vogt run it because you're afraid of losing a quarter of the market? To hell with the 25 percent, I decided. I'm going to run my own business.

I sent a telegram (no fax or voice mail or Internet in those days, thank God) to Tony Vogt, Bernard Vogt, and about fifteen other district buyers of A&P, plus the head buyer in New York City. The telegram simply said:

> *Please advise any of my Chun King representatives who may contact you that Chun King and the Great Atlantic and Pacific Tea Company are no longer doing business. Stop. Signed: Jeno F. Paulucci.*

My sales people thought I had gone bananas. I then sent copies of the telegram to the buyers of all the other supermarkets throughout the United States with a note: "Thought you'd like to know that I'm running this business to suit you, not the A&P Tea Company."

As a result, my business with the other 75 percent of the market grew steadily. In about a year,

Tony Vogt came to visit me in Duluth and we've done business ever since.

But my way, not Tony's!

> *Pointer from the Peddler: In business, you learn to play by the rules. You always provide the best product at the best value. But in a crisis, you do whatever's necessary, even if it means risking a big account in order to run your business your way.*

And sometimes you have to be lucky. Okay, and sometimes you have to bite the grasshopper . . . or swallow it.

Chapter 13

Where Do We Go from Here?

*L*ike most entrepreneurs—and all peddlers—I was never cut out to stick to one thing at a time. Diversification is sound business practice in any industry, of course, but for some of us, it's an obsession.

As soon as Chun King stood on a firm footing, I couldn't resist making one deal after another. One of the earliest took place in my new expanded headquarters at 525 Lake Avenue South, and my potential partner was the most unlikely person in the world.

"I'm going to make you a proposition," I said to my visitor. "Won't cost you a nickel."

He was in a business called Native Pie Filling, canning a variety of fruits—wild blueberries, raspberries, strawberries, sour cherries, and apples—that could be used as pie filling. All the homemaker had to do was pour a twenty-ounce can of her choice into a pie shell and bake it.

Great concept; great business. And this guy had it all to himself.

A radical 2% solution reveals Wilderness opportunity.

I took out a map and drew a bold line around all the states in his sales territory. "How much brokerage are you paying?"

"Five percent."

"What about cash discount?"

"Ten days, two percent."

"Tell you what I'm going to do for you," I said, standing up as tall as I could next to my lean-and-lanky guest.

"I'm going to sell for you. Strictly beyond the sales territory where you're now doing business, you understand. I'll open up brand new territory for you," I said, drawing another circle on the map. "We'll pay only four percent brokerage and one percent cash discount."

I paused before delivering the punch line. "I'll take that leftover two percent. You build your business without investing a cent, and I earn my money back."

A slow smile spread over his pale chops.

"Maybe so," my visitor concluded. "I'll get back to you."

With that, Norman LaPole grabbed my weekly payment on the settlement he had won in court, and left.

Yes, Norman LaPole, the vulture. Crazy as it sounds, I had offered to go back into partnership with the man who once all but ruined David Persha and me. He'd had good luck with this new business of his, and I was itching to get in on the action. And in the back of my mind . . .

Apparently a sucker had appeared out of the blue and asked LaPole to can these Native brand pie fillings. It was going great guns all over the Upper Midwest. Pretty soon LaPole had given up canning peas altogether, and the guy who had brought him this

new idea was no longer part of the picture. No doubt
he had been totally screwed, as I had been.

The next time he came by for his blood money, I
jumped to my feet, anxious to do business.

"Look, Norman," I said, "you even admitted once
that you don't deserve all this dough I've been paying you."

"So?"

"How about giving me a chance to get some of it
back?"

He looked at me as if I had asked him to goose
the Pope.

"Naw, I don't mean *give* it back," I assured him.
"I still owe you a few grand, and you'll get every
dime. This pie filling is a separate deal."

What can I say? Here this phony Abe Lincoln had
this great thing going, and I kept seeing in my mind
how I could make it even bigger and better. Also,
down the road, there just might be a chance to . . .

So that's how I came to make my pitch to him
and before I knew it, the two of us were once again
in bed together.

Selling LaPole's pie filling was . . . well . . . a
piece of cake.

A day's work, maybe, but I had my system in
place. In order to control freight charges, I stuck to
the neighboring midwestern states—outside his
original territory—as we had outlined on the map.
Norman provided me with free samples and copies of
his standard price sheet. To this I added my own one-
page flyer touting the wonders of Native brand.

I sent this package off to my regular Chun King
brokers with a handwritten message: "We now have

an exclusive line of pie fillings. Get out there and start selling."

The orders started rolling in. In three short months, I had brought the devil himself $250,000 worth of new business.

One day he called me up.

"Jeno," he shouted breezily, now that we were buddies again. "Just thought I'd let you know that I'm heading out to California on vacation. Ed Didier will be in charge for the next few weeks. I'll send you some oranges."

Ed Didier was an unpleasant memory. The man had worked in our Iron River factory until the trial in Superior, when he testified against David and me. Now, apparently, he was LaPole's right-hand man.

"Forget the oranges, but while I've got you on the line, maybe I could ask you about *my* check."

"Your check?"

LaPole seemed in the dark.

"Yeah, for the new orders. In case you haven't noticed, it's been over three months now, and . . ."

"Sure, sure. How much do you have coming?"

"Oh, about five," I said. I knew damn well he was playing dumb. How many times had he bragged about being an eagle-eyed accountant, and even hinted about keeping two sets of books—one for himself and the other for the IRS?

Although I wasn't crazy about the way he handled it, a check did arrive in the mail two days later, which was fine—until I opened the envelope. It was for "five" all right. Five hundred. The trouble was that 2 percent of the $250,000 worth of goods I had sold for him came to five *grand.*

No accountant I knew of ever made that kind of mistake by accident.

It was at that moment that my plan for getting back at LaPole crystalized.

No waiting until he got back from California. No waiting until tomorrow, after I had another lousy night's sleep. I grabbed the phone and got hold of Ed Didier, who had been left in charge of LaPole's office.

"Ed," I hollered into the receiver. "Boy, you won't believe this! I just got one hell of an order from National Tea in Chicago!"

"No kidding?"

I laid it on pretty good. "Listen, I don't know whether it'll all go on one truck or not, but I think we ought to give it a shot."

By that time, I was already running my own Orient Express rigs and I knew the legal limit for a semi-trailer was 40,000 pounds. I ran some quick numbers in my head. At two dozen cans each, a case of pie filling weighed about forty pounds. That meant about 1,000 cases to fill up a truck. If LaPole was selling those number-two cans for about $2.50 a dozen, a truckload had to be worth $5,000.

But I wanted more than that. I rattled off an order I had jotted down—so many cases of cherry, so many of raspberry, strawberry, and so forth—that came to a total of *2,000* cases.

"I'll have a truck over there in an hour," I told Ed. "They want the stuff on their dock in Chicago the day before yesterday."

"No problem," he gushed. "Whatever National Tea wants, National Tea gets."

Ed never had a clue.

When the truck came puffing back to our building that afternoon, after the pickup, my driver screamed at me from the cab, "Jeno, I can't take this load all the way to Chicago. There must be 80,000 pounds back there. I'll break down or get arrested or both!"

"You're right," I said with a broad smile. "But that truck ain't going to Chicago."

I pointed up the block.

"Unload it right over there. In my warehouse."

I couldn't wait to call Ed Didier back on the phone. This time I delivered an ultimatum: "Ed, I want you to get hold of your boss out there in those sunny California orange groves . . ."

"I don't think I can, Jeno," he started to whine. "Even his wife doesn't know where he is."

"Find him, Ed. And here's what you tell him. You say Jeno's got ten thousand dollars worth of his pie filling that he is holding hostage. And you tell him that if I don't hear from Norman personally, I'm going to dump this stuff in Native's juiciest markets—like the Twin Cities—at fifty cents on the dollar. One way or another I'm going to get the five grand that's coming to me."

"You wouldn't do that!" Ed pleaded.

"You've got twenty-four hours," I said and hung up.

Sure enough, before the day was over my sister Liz, who now worked in my office, announced that the vulture himself was on the line.

"How do those oranges taste?" I greeted him.

I kind of enjoyed the four-letter tirade that followed.

"Just trying to collect a bill," I replied innocently.

And that I did. LaPole at once agreed to have his attorney deliver a cashier's check for $4,500. In return, I gave him back his pie filling.

"What about our business arrangement?" he finally blurted.

"It's over," I said. "I've already notified every one of my brokers in the territory I opened up that we're no longer in the pie-filling business."

"You didn't . . ."

Well, he was right. But I planned to call them as soon as LaPole got off the phone.

"Hell, I'll just get that business back myself," he blustered.

And that's when I made up my mind to go through with my angry threat of years before. Even before I hung up, I had figured out exactly how I was going to break Norman LaPole.

I wasn't quitting the pie-filling business after all. Instead, I was going to start my own.

THE LESSON TO BE DRAWN from this next episode may be a little bit over and beyond the techniques I've discussed up to now. I don't know what to call it—How to Hold a Grudge? How to Close Out a Vendetta? How to Step on the Neck of the Son of a Bitch That Screwed You?

In good conscience, I'm not sure I should relate this at all.

Oh well, if you insist.

So I formed this new company—Northland Foods and Wilderness Fruit & Berry Pie Fillings. Long name. We just called it Northland Foods, Inc. And I formed it in 1950 for a single purpose—not to make money, but to get even with Norman LaPole.

Yes, David Persha and I had been dummies years ago. We should have stayed out of the Superior Court in Wisconsin, where LaPole was an elected supervisor in that county. And worse, we shouldn't have been taken in by those attorneys who kept saying we couldn't lose—and who demanded that we pay them in cash at the end of each week, or they wouldn't show up on Monday.

I'd like to see some attorney try that on me now. I'd have the son of a bitch disbarred, pronto!

The time had come for me to make good on my promise to LaPole that I'd break him. And the club I would use would be Northland Foods.

By 1951, I was doing well enough to move my entire Chun King operation into our own building in West Duluth. Our departure meant that 525 Lake Avenue South would need a major tenant, someone who could make use of all the food processing equipment that was already in place.

The opportunity was too good to pass up.

Once more I went to see Lennie Underdahl, who still represented the Madison-based landlords.

"Have you heard of Native pie filling, by any chance?" I began, expecting a tough sell.

Instead, I got lucky.

"Heard about it!" Lennie moaned. "I'm still kicking myself over that one."

"Really?"

"Yeah. That guy came to me first," he confessed sheepishly.

"What guy?"

"The one that had the original idea—the nut with all the fruits who was looking for a canner. He came to me before he went to LaPole."

Lennie started to blush. I never saw a more embarrassed look in my life. Obviously, he had followed the rise of Native pie filings with personal regrets second only to my own.

"Yeah, I could have had the whole thing. Instead I told him to screw himself with this crazy pie crap."

I told Lennie I was going to give him a second chance. And there was no stopping him. He persuaded his backers to put up the money (the fact that I promised to do all the selling probably had something to do with it) and we went into the pie filling business as fifty-fifty partners.

As I saw it, only one obstacle remained.

"They've got no competition out there," I began delicately in describing how I thought we should compete against LaPole. "And they've also got a top-notch product. We've got to learn how to make a damn good pie filling."

Lennie was way ahead of me. "Hell, that's easy," he said. "That fruitcake who came to see me originally is still around. I'll offer him a few bucks and get his recipes."

I had my doubts, but then Lennie said something that would make all the difference.

"You know why we can do that, don't you, Jeno? It's because I'll bet nobody bothered to patent anything. In fact, I'm sure of it.

"If they did, I'm the King of England and you're the next ambassador to China."

Lennie turned out to be right on all counts. La-Pole, who fancied himself to be so clever, had left the door wide open. Hadn't patented anything. So we went into business as Wilderness Fruit and Berry Pie Filling, division of Northland Foods, using exactly the same recipes Norman had.

The only hiccup was when I tried to use the same sixteen-ounce cans that I used in my Chinese food operation, in an attempt to save some bucks. I hadn't stopped to realize that sixteen ounces of filling didn't make much of a pie in a regular nine-inch pie pan. As soon as we matched Native's twenty-ounce cans, we were back on track.

My marketing strategy was a foregone conclusion.

LaPole was selling two dozen twenty-ounce cans at about $2.50 a dozen or $5 for a case of twenty-four cans. I figured his cost delivered to customers was about $4 a case, so he had a $1 a case sales margin. A nice business when you are selling more than a million cases a year. It wasn't going to be easy to bankrupt this guy.

My strategy was to send samples to all of Norman's Native brand customers and quote them a price lower than Norman's cost—about $3.50 a case—hoping like hell that Norman wouldn't wake up to my game, and that to protect his business he'd meet the price.

Sure enough, that's what he did.

Norman was telling the trade, "That guy Paulucci will be going broke soon with those prices, but I'll meet them for now."

Norman didn't realize that I wasn't selling much of anything; just sending samples and quoting my low, low prices. He still thought I was a dumb guy from the Iron Range, and he was cruising down the highway. But he was a few spark plugs short of a Ferrari, and on his way to a car wreck.

Instead of a profit margin of $1 a case, he now had a 50–cent loss on every case. By his way of thinking, he was keeping me away from his customers.

I did this everywhere Native was selling and kept it up by being persistent with the buyers at the retailers' outlets where Norman was getting his orders. I had my Chun King brokers go in with more samples, and I cut the price again to $3.25, this time market-wide. Again, Norman went down in price along with us.

You know something? I didn't sell much. Oh, maybe 50,000 cases the next two years. I lost $25,000 at most. So what? Norman was beginning to lose $500,000 a year or more.

Within three years, he was dead broke.

I had thought he would eventually figure out what we were doing, but it turned out he wasn't as smart as I thought, and not nearly as smart as he thought. I guess the only blessing for him was that he never lived to see the bankruptcy.

When word came that he died unexpectedly of a ruptured blood vessel in the brain, I tried to feel sorry for him. Tried hard. A month after his death, Native pie filling was liquidated at a loss.

We picked up Native's entire market share and the future for pie fillings was suddenly quite rosy, indeed. We then reversed our pricing tactics and started making money on my Wilderness Pie Filling because there was no more Native brand, just mine.

ABOUT THAT TIME I DECIDED I could save about 50 cents a case on cases of twenty-ounce cans of blueberry pie filling if I went from wild berries, which normally come from Canada, to domestic farm-grown berries. So, in 1953, I was lucky to become owner of a 700–acre blueberry farm in the Benton Harbor area of Michigan.

I never saw the farm, ever. But who in hell cared? I bought it at the right price and it produced one helluva harvest of thousands of pounds of blueberries each season. We'd freeze them in thirty- to fifty-pound tins (individually quick frozen) and store them year-round for canning Wilderness blueberry pie filling as needed.

I sold the farm at a nice profit years later, in 1980.

About a year after Wilderness started dominating the pie filling business, I had another talk with Lennie Underdahl.

"Look," I began, "we've made some money and had our fun with Wilderness. Now, I'd like to make a deal with your people in Wisconsin. I want to buy them out."

"That's a coincidence," he laughed. "They told me they want to buy *you* out."

"Well, I'm just thinking out loud here, but I'd hate to see all this come down to a lawsuit."

Lennie's eyebrows went up at the word *lawsuit,* as most people's did forty or fifty years ago, before going to court became almost a reflex.

"You really want the whole thing?"

I did.

And I correctly judged that Lennie's backers had lost too many times to risk going to court with me.

I got the company. I enjoyed that, but what I enjoyed even more was not having to spend a dime up front to do it. I paid them off in cash flow. In fact, Wilderness became so profitable that we had enough cash on hand not only to pay Lennie's backers for their 50 percent share of the business, but also $125,000 to buy the building at Lake Avenue South.

For most of the next twenty years, Wilderness brand stayed number one in the country and Northland Foods—a business I had started just to settle an old score—earned a minimum of a $1.5 million a year. When a new generation of cutthroat competitors—Comstock Brand from New York and Lucky Leaf—made it more trouble than it was worth, I sold the business to the Cherry Growers Cooperative in Benton Harbor, Michigan, for about $25 million in cash.

So I had fulfilled my promise to Mr. Norman La-Pole—*I'll break you, you son-of-a-bitching vulture!* And built a successful business on top of it. But somehow it was a hollow victory. I didn't feel like celebrating.

Maybe I was just being true to my Italian heritage and the vendetta that comes with it.

Pointer from the Peddler: As I've said, I'm not recommending this course of action to everyone. But there's nothing wrong with taking revenge when it's justified. But that doesn't mean you have to feel good about it.

Good-bye and good luck, Norman, wherever you are.

Chapter 14

Diversification and Its Dangers

*A*bout the time I was diversifying into the pie filling business, I was also diversifying into land. Back to the soil. After all, what better investment can you make than land? As is often said, they ain't making it any more.

So it was that I became a hands-on, plow the dirt, spread the fertilizer, get your boots dirty farmer, when I bought more than 5,000 acres of rich peat sandy loam soil about fifty miles northwest of Duluth in the towns of Zim, Sax, and Meadowlands.

When I was a kid, my mother took me to the Farmer's Market in Hibbing to buy huge, perfect home-grown vegetables. They came from local farms around those three tiny towns. And it was the dark Mesabi peat in those towns that caused the celery, cabbage, and cauliflower to reach fairy-tale size.

Remembering that, one day around 1954 I thought, hell, I can buy thousands of acres of that land that no one is now harvesting for about $10 an acre, and put it

Many restaurant concepts were tried and abandoned before Luigino's Pasta and Steak House brought success.

to work making money. I wanted to make Chun King as self-sufficient as possible. Every year we had to go all the way to Florida for the millions of pounds of celery we used in our chow mein and Chinese vegetables. Why not use all those rich peat bogs next door instead?

I could grow my own celery. I could get the strippings for nothing to blend with strippings I was getting from Florida Fresh. And maybe I'd sell the hearts to produce houses in the Twin Cities, Chicago, and Milwaukee.

We picked up 5,000 acres of idle, tax-forfeited land and named it Wilderness Valley Farms. Next we bought a beautiful yellow Caterpillar tractor, put my nephew Fred "Chub" Trepanier on top of it under a small umbrella for shade, and directed him to clear brush from the first 200 acres we needed to grow celery.

I was on the road at the time (where else?), but I was so excited about our plan that I called every few hours to see how Chub was doing. There was no telephone yet on the farm, but my secretary had him report in from a general store in nearby Sax.

"He's having some trouble, Jeno," my secretary reported the first time I called. "Chub thinks maybe we've got the wrong kind of tractor. It's starting to sink in the mud."

"Bullshit. Caterpillar is the best there is. He just doesn't have the hang of it yet. Tell him we've got to clear that land right away."

On my second call, I heard, "Still sinking, Jeno."

"Keep going," I ordered, wishing I could be there myself to drag the tractor out of the peat like I'd once dragged a garlic machine into my car.

On my third call, I heard, "Chub just called again from Sax. All you can see is the tip of that umbrella. The rest of the tractor has disappeared into the peat bog."

So we called in a salvage crew and raised that yellow Caterpillar out of the peat bog—our first crop—and sold it.

Then I bought four Oliver tractors—with wide instead of narrow tracks. With the brush taken care of, we dug drainage ditches and brought in huge Chrysler water pumps on wheels to irrigate our fields from a nearby lake.

My cash investment, at least, was growing nicely.

And so did the celery, for the first season. We had a fantastic harvest. Row after row of celery stretched to the horizon. Tractors rolled across those fields like waves of tanks. That first crop became trimming for chop suey, but the next season I decided to pack celery hearts as well. Heck, we were real farmers now.

We built a quonset hut on the farm with its own processing line and came up with a nifty logo and the name Krispi Celery Hearts.

And why stop at celery, there in the green acres?

We wrung every drop of value out of that acreage, let me tell you. We dug peat out of the bogs and sold it in fifty-pound burlap bags for gardening. We grew and sold sphagnum moss for lawns and landscaping. I set up a building for growing fresh mushrooms, and used the peat and sandy loam plus horse manure shipped in by rail car.

The cabbage and cauliflower we grew were exceptional in size and quality. And we started growing the most beautiful grass sod you've ever seen.

Then came more farm diversification. Justin Schmit, our director of farm operations, suggested growing wild rice. This had never been attempted before. The only local available crop came from the Ojibwe Indians, who harvested it in the wild. We invested hundreds of thousands of dollars and built the first, perhaps the finest, domestic wild rice operation this country has ever seen.

By means of dikes and dams, my people created our own paddy of wild rice lakes. Until that time, rice plants in the wild had to be harvested again and again, since the crop matured at different times. But our agronomist, Mr. Andrews, developed a different seed, a unique hybrid strain, that ripened all at once. We had this semi-automated harvesting machine that gathered it all in a single trip. Its riverboat-style paddle gently tapped the bumper crop into a giant hopper as it glided smoothly over the canals.

A farming paradise there in the wilderness of northern Minnesota.

Seemed too good to be true.

And it was.

We did have a promising first-year crop of wild rice in the making (and up to half of the wild rice sold today is grown following the fomula we pioneered, most of it in California). But our crop never went to market. What happened?

Wheat rust!

The agricultural experts couldn't explain what the hell wheat rust was doing in our rice paddies. They said we could eventually get rid of it. But that initial crop had to be destroyed.

I pulled the plug on the rice paddies.

Well, on to head lettuce. We tried a joint venture with a fellow by the name of Mr. Williams from Chula Vista, California, and had a tremendous crop of iceberg lettuce—about 500 acres—ready for harvest. Then it started to rain. That was okay, but after the rain came the hot sun.

Overnight, our 500 acres of iceberg head lettuce turned to absolute mush. Mr. Williams went back to California.

It was as if God was telling me what generations of failed homesteaders had learned before: The growing season in northeastern Minnesota is just too damn miserably short!

I found myself an expert on early frosts.

Eventually I could tell when one was coming by watching the changes in the moon. It took *three* killing frosts in succession to ruin a celery crop. Those rugged stalks could take one or two frosts.

But not a third.

Okay, but what were the odds of three in a row, right? Pretty high, apparently. After that first good season, we got frozen out every year. Always before Labor Day.

I remember that last time, during the seventh year when I drove out to our celery fields alone in my Chrysler Imperial. It was evening and those peat bogs already seemed as icy and remote as the North Pole. I sat there in the moonlight, knowing that the third frost was coming and there was nothing I could do about it. Not with all the money and technology in the world.

I thought back to how much fun I'd had when I was there doing the work myself—plowing the soil, working in the canals to provide irrigation, helping harvest. Harvesting mushrooms after shovelling manure-laden soil. Being a diversified farmer and getting every ounce of benefit from that soil, facing up to Mother Nature's whims and whams.

And now the celery business, the cauliflower and potato and mushroom business and the wild rice business . . . all hopeless. Maybe the heavy frosts didn't damage the lawn sod, but enough was enough.

To me, it was something out of the Old Testament. God was angry.

So was Jeno.

I started up the engine of my Chrysler and roared up and down those rows of celery. Back and forth I drove in the darkness, my headlights bouncing wildly. And I kept at it until it was all tramped down. All those hearbreakingly beautiful plants—destroyed.

That was my way of saying to hell with the entire farm business. I gave the farm and my research center there to the State of Minnesota in 1967 to use for further research. Too bad the state didn't maintain the 5,000 acres. It was a bonanza, but they screwed it up and all that remains is the growing of some sod by a Twin Cities firm on about 500 acres.

ANOTHER DIVERSIFICATION EXPERIMENT stands out in my memory. It was on a much smaller scale than creating a farm paradise in the north country, but it taught me a basic lesson in the advertising and marketing game.

You've heard that old axiom: "Sell the sizzle, not the steak." There's a lot to that, as I've found in most instances over the years. But this time I sold so much "sizzle" that I got all the "steaks" back for refunds.

In 1965, with Chun King an established leader in the marketplace, I decided to pack my mother Michelina's marvelous spaghetti sauce in cans.

Ragu was the leader in that field then, and I believe it is even today. But Ragu was packed in glass. I wanted my mother's sauce in cans because, believe it or not, the sauce tasted better after being sterilized in cans than when it was packed and sterilized in jars.

Our sauce was terrific. Everybody liked it. So I thought I had a real winner. I had our people at Chun King pack about 500,000 cases of twenty-four cans in two varieties. One was Jeno's Italiano Marinara, the other Italiano Meat Spaghetti Sauce. It was so good I decided there was no use trying it out in a so-called test market or two, just to see if consumers would buy it.

Hell, no. I never even asked a consumer, other than a few employees, whether they would buy it. I was much too mesmerized by how good it was coming out of the cans.

So I went national with a "sizzle" program. Free Fiat cars if a supermarket customer bought five truck-loads, about 10,000 cases. Free Vespa scooters with one truckload of at least 2,000 cases. Free Olivetti typewriters if you bought just a lousy 500 cases. And, as I remember it, free Italian derby hats with every hundred cases.

We went with the sizzle from coast to coast. Supermarket operators and wholesale grocers took our word, as well as our prizes, that this was the greatest authentic Italian sauce ever.

The sizzle worked. We gave away about 15 Fiats, more than 100 Vespa scooters, more than 200 Olivetti typewriters, and God only knows how many Italian derby hats.

Jeno's Italiano canned spaghetti sauce was on shelves and floor displays all over this nation!

But we had a wee bit of a problem.

The public wouldn't buy spaghetti sauce in cans. They were too accustomed to buying it in jars.

Before long I was getting demands from grocers: "Come pick up your sauce. It doesn't sell, no matter how good it is."

Of course my customers kept the Fiats, the Vespas, the typewriters, the hats. After all, that was the sizzle. I got back damn near every case I shipped of my delicious, authentic, Italiano sauce.

This diversification cost me about $3 million, a lot of money in those days and not exactly chump-change today . . . although I'm told Bill Gates of Microsoft gives that much in tips.

I learned my lesson. Before I dream up the sizzle, no matter how good my steaks, I now ask people whether they'd buy the damn stuff.

Today I sell the steak and add damn little sizzle. "Let the product speak for itself" is my motto.

FOR ABOUT THIRTY YEARS, I tried to diversify into the restaurant business. If I could make it big as a food manufacturer, why not get into the retail side? What could be more natural for a food expert like me?

So over the years I put on my chef's hat and became a restaurateur—over and over.

1. *Ricksha Inn.* Take-out only. Minneapolis, 1957.
Good Chinese food.
Good value.
Horrible location. I closed it after a month—should have taken the time to find a better location.
Failure due to poor location.

2. *Chop Chop House.* Take-out only. Blooming-ton, a Minneapolis suburb, 1960.
Great location.
Great asssortment of food from traditional Ital-ian pizza to Chinese.
We got a Rolls Royce sedan and painted it white for home delivery in style, before Domino's was even born.
But people wanted to eat on the premises. I'm stubborn; wouldn't allow it. In too much of a hurry to turn a profit. I made my point. No eating inside. My policy was enforced.
And now the building is a dry-cleaning estab-lishment.
Failure due to Jeno's stubborness and stupidity.

3. *Smorgasbord International.* Winter Park, Florida, 1961.
Foods of all nations, cafeteria style.
All you can eat for $2.95.
Great location.
Great food.
Incompetent manager.

I fired the manager and closed the restaurant, all within ninety days of opening, and rented the building to a steak house.

This experiment was a success down the line. I made money through rentals over twenty years and eventually sold the property at a profit.

The restaurant? A failure because I was too quick to hire an idiot for a manager.

4. *Riksha Inn.* Fern Park, Florida, 1962.
   A beautiful pagoda structure on two acres.
   Great concept for a Chinese restaurant.
   But the food was no good, because I used my own Chun King canned and frozen products in hot chafing dishes for self-service. The food quickly became mushy.

Again a measure of success, because once more I rented the property, which was used as a steak house for a number of years, and because the land and building sold twenty years later at five times the original investment.

But the restaurant was a failure because Jeno couldn't take the time to hire a good Chinese chef.

5. *Somebody's House.* Bloomington, Minnesota, 1965.
   Bought a concept by a woman who originated the idea of hamburgers with different and unusual toppings—like Fudruckers.
   Another great concept.
   Failure because Jeno had to fire a crooked manager, was too impatient to hire another manager, and closed the place.

It was small consolation that I again sold the building and land for a nice profit.

6. *Pizza Kwik, Inc.* Orlando area, 1986.
I organized pizzeria operators who would make the pizza to our specifications that we in turn would sell for home delivery under the Pizza Kwik name. We'd take phone orders citywide and send them by fax to our nearest affiliate for delivery through an independent driver pool.

No overhead. Just collect a profit for each pizza sold over cost to pizzerias.

Not a bad idea, right?

However, it turned out to be a great failure because individual pizzeria owners got greedy and started to cheat on the quality of the pizzas. That's when Jeno's temper got out of control.

I told them all to go to hell. No more Pizza Kwik.

7. *China Kwik* was next. Orlando area, 1987.
Same great concept, but for Chinese food. Unfortunately, I found that Chinese food operators were just as greedy as the pizzerias.

Goodbye, China Kwik.

8. *Pasta Lovers,* restaurant franchising. Sanford, Florida, 1989.
Franchised some ten Pasta Lovers restaurants and ended up with twenty lawsuits. To hell with franchising.

9. *Pasta Bowl, Inc.* Florida Mall, Orlando, 1989.

Designed for small fast-food operators in shopping centers.

Turned out to be small operators, all right. But big losses.

So goodbye Pasta Bowls. They were money bowls going out the door.

10. *Luigino's Pasta and Steak House.*

After thirty-seven years of really trying, I finally had a smashing success with this restaurant, opened as Pasta Lovers in 1988 in the shopping center at Heathrow, Florida, the town built by my family.

The reason it's a success is because I finally was able to discipline myself. No longer did I demand an immediate profit. Instead, I told my management: "Look, I don't want to know what your food costs are, nor your labor costs. Just put out the best quality food possible. If I lose $100,000 a year for a couple of years, that's okay. We're building for the future."

The fact is, this restaurant turned a profit within a couple of years.

So if you drop into Luigino's Pasta and Steak House in Heathrow, Florida . . . tell them Jeno sent you!

UNTIL THIS LATEST VENTURE, my career as a restaurateur had been fairly comical. So I can't resist telling about the greatest of all the ones that got away.

One summer day in 1983, while I still ran Jeno's, Inc., my secretary, Gail Bukowski, stuck her head into my office.

"Mr. Thomas Monaghan to see you, boss."

The name didn't ring any bells. "Who's he?"

"Well," she huffed, "he just happens to own Domino's Pizza."

"What's that?"

Gail was flabbergasted.

"Why, it's that outfit that delivers pizza in thirty minutes or less, Jeno. They're everywhere. You must have heard of them."

I swear to God, I hadn't.

But that wasn't surprising. I tend to get so lost in my own affairs that the world's business culture is just so much white noise.

I asked Gail to show my visitor in. He was roughly dressed, as though he'd just wandered in from the woods. Which he had.

"Please excuse my appearance," the stranger apologized cheerfully. "I've been on a canoe trip in your wonderful Minnesota north country for the past ten days. But I've heard a lot about you—may I call you Jeno?—and just had to stop by and say hello. One pizza man to another."

I nodded politely as we shook hands.

Jeno's Frozen Pizzas were flying high in those days, and Tom Monaghan and I had a pleasant conversation about business during which he mentioned that he owned about 1,500 take-out places, doing more than a billion dollars in combined annual sales.

"I just turned down an offer of $200 million for the company," he sighed.

"No kidding?"

And then it struck me—I'd really been asleep.

This unassuming guy standing before me—unshaven, wearing Bermuda shorts and an open-collar sports shirt, telling me in a nice way how rich he was—made me feel like a real dumbell. He had taken an idea for marketing restaurant food to the home market, and made a fortune out of it.

Home delivery pizza! I'd had the same idea decades ago! And I'd gone to all the trouble of starting such a business—Chop Chop House in Bloomington, Minnesota, complete with white Rolls Royce for home delivery—and had given it up in anger.

As our conversation ended and Tom Monaghan was leaving, I shook his hand.

"Nice to meet you, Tom."

"You too, Jeno. Good luck."

But I'd already thrown away that particular piece of good luck.

Pointer from the Peddler: Like any chance you take, diversification has its downside and its upside. But not taking a chance is the worst mistake you can make. Good luck grows out of good ideas. If you think you've got a winner, bet on it. Pursue it and don't ever give up. Otherwise your great idea might end up like one of mine—the site of a dry-cleaning establishment.

Chapter 15

"Human Resources" Are People

*F*or some reason, demanding SOB that I am, people like to work for me. Probably has something to do with the fact that they can earn a lot of money doing it.

Executives and managers get above-average salaries, with generous bonuses for those who deserve them, and a variety of other financial extras but no perks.

People in the factories, on the canning lines, and those performing all the routine work that is the heart of any business–blue collar, they're called, although I don't give a damn what kind of shirt they wear—are represented by strong unions.

I believe in unions, and they're entitled to negotiate every last dollar they can get out of me—though the negotiations may be tough. So here's my take on human resources, which used to be called personnel but, in case you hadn't noticed, are just people.

I'M THINKING BACK A FEW YEARS AGO, to the formation of my current company, Luigino's Inc. I'd

Jeno's Credo:

Lest you forget . . .
We are here for only one reason. . .
And that is to make money . . .
But let's have fun doing it!

been laying low in the food business for a while because of non-compete agreements, and I'd been out of touch with many of the wonderful people who'd helped me build and sell Chun King and later, Jeno's.

Then, out from under the non-compete, I saw this great opportunity in microwavable frozen entrees. By any measure, Michelina's is a huge success, but I sure didn't do it alone.

While the new company was still an idea in my head, I got on the phone and hired back what became known as The Gang Who Wouldn't Retire. Men like Jim Tills, Dave Ahlgren, Joe Scinocca, and many more, whose experience in my many businesses totaled some 700 years.

These were people I could count on. And they knew the drill: No minor frills such as leased cars, country club memberships, subscriptions to the *Wall Street Journal* or cellular phones. A 401(k) program, sure; hospitalization and insurance benefits, sure. But no pensions.

Instead, top-dollar salaries and the opportunity to earn *up to 100 percent bonuses* when we made sales and profit goals.

As the business was getting on its feet, a magazine called *Corporate Report* sent out a survey, looking for the "best places to work" in Minnesota. They asked about benefits, vacations, dress code, and so on and so forth. The survey came to my desk, so I scribbled out an answer to be typed up and sent to the editor.

I told them about all the conventional corporate perks that weren't available, the salaries and bonuses that *were* available. I even mentioned that an extra benefit was a biennial trip to our Wilderness Village fishing camp up in the north woods—maybe not attractive to some people, but for others, the best benefit of all.

Then I made these other points:

"Play politics and you're out."

"No play, play, play with your laptop. Work a full day or get out."

"Each your lunch fast; we've got work to do. Work hard and smart and you can double your income. But don't pester me with headbolt heaters [the wintertime engine warmers for cars here in the north country] or soccer teams."

I also noted: "There's a four-ring circus around here every day, not only at Luigino's but also our other companies from Republic Banks to Etor Real Estate to Self Serve Foods, Inc. through dot.com and internet operations, hotels, restaurants and what the hell else I don't remember right now. Nothing staid, nothing routine, and none of that corporate drivel."

"The sky's the limit on salaries, bonuses and promotions."

I quoted a credo, which I've been posting in our offices for forty years:

> *Lest you forget . . .*
> *We are here for only one reason . . .*
> *And that is to make money . . .*
> *But let's have fun doing it!*

To my surprise the magazine printed in full the memo they'd received from "irascible entrepreneur Jeno Paulucci." They quoted my comments on a full-page layout with my picture and called it "a priceless antidote to today's employee-is-king environment."

I wrote back to thank them and to say, "We may not make the 10 best, but we hope to be *first* of the *worst,* and we aren't going to change. And it's still fun for all of us!"

Believe me, this kind of policy works for us . . . and for a growing number of other companies around the country that are returning to reality.

SO MUCH FOR THE WHITE COLLAR environment. Now let's talk about workers, and unions.

If you don't think unions are useful, I'd like to tell you what it was like when we didn't have any.

No labor unions protected workers like my father when they toiled in the mines in the first decades of the twentieth century. I learned that first-hand. At age eleven, I was chosen to ride with my uncle Rinaldo Pagliarini in his horse and cart to Dupont Lake five miles away. Because he didn't speak English, it was my job to talk the Dupont Explosive Company into hiring him. I served as translator during the interview.

Uncle Rinaldo went to work the very next day. I felt proud of the help I had given him.

The day after that he was fired.

It didn't take the family long to figure out what had happened. Once, in passing, Uncle Rinaldo had talked about unions—in his native Italian, for God's sake—and as a result he was no longer permitted in the mines.

His name was on the blacklist.

No one beholden to Oliver Mining—as was this explosives outfit—dared offer him work. Men like my uncle, and my father, lived in terror of that unseen list.

When I went into business for myself, that hostile attitude toward unions came with the territory.

When David Persha and I started canning bean sprouts and chop suey vegetables for the Chun King brand in the little cannery we fixed up in Iron River—doomed to be burned down a couple years later—we employed about seventy-five women and twenty-five men. Canning wages in those days were about 50 cents an hour. Doesn't sound like much, but that would be around $10 an hour today.

One day Dave phoned me while I was on the road selling, and said, "Jeno, that son of a bitch Elmer Foster wants to try to unionize our plant!"

Elmer Foster was the agent for the Retail Clerks and Food Handlers. Dave had had a run-in with him earlier, when he had the City Markets stores.

"Jeno, you've got to help me stop Elmer!"

I saw it as a personal vendetta between David and Elmer, so I went to the plant out of sympathy for David and all the grief Elmer and his union had given David in the old days. I made speeches to the employees, telling them, "You don't want or need a union." The people listened to me. When the day came for the election to choose a union or no union, they voted damn near unanimously against the union.

Everybody was happy.

Except me.

Here's why. The next day when I drove to the plant the employees greeted me with great big smiles. It was "Hello, Jeno," "Great to see you, Jeno." Implied was: "We did you a favor, Jeno."

Some of the people were sitting around smoking cigarettes. Others were running the two canning lines at about half-speed.

I thought to myself Hello Chapter 7 or come 11.

If this continues, I thought, how in hell are we going to get these people back to a productive workday, like we'd had before the "no union" vote? This is now one big happy family of a hundred women and men at their leisure.

On my return to our cubbyhole offices behind the butcher shop on First Street in Duluth, where we grew the bean sprouts indoors, I told David that we had made a mistake. I felt we should be unionized, Elmer or no Elmer.

David warned me that Elmer was a tough, crooked son of a bitch.

"All the more reason why he will be a good agent to represent our employees in a union, once we negotiate a contract," I said. "I'll make damn sure that Elmer and his people live up to that contract."

David gave up. "Okay, young man," he told me, "go ahead and see what happens."

I asked Elmer to bring the terms of the contract that he had promised our people if they voted for his Retail Clerks and Food Handlers. Elmer and I went over the contract, negotiated it further, and then I told him, "Soon as it's legal, call another election. David and I won't discourage you."

It was done shortly afterward, and we became the only unionized Oriental food packer in the country, with a contract that let both sides know what they had to do to keep us in business. Elmer was in charge for some twenty years and was always true to his word—tough, but fair and honest. We have that union in some of our plants to this day, with no work stoppages ever.

Over the years I learned to bargain with anybody—the Retail Clerks and Food Handlers; the United Packinghouse, Food and Allied Workers; the Amalgamated Meat Cutters and Butcher Workmen of North America; the Steam Fitters; the Construction Workers; the Teamsters; and even District 50 of John L. Lewis's United Mine Workers, who for a short time were desperate enough to organize my food processors in Ohio.

OVER TIME, I'VE DISCOVERED that more often than not, the problem in union–management relations isn't that the unions are being unreasonable. It's those weak-kneed, kiss-your-butt Pollyannas in management who are afraid to negotiate in a tough but fair manner.

It's "Don't rock our boat—it might affect my bonus."

As a result, more than a few companies have failed to protect their competitive status within their industries, and have had to go bankrupt or reorganize. We've seen it in the airlines, in the auto industry, all over.

Effective negotiation means listening carefully at contract time to evaluate union demands. Just let them talk until all issues have been put on the table. Don't give in on one issue or compromise until you know all the issues. Then don't be too timid to say, "No, my competitive position in this industry won't afford your demands."

And keep in mind that you want the money to go to the workers, not their often overpaid representatives and the union pension funds.

This is never easy, but it's a hell of lot less difficult if you realize that contract time isn't just every three or four years. It's every day. Each member is an individual.

If you can't be there yourself, have somebody else on plant and factory floors asking employees how they feel. Any work problems? Any personal problems?

Here are a few examples to prove my point.

One involved the Union of Stationary Engineers— a large name for the small group of employees who take care of the high-pressure steam boilers in food plants, even though most were then and are today automatically powered by fuel oil or natural gas.

Around 1952, our oil boiler men (about six per plant) decided to join the Stationary Engineers. Okay, let's negotiate a contract.

In comes a seasoned union rep. He's around sixty; about double my age. He laid his demands on the table: hourly pay, benefits, working conditons, seniority, and so on.

He was asking for way too much. So I started to expound and made an ass of myself trying to out-negotiate this seasoned negotiator.

He just sat back and let me talk on and on about how I couldn't do this, couldn't pay that type of increase, and so on. Well, he didn't say anything for about two hours while Jeno was doing all the talking.

I started out by saying, "Your demands will cost us over fifty cents an hour. All I can give is ten cents."

That was the first half-hour. Next half-hour I was still talking. "Maybe I can make it twenty cents." He just sat there looking at me, so I went up to 25 cents without him saying a whisper of a word.

Finally, after getting myself up to 30 cents an hour, I realized that I was negotiating *with myself!*

"Shut up, Jeno," I said to myself. "He is out-smarting you by not talking and letting you make a damn fool of yourself."

What did I do? I said, "Sorry, I've just got to leave. How about if we meet tomorrow? My last offer is off the table. Since you don't accept that, I want to study this further. Maybe I can't afford even that."

The next day I said, "Sorry, I got carried away yesterday. Let's start from scratch."

Then he did the talking . . . the talking . . . the talking . . . while I laid my head back and just nodded. After a couple of hours he gave up and we settled for a total increase costing 15 cents an hour.

> *Pointer from the Peddler: Just shut up and let the other guy negotiate with himself; a lesson I often used in the future.*

A couple of years later, 1954 I believe it was, we had a confrontation with the United Mine Workers at our plant in Jackson, Ohio. We had the Food Handlers there, the same as in our two plants in Duluth.

All at once we got notice that District 50 of John L. Lewis's coal miners' union had petitioned the National Labor Relations Board for an election to determine whether our employees wanted to shift unions from Food Handlers to Coal Miners.

Jackson is in a coal mining region of Ohio, and District 50 was very important and active in that area. I never met John L. Lewis but learned that he was calling the shots for a fellow named Dan Sandy, who was the agent trying to persuade my employees to switch unions by offering them large wage and benefit increases.

It was crazy. Hell, I wasn't operating a coal mine! Just a Chinese frozen food packing plant employing some 250 people. So I naively thought that my people weren't going to join a coal miners' union.

Wrong.

I remember a National Labor Relations Board official saying to Dan Sandy of the union, "Tell me, Mr. Sandy, what in hell business does a coal miners' union have to do with organizing a Chinese food packer?"

"Just as much," Sandy replied, "as that Italian, Paulucci, has in owning it."

That's what America is all about, and rightfully so.

After the NLRB votes were counted, District 50 was declared the victor. But they weren't too successful. They had promised too much. I sure as hell wasn't going to bow to these demands. I simply let them ask and ask and ask and ask. I'd learned that lesson well from the steam boilers.

When they finally got tired of talking and trying to get me to yield, I told them to go to hell, John L. Lewis or no John L. Lewis. They soon folded up their tent and the union that had been voted out, the Food Handlers, had to be called back by the NLRB.

Then there was an encounter later on with the Meat Cutters Union in a plant we'd opened in Cambridge, Maryland. When the time came for new contract negotiations, they demanded butchers' wages for food processing employees. Just nuts.

So I asked our personnel man, George Mueller, to go to Cambridge and meet with the union agent. I told George to let him talk; just listen.

After a couple of days, he called me and said, "Jeno, they are through talking. What should I do now? Give them our counter-offer?"

"No, no," I answered. "Let them talk for a few more days."

"What if they won't?"

"In that case, George, you start talking about your family, the weather, politics, hunting, fishing, whatever . . . but no counter-offer."

Believe it or not, George kept it up for eight solid days.

Finally, they made a modified offer. We countered and settled it all in an hour. Everybody had become exhausted. Except me. I wasn't there.

ANOTHER MEMORABLE UNION ENCOUNTER was my run-in with Jimmy Hoffa, the legendary Teamsters boss, allegedly mob-related, who was later killed (although his body was never found).

I had set up this separate trucking company, the Orient Express, that hauled finished products from our plants to our customers and returned with raw materials—a fleet of about fifty tractors and semi-trailers. The Teamsters Union represented all my drivers and they were tougher than hell to deal with. But we got along.

Then I got a notice that the Teamsters wanted to take over my Duluth, Jackson, and Cambridge plants, even though we had current contracts with the Food Handlers and Meat Cutters.

The Teamsters didn't care about contracts. They said, "We'll take over your warehouses first at each plant and then, in a little while, all the operations."

I said, "No way am I violating our contracts with the other unions."

We got a call from Gil Eiver, the Teamsters head in Duluth, saying that he and Frank Demeria—who was his assistant, I believe—wanted to meet on a certain day and time on the mezzanine of the Hotel Duluth.

I told Bill Olsen, our personnel director at the time, "Okay, let's go meet these two." The meeting, as I recall, was for eight A.M. Bill and I were in the hotel lobby by seven forty-five, ready for the meeting, when we heard this announcement over the hotel's loud speaker:

"Paging Mr. Hoffa . . . paging Mr. Hoffa."

Bill and I went up to the mezzanine.

Lo and behold, there was a man we immediately recognized from all the publicity he was getting: Jimmy Hoffa.

With him were Gil Eiver, Frank Demeria, and a Teamsters agent from the Twin Cities (who later went to jail for using a gun to persuade someone to do his bidding, whatever it was).

Gil introduced me to Hoffa and his Minneapolis guy and we all sat down to talk. But it was Jimmy Hoffa doing the talking in a strong voice.

"Paulucci," he said, "I've heard you are resisting our people taking over your plants. Now, I'm not going to take a lot of time to tell you what's what."

He lifted his arm, bent it, and clenched his fist. He showed me his muscle, tapped it with his hand, and said, "You see this, Paulucci? That's what we've got. Muscle. Now I'm going to give you twenty minutes to make up your mind and dance to our music. If you don't turn over your plants to us, we will secondary boycott your plants and products all over the country, legal or not. You got that?"

I answered, "Are you through, Mr. Hoffa?"

He nodded yes.

"Okay. Mr. Hoffa, I don't need twenty minutes. I ain't going to dance to your music.

"If you know so much about me," I continued, "why don't you ask our mutual friend, Abner Wolf of Detroit, about me?" Abner was a good customer of mine with Abner Wolf Wholesale and I knew he was a good friend of Hoffa's.

"Why should I do that?"

"Because Abner will tell you that I'm the only union organized packer of Chinese foods in the United States, and I'm honest and treat my people right . . . and I don't run scared for anyone."

Hoffa said, "You mean to tell me you're the only Chinese food packer that's unionized?"

"Hell, yes. I'm proud of it, but I ain't no pushover."

That evidently impressed Hoffa, who said, "Okay, we'll wait until I return to Detroit and talk to Abner. But if you're lying, God help you!"

Two weeks later to the day I got a call from Jimmy Hoffa.

"I talked to Abner," he said. "He verified what you told me, and he said, 'Paulucci's all right, leave him alone.' "

Hoffa closed by saying, "Paulucci, we will never bother you again."

He kept his word, right to the day of his tragic end.

IT SEEMS TO ME THAT MOST employers resist or dislike—even hate—unions, but put up with them as a necessary evil.

Not me.

Ever since the days on the Iron Range when my father and my uncle and others working for the mining companies couldn't even *talk* union or they would be fired and blacklisted, I have felt that the working man and woman needed a spokesman.

However, the unions and their officials and agents, while doing the best they can for their members, must never forget to judge employers and negotiate with them within the boundaries and limitations of the industry. A union can't expect steelworker wages for employees of a grocery store, a food processing plant, or other types of businesses.

That's the guide I've used in union negotiations since 1944, in the United States and abroad.

Looking back now at almost sixty years of being as tough as I dared and as fair as I could be in countless negotiations with unions of all kinds, I'm proud of my record of employing tens of thousands of union people and *never having suffered through one hour of work stoppage or strike . . . anywhere . . . ever.*

A POSTCRIPT: Maybe I'd better admit that there was just this one time when I ran into a union man I couldn't reason with. You may or may not be surprised to learn he was a relative of mine.

It was during that terrible 1950 depression on the Iron Range that my mother called me about this young man from the town of Chisholm, a miner who'd been left without work. His father, my mother's cousin, had also immigrated from Bellisio Solfare in northern Italy, so he was some kind of cousin.

"Jeno," my mother asked, "could you find young Renzalia a job?"

"Sure Mom. Send him down."

When my cousin showed up at the plant in Duluth, he said he liked machines. So I put him to work greasing the can-sealing equiment on our processing lines after the second shift at night.

In those days I routinely arrived at the plant at four A.M. Well, pretty soon there was Renzalia every morning too, grease gun in hand. He started following me around. I couldn't get rid of the little guy (he was even shorter than me). What could he possibly want?

Simple. He thought he deserved a better job.

I suggested maybe we take this one step at a time. That first he should prove he was good at what he was doing. But no, Renzalia didn't see it that way.

"Jeno, I want to do what you do. Why don't you give me the chance?"

He was like the plague. Outside my office. Everywhere I went, it seemed, my little cousin popped up at my side.

One day he followed me right into the men's room. That was the last straw.

"Come here, Renzalia," I ordered. "You say you want to do what I do? Watch this."

I had noticed a brown stain in the toilet bowl from all the iron in the water. No one had cleaned it recently. I found a brush, went into the stall, got down on my hands and knees, and proceeded to get rid of that toilet bowl ring.

When I was done, I stood up, flushed the toilet, put away the brush, and washed my hands. I turned to my cousin.

"That's what I do around here, Renzalia," I announced. "Whatever it takes to keep things going. Whatever's best for Chun King at any given moment on any given day."

I wiped my hands and tossed the paper towel in the basket before looking him in the eye.

"And the best thing you can do for Chun King right now is grease those damn machines. So get the hell out of my sight and stay out of it. I don't want to see your face any more!"

For a while I didn't. Then word came back that things were no longer going smoothly at the monthly union meetings held in the plant. Lots of griping and dissatisfaction over wages, working conditions, and the lack of promotions.

All of a sudden, nothing was good enough.

"Are we doing something different?" I asked some of the employees, who were as concerned as I was.

They all shook their heads. "Nothing we know of, Jeno."

A silence fell.

"Well, who's causing all this ruckus?" I finally asked.

They all looked at one another. Nobody wanted to speak up. Then it dawned on me.

"Is it *one* person?" I asked, holding out my hand to indicate a very short person.

They nodded solemnly.

The next morning I made sure I was at the plant at three-thirty A.M. I tracked down Renzalia and his grease gun. Before he could open his mouth, I grabbed him by the throat and shook him up and down.

"Listen, you son of a bitch," I screamed. "I'm through putting up with this crap from you. I hired you in the first place as a favor to my mother, and not only do you bug me morning and night about a better job than you deserve, but now you turn out to be some kind of agitator with a screw loose . . ."

His eyes glazed over and he slumped to the floor. I was so angry I yanked him to his feet by his jacket.

"Damn it, don't faint on me!" I yelled, slapping him alongside the face to wake him up. "I'm not through talking to you yet!"

But apparently I had done enough talking for Renzalia. My little cousin turned in his grease gun and quit.

Later on Renzalia got a job working for the Port Authority of Duluth. Whenever I ran into him, we both laughed about the incident. We figured it was just one of those things that happen along the way.

> *Pointer from the Peddler: Come to think of it, maybe that's all you need to know about "human resources" in the workplace.*

Chapter 16

The Poor Man's Guide To Advertising Success

*A*dvertising is the greatest tool ever invented for building a business. Everybody says so, especially the advertising agencies that want your billings.

But *not* advertising is even better–if you can get away with it.

Today, I can. You won't see Michelina's or Budget Gourmet on TV or on display ads in the print media. That's because at the start, I went to the biggest supermarket chains in the country and offered them a deal: I don't advertise in the media, just help you with in-store promotions, and I pass along the savings to you.

As a result, the supermakets could sell our products at unheard of low prices that get people in the store.

The supermarket chains bought into this radical idea because I had a long record in the food business. They knew me, and trusted me.

Stan Freberg proved to Jeno that advertising is the greatest tool ever invented for building a business, and the ad man won this rickshaw ride

But back in 1947, trying to promote this new company called Chun King, nobody knew me or my products.

I knew I had to advertise, so I did.

Fifteen choice ingredients–
One delicious dish!

That was the message in one tiny newspaper ad cooked up by me and a woman starting her own agency with my account.

As ads went, it was okay. But there was just no way that one little ad was going to help me compete against the big boys in the industry.

Maybe I could find a way to get more clout— maybe by *joining* the big boys.

I CALLED UP LaChoy, which was based in Ohio and was far and away the leading Chinese food producer. Got French Jenkins, their president, on the phone.

"Oh, you're that Italian fellow up in Duluth who's trying to put us out of business," said Jenkins.

I laughed and said I'd like some advice.

"Mr. Jenkins, I was just sitting here tossing a few ideas around, trying to figure out how we could get more people interested in trying our products, broaden our overall market, you might say. Now, you've been in the business much longer than I have, of course . . ."

"No doubt about that."

I made my pitch. "Well, do you think there's any merit at all in the notion of us Chinese food outfits banding together and forming our own association?"

"We tried that years ago," Jenkins dismissed me in a world-weary voice. "It didn't work."

But as a result of my persistence, we all—large and small producers alike—did meet in Chicago and eventually formed what our consultant chose to call the Chop Suey Institute.

Everybody wanted to gripe about the price wars that were killing the smaller outfits, and hurting the margins of the bigger firms. My concern, on the other hand, was to improve our product standards so whatever brand Americans tried, it would still be tasty enough to keep them eating Chinese food on occasion.

Yet when all was said and done, there was only one reason, in my mind, that we were all gathered around the table. If I wanted any national promotion for Chun King's products, we had to do it together.

Otherwise I simply couldn't afford it. I could pay for a fraction of a national ad, which promoted Chinese food in general, but there was no way I could buy anything like that on my own for Chun King.

Until then, none of my competitors even bothered to advertise. They relied on the local grocer's hit-and-miss ads given in return for the "promotional discount" each buyer received.

But finally I won them over, and we all agreed to contribute 1 percent of our total sales to a fund for national advertising and promotion. Only our consultant knew what each firm was actually shelling out, but there was no doubt where the lion's share came from: LaChoy and its forward-thinking president, French Jenkins.

That fund became the war chest for an all-out Tonight's the Night campaign that for the first time put displays of Chinese foods into supermarkets across the United States and let the public know we were there.

As a result of that, and subsequent promotions, Chun King at last established a foothold in the national market.

Three years later, the wrangling was still going on among smaller institute members over their own cut-throat pricing. For anti-trust reasons, obviously, we couldn't do anything about that. The moment we agreed to fix prices, the Justice Department would have been all over us, and rightfully so.

Because Chun King had become a more formidable competitor, some of the members started complaining that we were the only ones who did not concede every buyer a fixed 5 percent "promotional discount" on all shipments.

All the others, along with the Federal Trade Commission, wanted to force us to offer the same unworkable deal. To me the Chop Suey Institute had outlived its usefulness.

I walked out.

From that day forward Chun King would advertise and promote on its own.

Pointer from the Peddler: In advertising, if you can't beat 'em, join 'em. Then when you're ready, resign from the group—and then beat 'em.

WE STARTED OUT with established ad agencies like Campbell Mithun out of Minneapolis. By 1954, thanks to increasing sales, our overall budget for promotion included $1 million for advertising. That was a healthy budget for a Chinese foods producer, but anemic in comparison to the food giants like Kraft or General Foods. And after all, we were competing against everyone for a share of the great American stomach.

That summer, daytime TV host Gary Moore advertised Chun King on more than seventy channels. We ran a nationwide promotion giving away 20 million cans of chow mein noodles.

The public, if you'll pardon the expression, ate it up.

Suddenly I was dealing with big-time outfits like J. Walter Thompson out of Chicago, and Batten, Barton, Durstine and Osborn in New York.

Over the years we must have gone though at least a dozen ad agencies, some of them more than once. Chun King's sales were going up all the time, and the ad men, of course, were more than willing to take the credit. In the end, however, the problems of one kind or another became so great that I had to fire every one of them.

We needed something different, some attention-getting ads that would make the most of our limited advertising dollars.

AND THEN I GOT IN TOUCH with a young man named Stan Freberg. I'd heard of him vaguely: a comedian, with best-selling records such as a takeoff on *The Yellow Rose of Texas.* Now he was a budding advertising genius in Los Angeles. I don't remember whether he called me or I called him. But he had some ideas about Chun King.

When BBD&O's creative well finally dried up, I decided to take the plunge with this self-confident, slightly arrogant Freberg kid. We started with a radio spot, on trial.

To tell the honest truth, I never knew whether Stan's commercials were funny or not. When I got his first script, I didn't know what to make of it. The scene was a Chun King board meeting called by "Jeno," the president, to find out why not enough people were eating chow mein. That part I understood, but was it funny?

Tom Scanlon from my staff and I locked ourselves in the conference room and read the script into a portable tape recorder, adding "table-pounding" sound effects. We took the finished production out and played it for everyone in the office.

Nobody laughed.

"Hell, we aren't actors, Tom," I said, coming to my senses. "Tell Freberg to go ahead and make some commercials."

Nevertheless, the prospect of building a national merchandising campaign around sixty seconds of satire worried me.

I had to get away. I promptly went moose hunting up in northern Canada. There wasn't even a radio phone up there to give me static about the commercials, or anything else.

When I got back, I found a stack of messages to call Tom in Beverly Hills, where Stan had his studio.

"What's wrong?" I asked, more anxious than ever.

"It's Freberg. He changed his mind. He decided he didn't like the commercials we approved."

"And?"

"He wrote these new ones. He thought they were funnier."

"Can you tell me what they're about?" I asked, not sure I was in the mood to laugh.

Tom gave it his best long-distance shot. "One has a Chinaman being questioned about what he'd like for dinner tonight. And the Chinaman says, with this funny accent, 'Hot dog!' And the interviewer replies, 'No, I'm glad you're excited, but what would you like to eat?' And the Chinaman repeats: 'Hot dog!' "

I began to get a little confused.

"Geez, we're not selling hot dogs! Tell Stan to forget that and use the scripts we already okayed."

"I was afraid you'd say that," Tom groaned.

"What's the matter?"

"The new ones are already in production. I thought . . . well, hell, they sounded funny to me."

We test-marketed the new spots on radio stations in Duluth and Minneapolis. But rather than ask people what they thought of them (and prejudice their response), we decided to see if anybody called us first.

The phones rang off the hook.

"Congratulations on being willing to make a little fun of yourselves!"

"A real breath of fresh air!"

Comments like that, over and over.

Tom and I nodded at one another and felt like geniuses.

With the radio spots in national circulation, and very well received, we gave Freberg the go-ahead to produce one-minute commercials for television as well.

And then I got worried all over again.

Looking at the finished pieces, I couldn't make heads or tails of them. Just before we launched our new TV campaign, I flew out to Los Angeles for a last-minute talk with Stan himself.

"Maybe we're making a big mistake here," I said, confessing my uncertainty. "All this dwelling on how few customers we've really got out there . . ."

I guess I shouldn't have been surprised with the latest theme. After all, it was the premise of every one of Stan's commercials—only a minority of Americans ever ate Chinese food. He was turning a marketing disadvantage into an advertising advantage.

One of the ads began: "Nine out of ten doctors recommend you eat chow mein for dinner." The camera opened on ten men in white coats, then panned slowly over our smiling medical corps.

Nine of the ten doctors were Chinese.

Maybe this was funny, but . . . "I know you like to break the rules, Stan," I said, "but . . ."

"Trust me," Stan interrupted. "I'm so sure these commercials are going to work, Jeno . . . I am so sure sales will go up, say twenty-five percent, that I'll . . . I'll . . ."

He glanced out the window of his Beverly Hills suite and pointed to the street below.

"If I'm wrong, I'll personally pull you down La Cienega Boulevard, right past restaurant row . . . in a rickshaw."

Now even I thought that was funny.

"You're on!" I roared. "And if sales do go up, *I'll pull you.*"

The commercials went on the air.

Almost immediately our sales in targeted markets across the country jumped an unbelievable thirty percent. And on my next trip to Los Angeles, with photographers' flashbulbs popping, I performed as Stan's coolie for the day.

IN THE LIGHT OF OUR SUCCESS, Stan proposed we do an hour TV special together.

After some thought, I gave him the go-ahead on one condition. He had to tie the show in with Chun King's biggest annual promotion. Beginning in February, the Chinese people celebrate the start of their new year. Each year is identified by a different sacred animal—the Year of the Snake, Dog, Dragon, Ram, and others. Their observance might last a week.

Every year, our corresponding national campaign grew—until it stretched out into an entire month of hoopla and gala festivities.

Our efforts did not go unreported in the Chinese-American community. A full-page editorial in a newpaper in New York's Chinatown summed up their reaction:

Shame on us! How can we allow an Italian by the name of Jeno Paulucci, whose canned foods are not

*even authentic Chinese dishes, to steal our national
holiday from us?*

In effect, we had "hijacked" the Chinese New
Year. And in the process, we finally knocked LaChoy
from the top spot in sales. Even with all our success,
however, research told us we were still reaching only
a little over half of the people who watched television.

Why not go for broke?

The Year of the Tiger would begin on the eve of
February 5, 1962. For $250,000, we bought a whole
hour that evening on the ABC network. (Today, a thirty-
second commercial costs as much or more.) This time,
however, I was determined to play it smart. In addition
to my initial condition, we agreed on the program title
Stan Freberg presents the Chun King Hour.

Otherwise I left Stan completely alone. I didn't
ask to see a thing.

For nine months our people planned our block-
buster displays of pagodas, lanterns, gongs, and
coolie hats and talked up the Freberg TV special that
was in the works. But then, on the big night, as Lois
and I sat down in a Minneapolis hotel room to watch
the live television broadcast—with a Minnesota bliz-
zard raging outside—why was I suddenly feeling
nervous all over again?

"I'm sure it can't miss," I said without conviction.
"It'll probably be a big musical spectacular. Sort of
like Perry Como, maybe."

The next hour passed in silence.

When Stan himself came onto the screen riding a
bicycle early in the show, Lois and I smiled at one another. That was as close as we came to laughing.

"Nobody's going to think that stuff was funny," I sighed, switching the set off in disgust, once the special was finally over.

"That's for sure," Lois agreed, dashing any lingering hopes. "I thought it was terrible."

A disaster, I decided woefully.

Somehow I managed to restrain my disappointment in the telegram I sent to Stan from the hotel room: "No doubt the critics will love it. Thanks for all your efforts. Highest regards. Jeno."

The scene at our offices in Duluth the next day took me completely by surprise.

Smiling faces all around. A celebration, as if we'd won the World Series. The rave reviews were pouring in: "Vintage Freberg!" From *Variety* and the New York and Los Angeles newspapers on down, the media were all choking themselves with superlatives. Audience ratings came in over the top. Food brokers around the country reported how the trade loved the show and our merchandising job. Thousands upon thousands of dollars of products were going out the door.

Once again we were all comic geniuses.

One final incident stands out from those crazy years.

A go-getter of a publicist in New York by the name of Vernon Pope had arranged for my appearance as a contestant on the long-running television quiz show *What's My Line?* None of the panelists successfully guessed that I packed Chinese foods in Duluth for a living.

So what else was new?

But when Arlene Francis, the charming Broadway personality who had been with the show for years, heard me answer that yes, I was Jeno, she ad-libbed a line that won my heart forever: "Chun King? Why, they've got the best commercials in the world!"

Atta girl, Arlene!

Pointer from the Peddler: As you go along, you'll learn what kind of advertising works best for the least money. You'll get to be good at it, and you'll enjoy it. But if you ever find yourself working with a wizard like Stan Freberg, just keep out of the way.

So what if I was the last person to laugh at Stan's work. Nothing wrong with having the last laugh, is there?

Chapter 17

Build 'Em to Sell 'Em . . . Not to Go to Bed with 'Em

*O*nly entrepreneurs create companies. In doing so, entrepreneurs create most of America's jobs and wealth.

Not many large corporations started with the configuration of products the corporation is presently selling. More often than not, corporations simply acquire companies started by entrepreneurs, then plug them into their computers and start tinkering.

All too often, they heap on overhead, puzzle over their computers, and wonder why this good business they bought isn't so good any more.

Why? Because they keep on hiring pricey executives and enriching them with pensions up to 75 or 100 percent of their salaries, payable after the age of fifty-five or sixty-five. They pay bonuses of $100 million or more to chief executives. Their perks run the gamut from golf and country club memberships, limousines and Gulfstreams, to working four days

In his Chun King office, Jeno ponders whether his decision to walk away from the $40 million offered for his company will work out.

and playing three . . . plus month-long vacations a couple of times a year.

Believe it or not, that's how chief executives run large corporations today, and they have a "golden parachute" when they leave.

And what fuels the economy? Money, of course. Money from shareholders; man-on-the-street investors. Once they buy, they're stuck with paying for all those gratuities to top brass.

That's why small entrepreneurial firms, such as mine, keep growing and growing and can outperform, outmaneuver, and outlast those large corporations.

As just one example, let's look at a recent transaction involving this current major company of mine, Luigino's. From the start, it was a David versus Goliath situation.

We drove the Philip Morris company crazy by competing with its Kraft Foods division, which sold Budget Gourmet frozen entrees. We beat Budget Gourmet at every turn and wore out three of Kraft's frozen foods presidents. They were fired.

They finally sold Budget Gourmet to Heinz for $185 million, taking a loss of $215 million from the $400 million they'd paid for the brand not many years earlier. After that, we wore out two more Budget Gourmet presidents, this time for Heinz.

Maybe their investment advisors eventually said, "Dummies! Either sell Budget Gourmet to Jeno at a discount or buy the son of a bitch out!" Heinz chose the former, taking a $120 million write-off from their $185 million purchase of Budget Gourmet as they sold it to us for $65 million.

That's proof positive that if he has the guts to fight on, an entrepreneur can outsmart and outwork a big corporation, and overcome all the obstacles it can throw in his path. When the corporate executive says the hell with it, the entrepreneur goes on from there, having won the battle.

And yes, one day Luigino's also will be up for sale, because as I've said, I build companies to sell 'em, not to go to bed with 'em.

Right or wrong, that's what I've done time and again over fifty years . . . built companies from nothing to multimillion-dollar entities, about a billion dollars worth to date.

Maybe I've just been enamored with those two lovely words: *capital gains.*

Why don't I just keep these companies and watch them grow indefinitely?

Well, after you build a company to a certain size, it becomes too cumbersome to manage and the more management you have to hire on the executive level the more problems you encounter. Too many people, too many details. At that point, when I've built a nationwide or worldwide company, I realize that my education in high finance is limited. I find it hard to cope with the mergers and acquisitions necessary to build a true empire, whether privately owned or publicly held.

Could I turn it all over to computers, let them make the decisions? Not likely. In today's computer age, there's a real danger that you won't manage the business; the goddamn computers will. Computer-illiterate I may be, knowing little about Web sites and the Internet and all that, but I'd rather trust my own judgment.

You may recall the headlines a few years ago when a famous chess master faced off against a computer. They played even for several matches, but eventually the computer was declared the winner. I thought the human race was the loser.

Also, I keep reading that Bill Gates of Microsoft is going to make me and others like me seem even more illiterate with his so-called "paperless society" so he can make a few more billion for himself. I predict it will be a brainless society as well.

I understand that the Age of Information is revolutionizing the world, and I respect computers. I also hate them. I'm so ignorant that until a couple of years ago, I was wondering why a guy like Bill Gates could make all those billions just selling windows. I thought he was in the construction business.

I've never liked having to reorganize our planning style to fit the computer's format, whether it's for us or for our customers.

Others who are more computer literate and no doubt more intelligent than I (at least more schooled) can take companies I have created and sold to them, and then try to run those companies to the dictates of the computer. Usually they run them into the ground after a few years, but I don't give a damn because by then I've cashed in my chips, paid off capital gains taxes, and started another company . . . with damn little help from the computer.

What it comes down to, I guess, is that I don't like to run big companies. I like to create, to build, and then sell, sell, sell . . . first the products of my creation and then eventually the companies I've created that produce those products.

The best explanation of this attitude is my self-styled job description: *I'm a peddler from the Iron Range.*

Pointer from the Peddler. When all is said and done, my history has been that I create something, I peddle it one way or another, and then I start all over again. That's the fun in my game of life. Try it; you'll like it.

ALL THAT BEING SAID, it's true that for some years I was reluctant to complete my first big sale of assets—that of Chun King Corporation. Hell, it was my first-born!

Sure, it was flattering, all those offers that came in thick and fast as soon as Chun King became successful. As early as the 1950s, a group of Duluth businessmen approached me. They included Herschel Fryberger, the attorney who earlier had turned down the chance for a fifty-fifty partnership for $25,000.

"How much do you want for your company? A couple hundred thousand?"

I couldn't help but smile.

"We just turned down American Home Foods," I said, mentally thumbing my nose. "They offered four *million.*"

Others quickly followed, offering more. Why not? We had a solid, sound, and solvent company. Also, the economy of the 1960s encouraged acquisitions. Large corporations, desperate to diversify to keep on growing, were buying up profitable companies right and left.

Bargain hunters were offering ridiculously low prices. Other giants threatened to drive us out of business if we didn't knuckle under. And still others showed up with balance sheets far inferior to our own. "If you and I merge," I told one guy, "*I* should be in charge."

Once the board chairman of Colgate-Palmolive came out to see me in Duluth. Never one to stand on ceremony, I ordered him a ham sandwich for lunch so we could keep talking in my office. My visitor became offended, and as far as I was concerned, the negotiations were over.

But a year later, after returning from a fishing trip to the remote Northwest Territories, I got a call from a local banker.

"Good to hear your voice, Jeno," he greeted me, sounding relieved. "We heard a rumor you'd been killed up there in Canada."

There had been an accident, but in another fishing party.

"Where did that rumor come from?" I laughed.

"New York, of all places. Remember Colgate? I've been working with them, you know. They called and said if you were really dead, they wanted to reopen talks for Chun King."

I couldn't resist wiring the board chairman—Mr. Little, I believe was his name: "Sorry to disappoint you. Still alive and kicking. No deal, but stop by for a sandwich anytime. Regards, Jeno."

But in good time I did sell Chun King. Sold it to R. J. Reynolds Tobacco—twice.

THE FIRST TIME WAS in 1965. The price was $40 million. That was when a million dollars was a lot of money. Now all you hear about is billions. Millions are chicken feed (but not to me).

After some twenty years of building plants, buying out competitors, growing and growing, I got tired of it and wanted something new to create and build. The tobacco company approached me with a buyout offer as part of their entry into the food business as R. J. Reynolds Foods of New York City.

They wanted to diversify from tobacco for obvious reasons. I accepted their offer of $40 million cash.

So my attorney from Minneapolis, by the name of West (I forget his first name), and I go to New York to sign papers and get my check for $40 million. When we reached the suite of these New York City attorneys, on about the thirtieth floor, we walked into a large conference room. It seemed a block long. Documents were piled all over. You'd think the tobacco people were buying the City of New York and maybe half of New Jersey.

There were at least ten attorneys and paralegals there. They were dressed to kill . . . three-piece suits, fancy vests, watch chains with a dangling elk's tooth, and so on. Jesus, it was a dress parade.

Here I am with cowboy boots, leather jacket, shirt, sweater, and jeans.

I sat in a far corner waiting for my check.

Three or four hours later, I'm still being ignored while these fancy pants attorneys are carving up the carcass of my Chun King Corporation, my Orient Express trucking company, and my Florida Fresh celery company.

My attorney was over there chattering with these morticians. Finally I called out, "What in hell's going on, West?"

"Oh, Mr. Paulucci, these matters take time and a lot of detail. Just sit there and we'll take care of it all."

Jesus! Now he's calling me Mr. Paulucci. On the way over from Minnesota it was "Jeno." Is he getting brainwashed?

I thought to myself that the son of a bitch had joined the other ten; he was playing their game. Too bad he didn't have a vest and watch chain.

Besides that, I was being treated like an outsider . . . and it was my $40 million! Nobody offered me a glass of water, a cup of coffee, a soft drink, or even a place to piss. So I was getting my hair-trigger temper revved up.

Soon I heard one fancy pants, looking at some papers, say to another one, "Oh, Tom, I see you're a graduate of Harvard, Class of 1932? I'm Yale, '34."

Another one piped up, "Gosh, that's a coincidence. I'm Harvard, too, but '33."

I'd had enough!

I got up and hollered, "Gentlemen! Gentlemen!"

They stopped talking and looked at me as if wondering who in hell this peasant was. So I told them.

"I want you to know that I am Luigino Francesco Paulucci. I am a graduate of Hibbing High School, Class of 1935, and you can take your forty million dollars and shove it right up your fancy asses."

I walked out.

My brainwashed attorney followed me, his face flushed.

"You can't do that, Jeno," he said sternly. "If you do, I resign."

"Fine," I said. "I was going to fire you anyway."

And that was how—even though I build companies to sell 'em—I turned my back on $40 million cash.

> *Pointer from the Peddler: When somebody wants to buy your company but insults you in the process, just walk away. It's a matter of self-respect, and my self-respect was worth one hell of a lot more than $40 million—so they could shove it.*

I didn't plan it that way, but sticking to my principles turned out to be a great financial move. Fortune smiled. A year later, our sales and profits were up, and so was the Dow-Jones. Chun King was worth some $23 million more than that $40 million I'd left on the table.

Chapter 18

From One Company to Another

*T*he next year I sold Chun King to R. J. Reynolds all over again, and this time it stayed sold. Well, more or less.

The lesson we're looking at here is this: When you're selling one company, if you work out the details correctly, you can use the sale itself as the groundwork for your next company. That may sound unlikely, but it's true.

Our canned and frozen Chinese foods were well-established as the number one seller in the United States. Much credit goes to the creative advertising genius of Stan Freberg. Also, of course, we produced some of the best Chinese foods ever packed. I was seasoning the Chinese dishes with garlic and chicken broth and other choice ingredients, just as my mother Michelina did with Italian foods. They tasted great and were a good value.

We had canned and frozen packing operations in Duluth; Jackson, Ohio; Los Angeles; Cambridge, Maryland; and in Canada in Windsor, Ontario.

Entrepreneurs whose brands formed the nucleus of R. J. Reynolds Foods, Inc.-Hawaiian Punch, Chun King, College Inn, Vermont Maid, Patio Mexican entrees, My-T-Fine dessert mixes, Filler's Snacks, Davis Baking Powder, and Br'er Rabbit Molasses—gather to launch the venture with Jeno (second from left) as chairman and John Phillips (second from right) as president. Later, Jeno marched on to create Jeno's, Inc. and split a dollar with John Phillips that opened the future.

Still, I knew it was only a matter of time before I did sell—and for more money than Reynolds had offered the first time.

Two things prompted me to do it—two tiny things that stuck in my mind one day as I emerged from a long executive committee meeting.

One was the complaint that having office people work a half-day on Saturdays, as we had always done, had become, as someone put it, "a barbaric hardship." Apparently the rest of the civilized world had gone to a five-day week.

The other was insistence on installing power connections for heaters in the company parking lot—headbolt heaters—to make it easier to start cars in the winter.

Reasonable requests, some might say. But they went against the grain.

Well, did I have to sell the company, after all? How about offering stock, taking it public?

I remembered a few years earlier I'd come across an article from the *Wall Street Journal.* The story was an account of the annual meeting of a coffee-shop chain called Chock-Full-O'-Nuts. The executives reported a healthy 20 percent increase in sales, but stockholders still attacked the podium.

- Why didn't the company make more rye and pumpernickel bread, demanded a lady who didn't like whole wheat.
- Another shareholder complained that the company's coffee left sediment in the cup.
- Another guy thought the coffeecake was too soft.

- Still another wondered why "his" take-out place had been out of insulated containers on his last visit.

I had the article blown up and framed for our conference room, and scrawled across the top: "Why Not to Have Shareholders."

I know that publicly owned securities form the lion's share of the economy. But if I'm able to finance everything on my own—no thanks.

More to the point, if I was going to have to deal with requests of "no work on Saturdays" and "head-bolt heaters" from employees, how different was that from having shareholders?

THAT WAS THE QUESTION I was wrestling with when one man finally convinced me that it was time to move on.

Years before, I'd been impressed with John Phillips, a vice president with American Home Products, the parent firm of Chef Boy-Ar-Dee. An entrepreneur . . . a peddler . . . like me, John had co-founded his own company called Wisconsin Cheese, which he sold to Armour. He'd negotiated with me to buy Chun King, but the negotiations fell apart when his boss refused to meet my asking price.

Afterwards, John stopped by the Pierre Hotel in New York to let me know how personally disappointed he was.

"Someday when you're running your own food company again," I told him, tearing a dollar bill in two and handing him half, "give me a call."

About a year after I left the $40 million at the Reynolds altar in New York, he did just that.

"Jeno, I've still got my half of the dollar bill," he reminded me at once.

"What's up?"

"R. J. Reynolds has just made me president of the new food division they are going to be creating here in New York."

I congratulated him.

"They've been acquiring top-notch companies from all over the country. They want Chun King."

"I turned them down once, you know."

"I know, but they're still very interested in Chun King."

John didn't take part in the direct negotiations that followed, except at the end. But it was his enthusiasm for what this new division of R. J. Reynolds might become that persuaded me to join him in New York as part of the team. I admired his determination to corral other successful entrepreneurs—Rueben Hughes from Pacific-Hawaiian Products (who had come up with Hawaiian Punch); I. J. Filler from Filler's Products, who had created a line of snacks; and Texan Louis Stumberg and his brother with their Patio Foods line of Mexican dinners.

Once again the terms were set. The R. J. Reynolds people came to Duluth again, and this time very, very humbly offered me:

- $63 million in cash, up $23 million from less than two years earlier.
- The position of chairman of their new food company in New York with a nice salary.

- And there was another provision, put in there in an informal letter. Reynolds agreed to pack for me any new product I might come up with, at cost plus 5 percent.

That was a provision that the Reynolds people sort of overlooked. Pretty soon they'd have to be reminded of it.

Sure, I accepted. I'm not stupid.

I had the birth of my next company assured with no plant or capital investment, and I had $63 million—before capital gains taxes, of course.

The very next day I planned to make the formal announcement of the sale to my employees in Duluth. But I got a last-minute call from Reynolds headquarters in Winston-Salem, North Carolina. Suddenly, the Reynolds people wanted me to hold off until they announced the formation of R. J. Reynolds Foods, and then my appointment as chairman.

Sounded to me like it was going to screw up the morale of my employees even more.

Reynolds wanted to discuss it further, as large companies always do. Finally, I got upset and told them to go to hell once again.

After spreading the word that the deal was off, Lois and I left for Florida.

By the time we landed, John Phillips himself was waiting at our door with David Peoples, the treasurer from Winston-Salem. Both men admitted they had made a mistake. Once again, I was moved by John's integrity.

The next day, Lois and I flew to New Jersey, where this time I signed my name with a flourish. After going numb for a moment, an odd thought struck me.

I had to find a telephone and call Gail Bukowski, my wonderful secretary of many years in Duluth.

"Gail," I said, "I guess you don't have to do it anymore."

"What's that, Jeno?" she asked faithfully.

"The taste test. There'll probably be a new procedure."

Four times a day for as long as I could remember, I had tested all Chun King products personally at the plant. In recent years, Gail had filled in for me when I was gone.

Would either of us ever touch chow mein again? That's what I wondered on that day, November 28, 1966.

After more than twenty years, it was really over.

That evening Lois and I had dinner with John Phillips and his wife, Estelle, at the Four Seasons in New York. I was going to start work as chairman of the division the very next day. We had a fine time discussing how we were going to build a successful food empire together.

Finally John, a soft-spoken, dignified man, brought up a matter he had clearly been reluctant to speak about until that point.

"Jeno, we're going to be working pretty closely together in the years to come," he began uncomfortably. "Your style is a little different from mine, you know. No offense now, but you've got a reputation for liking to holler a lot.

"Me, I'm pretty quiet. But on occasion I've been known to give it to someone pretty good myself."

I had to smile. No doubt the knowledge of my temper had preceded me.

But John had thought of that. "How about if we have a private understanding that we aren't going to holler at one another?"

Before I could answer, he raised a finger.

"Except here's the good part. We each are entitled to one free holler. I get one. You get one. But only one. So you've got to make sure you're really mad before you use it, okay?"

"You've got a deal. One holler apiece." We all had a good laugh.

And as we shook hands across the table that night, I thought I might never holler about anything again as long as I lived. At age forty-eight, I had just sold a company for $63 million in cash, and the Dow Jones was just 650 (the equivalent of $1 billion today)—better than 50 percent more than I'd have been paid if I hadn't taken that first "holler" with my boots on in New York the year before.

I had no idea yet how that kind of money can change your life forever.

SO HERE I WAS, A MULTIMILLIONAIRE who'd sold one company and was starting another, while staying on as chairman of a food conglomerate.

Now the typical pattern for entrepreneurs with a newfound fortune is to squander some of it in investments they should have avoided like the plague. But a street-smart guy like Jeno would never do a thing like that, would he?

Well . . . yes, to some extent, as will be seen later in a few stories I'm not especially looking forward to telling.

Meanwhile, it was a great moment—a triumph. But I knew I sure hadn't done it all by myself.

I'd had my wife Lois, who had faith in me and kept on encouraging me not to give up.

And I'd had a core of people who'd helped to build the company and bring the ideas to market.

Without good people, you just have an idea. Products don't build a company . . . good people do.

When I think back on those years and the years to come, I remember all these wonderful individuals I've been privileged to work with.

I think of Joe Scinocca, Sr., who was married to my sister Elizabeth—both of them were involved during those early days. He passed away many years ago. His son, Joe Scinocca, Jr., has been a valued plant manager in Duluth. Jim Bingham was my first plant manager and engineer and has since passed on. Lee Vann was a trusted associate and a true friend throughout many of my enterprises.

There was Kelly Cardiff, Sr., whose son, Kelly "Toby" Cardiff is still a valued employee . . . Jim Lee, our first sales manager . . . Harvey Ramsey, our second sales manager . . . Jack Jurmain, in charge of Eastern Sales . . . Bill Rinker . . . Bill Bischoff . . . Virgil Kordahl . . . all gone now, and yet I keep going. It gives me a strange feeling.

I was so grateful that, to show our appreciation, Lois and I gave $2 million in tax-free gifts to Chun King employees at the time of the sale.

Today there is still Dave Ahlgren, invaluable as head of Research and Development and Quality Control (he recently retired after working with me for more than thirty years (but has come back on a consulting basis to help me kick off my next company) . . . Tom Bradseth, Don Wirtanen, Gail Bukowski, Les Eskola, Jim Boosalis, Mike Raiola, Harry Barton.

And Jim Tills, great public relations man—savvy, sensitive, and sensible—who is helping me edit this book.

And a lot of others. I apologize to those whose names don't come immediately to mind.

Pointer from the Peddler: If you're a successful entrepreneur and you think you did it all on your own, you've lost touch with reality. You were just lucky as hell to have the people around you who boosted you on the ladder to success, and gave you an extra nudge when you stumbled.

WHEN I WENT TO NEW YORK as the exalted chairman of this new R. J. Reynolds Foods, I was in for a helluva surprise. In fact, a helluva lot of surprises.

The office was on East 43rd Street, just off Park Avenue. I was anxious to get started, so I hurried from my apartment at 61st Street and Madison and arrived at five-thirty A.M. The security guard stopped me from getting into the elevator.

"Where the hell do you think you're going at this hour?" he asked in an officious tone. I explained to him that I was the new chairman of R. J. Reynolds Foods, that I had my keys, and wanted to go up to the twelfth floor (I believe it was) and start my day.

"I just sold my Chun King Corporation," I beamed.

The guard scowled. "I don't give a damn if you're Charlie Chan. Get the hell out of here and don't come back until eight-thirty."

Welcome to the New York work ethic.

So my first day wasn't so good for me. Nor for the guard, who got transferred to dog-catcher detail shortly thereafter.

I'm still wondering how in hell Reynolds or any other New York company ever got anything done in those days. Productivity was nil. I'd see employees come in at nine or nine-thirty, take off their coats, then go down the elevator to get coffee and a roll. Maybe they'd start work about ten o'clock or so.

Around eleven or noon, down all would go for lunch. They'd come back between one and three o'clock, depending on the type of work they did or how many martinis they'd had with lunch. Around four-thirty, down they'd go again to catch the commuter train or the subway or maybe another martini. Jesus! What a way to run a business.

And no use firing any of them because whomever you hired to replace them would have the same bad habits.

In all fairness, I think it's not quite that bad anymore. New York has made some strides in catching up with the rest of the country, and you often see even highly placed executives coming to work at . . . well, maybe nine or nine-thirty. Some even stay on after hours for a meeting and catch the later train. What dedication!

I could go on telling you how much I hated working in New York City, trying to run that new food company, but suffice it to say that I did my part and helped put R. J. Reynolds Foods on a successful course. Then I left. And I sure was grateful to get back to Duluth full-time, where workers are workers at all levels.

To John Phillips' credit, the company eventually became the second largest food conglomerate in the world behind Philip Morris' General Foods division. And later as RJR-Nabisco, about to be spun off again, it somehow kept rolling along.

While working in New York, I had another business back in Duluth. I had hung onto Northland Foods. That wasn't part of the sale.

After selling off the pie-filling end of the business, the operation consisted of little more than Jeno's Pizza Mix and attempts to market my mother's spaghetti sauce. But as great as her home cooking was, I started to see America's eating habits heading in a new direction. Everywhere I looked there were families on the run with no time for knives and forks or mixing bowls. I could see a time when people would eat food right out of their hands, at home, in the car, or literally on the move. "Finger food"— that's what I saw down the road.

Although a standard non-compete agreement with Reynolds barred me from returning to the Chinese food business, I still had that "escape clause" in the final letter of the contract. The sale of Chun King had closed at the end of November 1966, and by the following March, my plans were well under way. Not only did I have packaging in hand, but also $100,000 worth of Stan Freberg commercials (make that a $1.5 million in today's dollars) all set for national television.

The old Northland Foods signboard on the 525 Lake Avenue South building had been replaced by a brand-new Jeno's, Inc.

A new era had begun.

But Reynolds Foods was in for a big surprise.

Chapter 19
Pizza Rolls: They're Not Danish

*B*ack in New York one day, the chairman of Reynolds Foods (me) stepped into the office of the president and CEO (John Phillips) and dropped a sheet of paper on his desk.

"Here's my order for . . ."

"Pizza rolls?" he cried, looking at the paper. "What the hell are they?"

My cards were on the table at last.

In order to refresh his memory, John had to pull out the informal letter we had added to the original sales contract. As a concession, Reynolds had agreed to my request to pack pizza rolls.

The letter even identified the specific product as pizza rolls. At the time, John had carefully added a provision of his own, making sure I had to put up the capital for any new equipment required by such "experimental ventures."

Jeno's pizza rolls established the "hot snacks" category.

"Okay, Jeno," he said, tossing the letter aside in disgust. "You've got me. It looks like we do have to pack your 'pizza rolls' for you."

"Don't worry, John," I said, trying to be helpful. "There's nothing to it. I've already shipped the packaging to your plant in Ohio."

The order I dropped on his desk called for 50,000 cases in May, another 50,000 in June. Maybe 200,000 cases in all.

"Now wait a minute!" he protested. "We can't move that fast on all this!"

"Why not?" I asked innocently.

"You expect us to be in production next month, for God's sake? What about all the equipment we'll need. You know how much time a new line takes to install." He gave me a suspicious glance. "Don't forget you're picking up the tab for all this equipment."

"That's the beauty of it, John. We don't need any new equipment."

"Come again?"

"We've already got everything we need down there," I explained. "It's the same line we use for Chun King egg rolls."

"How can that be?"

"Look at the formulas for the pizza rolls," I suggested, offering a second sheet of paper. "Only the fillings are different."

John took a minute to read it over, before looking me coldly in the eye.

"You mean to tell me a pizza roll is just a god-damn egg roll with a pizza filling?"

It was true.

My new "finger food" frozen snack used the same shell as the Chinese egg rolls he had inherited from Chun King.

"What do I tell the people at corporate headquarters in Winston-Salem?" he sighed, throwing up his hands at last.

"Just tell them what I told you," I replied. "I'm not pulling a fast one here. After all, they signed the papers. The letter expressly says pizza rolls are a possibility."

"Hell, I don't know what I was thinking"—his eyes rolled skyward—"I guess I thought a pizza roll was, you know, something like a Danish. A hunk of pastry with a pizza topping."

Anyhow, Reynolds went through with our arrangement and began packing the pizza rolls for me. There was no way on earth I could have started my own plant that cheaply. And here I had a ridiculously low fixed ceiling of 5 percent.

It was a wonderful deal. But it wasn't all smooth sailing, of course.

Even being a senior member of management, I could never get the Ohio plant to give me the quality I wanted. After I resigned from Reynolds to devote full-time to Jeno's, Inc., our running dispute only worsened. Because Reynolds didn't make any money on my line, their heart wasn't in it. My complaints, even to John himself, fell on deaf ears.

Finally, I'd had enough.

I filed a lawsuit against the corporation for failing to pack my pizza rolls in a responsible manner.

The reaction was not what I expected.

One morning John Phillips burst into my office at Jeno's, Inc. 525 Lake Avenue South in Duluth. Without any ceremony whatsoever, he leaned across my desk and used up his one "holler" we had agreed to years before.

"Jeno, how could you do this to me?" he raved, pounding his fists. Truthfully, I had never seen a man so angry.

"Here I was the one who brought you into the company in the first place. And what do you turn around and do? You make me look like a godamn fool in front of everybody in the place!"

Finally, he calmed down enough to add, "Besides, you and I, of all people, could have worked out those quality problems without resorting to more lawyers, for God's sake. I'm terribly disappointed, Jeno."

John didn't have to say more.

The very next week I met with the general counsel of R. J. Reynolds in Winston-Salem and agreed to drop the lawsuit. To settle the packing problem with Reynolds, I did what I should have done a long time ago.

Jeno's, Inc., took over manufacturing its own pizza rolls and moved the entire operation back to Duluth. Even though it meant surrendering our dream cost plus 5 percent arrangement, we were enjoying such a whopping gross margin on sales—better than 60 percent—that we easily absorbed the costs of managing our own facilities.

On top of that, I was able to hire back many of the experienced people who had set up those same egg-roll lines for Chun King in the first place.

Meanwhile, the success of Jeno's Pizza Rolls was little short of phenomenal. We had put the right product on the market at the right time.

A peddler had once again shown those giant corporations how to create a company.

But there was more expansion in store for Jeno's. And it was no cake-walk, nor was it an egg-roll.

I NEVER INTENDED to get into the frozen-pizza game.

It didn't seem like a good bet. In the late 1960s, 50 different companies must have been competing for freezer space in the supermarkets. They came in as many varieties as they did sizes.

American Home Foods' Chef Boy-Ar-Dee ranked number one in the United States, but Celentano was popular in New York. In the Midwest, John's Pizza seemed to be everywhere. Tombstone was becoming big in and around Wisconsin and was talking about going national. Marvin Schwan's brand, Tony's, was starting up, and doing well, and it went on and on.

But my people talked me into it, and we got into frozen pizza. I became convinced that there was only one way Jeno's could survive in such a crowded market: We had to have a highly automated system that used our own ingredients and made the entire pizza, with no waste whatsoever.

If we had a good product and were the low-cost producer, we had a chance.

One small hitch. Nowhere on God's earth did there exist a machine that could make good-enough pizza crust. After searching engineering firms all over the country, the best my people could come up with was right here in Duluth. A tiny outfit called Moline Bakery Equipment Supply Company.

"Hell!" I exploded, "I didn't need to pay you guys to tell me about Moline. I knew Harry before he started the damn place."

Harry Moline had been a faithful customer back in my Hancock Nelson selling days. He was someone who could always be counted on to take a few cases of canned fruit for his bakery.

As I was well aware, Harry was also a genius at automating the procedures that went into baking. Throughout the years, he would show me what he had come up with.

"But Harry's no longer there, Jeno."

"I know that. He died of a heart attack years ago. That's the only reason I didn't suggest Moline in the first place."

Harry's son Don and brother Roy had carried on the business. And Roy had assured our engineer, Dan Kussy, that they could give us exactly what we wanted—an automated sheeted crust machine with no waste.

Don Wirtanen, the president of Jeno's, met with the new owners of Moline and came back with a deal. We would put up $700,000 to cover the cost of any experimental model. If we went into actual production, they received a royalty for a fixed period on each crust we turned out.

I asked Don one question. "What will this machine do for our costs?"

"We'll save a nickel on every crust we make."

We sold pizzas in those days for about $6 a dozen. A 10 percent savings offered us a tremendous edge.

"Let's do it," I told him.

When we wrote up the contract, I made sure we added a couple of provisions. For underwriting the project, we were entitled to all patent rights. This would include, I specified after a moment's reflection, "any future improvements" to the machine.

The Moline machine worked like a dream.

The dough, after being mixed in a hopper and pressed between rollers, could be cut into shells of any size or thickness, with whatever was left over flowing back to the mixing vat, to become part of a future crust.

Our own engineers designed the rest of the system. A series of "waterfalls" poured the topping on the shells in prescribed amounts. Any overflow of topping also returned automatically to the dispensers.

Little more than a year after starting development, we had three lines producing "automated sheeted crusts" at a plant across the bay in Superior. Nobody else had anything like it.

But even with a superior product and a built-in cost advantage, it was still a tough market to crack. Too often we had to buy our way into the bigger supermarket chains. This could mean shipping a chain of 300 stores at least a hundred free cases per store right off the bat. And once the chain started ordering, they still wanted a freebie along with every one they paid for.

One morning in the fall of 1969, I added up all the orders we had received for frozen pizzas the previous day across the United States. It came to 107 cases of pizza sold, and 155 cases given away.

That's how cutthroat the competition was from the very beginning.

But in the end, a determined effort from top to bottom—coupled with low costs—won out. Jeno's, Inc. rose to number one in the country, with a 30 percent share of the frozen pizza market.

Chun King was history, as far as I was concerned. Jeno's, Inc. was a new force in the food business nationwide. But much more fun was to come.

Pointer from the Peddler: The time to sell your company is the time to pave the way for your next company.

Chapter 20

Building a Business Is Fine—But There's More to Do

I can't close out this discussion of building and selling businesses without some comments on what I believe to be a closely related subject that, for lack of a better word, let's call *activism.*

Getting rich is a worthy goal, but it's not enough. From the start, you owe it to yourself to spend time—and money—finding ways to improve and enrich the place where you do business. Later on, maybe you can do the same thing on a national and international scale.

It's not easy, and you'll make as many enemies as friends along the way. But looking back, you'll be proud of what you did or tried to do. And what the hell, it's fun!

MY SECOND CAREER AS AN "ACTIVIST" started back in the late 1950s, just as soon as Chun King was

Taconite Amendment
By Roger Skophammer

PEOPLE OF MINNESOTA...

YOUR CHOICE:
ACT NOW OR
YOU'LL PAY EVEN
HIGHER TAXES!

DULUTH
NEWS-TRIBUNE
SEPT. 25, 1966

pages in the history of the amendment.

The first talks about a taconite amendment were among a group of Duluth and Iron Range men who included both Democrats and Republicans as well as independents. Only one of them, Rep. Fred A. Cina of Aurora, held public office.

Other people involved in the initial stages of the talks were Jeno Paulucci, Chun King Corp. president; Christian F. Beukema of U. S. Steel Corp; Everett Joppa of Pickands Mather & Co.; Gerald W. Heaney, DFL leader and attorney for labor unions, and Richard Hastings, attorney for mining companies.

The first key meeting was a gathering in Paulucci's office in the summer of 1960. Most of all of those mentioned above were present. This meeting is said to be the birthplace of the Taconite Amendment.

Wake up!
We're 100 years
too late.

Let's stop giving away our future.

N·E·MINN. ORGANIZATION FOR ECONOMIC EDUCATION

it's up to ALL OF US in "64"
TO GET STATE WIDE SUPPORT FOR THE
TACONITE AMENDMENT VOTE!

nemo inc.

NEMO ACTION BOARD

NEMO, Inc., spearheaded the Minnesota Taconite Amendment campaign, which brought thousands of jobs to the depressed mining region.

successful enough for me to pry some time away in the evening or early mornings or weekends. I founded a group called NEMO, Inc. (the North Eastern Minnesota Organization for Economic Education), and installed my valued assistant Lee Vann as executive vice president. The purpose was to bring back jobs to the Iron Range and Duluth.

The high-grade iron ore had run out and miners were out of jobs. The unemployment rate on the Range was in double-digits. We were losing our most valuable asset—our youth—who had to leave the area to make a living.

After a while, Lee and I were sick and tired of the vacillation and indifference we ran into. It was clear we weren't going to get any help from the old-line wealthy, or formerly wealthy, people centered in Duluth's musty old Kitchi Gammi Club, who didn't give a damn what happened to the people on the Range.

One company, Reserve Mining, was processing iron-bearing taconite rock successfully, and employing more than 600 people year-round. But extracting iron from taconite rock is an expensive process. It cost about a billion dollars to build the plant.

Still, the Iron Range could have a real future if we could get the other mining companies to build new high-technology taconite plants as Reserve Mining had done.

They weren't against the idea, those companies, but they worried that if they made the investment, the local communities, the county, and the State of Minnesota would tax them out of business.

I thought their fears were justified. That was going to be a problem. What we needed was an amendment to the Minnesota Constitution that would set the ground rules, fair to industry and labor, for a new taconite industry in our state.

Lee Vann and I visited with Christian F. Beukema of U.S. Steel; with Representative Fred Cina of Aurora, who was chairman of the State Tax Committee; and with Nick Krmpotich of Coleraine, director of U.S. Steelworkers District 33.

We made little progress. So using my powers of persuasion—a peddler on a different cause—I got the key people together in my Chun King offices in West Duluth on December 31, New Year's Eve, 1960.

Present were Representative Cina; Chris Beukema of U.S. Steel; Everett Joppa of Pickards Mather & Co., which managed the mining operations for various investors; Gerald W. Heaney, Democratic-Farmer-Labor party leader and an attorney for labor unions (later Eighth District Appellate Court Judge); Richard Hastings, attorney for mining companies; Lee Vann; and me.

We started about two P.M. I locked the door—to the raised eyebrows of my guests, who wondered what they hell they were getting into—and stated that we were not going to leave until we had a consensus. Sandwiches and coffee were available.

It's interesting, what happens when you get adversaries together in a room and lock them in. First, polite conversation, suspicious glances, frost in the air. Then, little by little, they started loosening up and talking to each other. Maybe they hoped to God they'd be let loose in time to celebrate the new year.

By about nine P.M. we had reached consensus. We agreed that we would work together to convince the public—most especially the dyed-in-the-wool "I hate mining companies" people on the Iron Range— of the need for a Taconite Amendment to the Minnesota Constitution. The amendment would last some twenty to twenty-five years. It would be based on fair treatment of mining companies' billion-dollar investments, but it would not cave in with any odious concessions.

That's how we got started together on the Taconite Amendment. But it was slow going. Getting it approved and passed by the legislature was going to be a battle.

The unions were worried about taxes being too low. The industry, with Chris Beukema of U.S. Steel as spokesman, wanted to get the production tax included in the amendment, and frozen at the then-current five cents a ton.

I well remember a call from Fred Cina, the representative who headed the Tax Committee and was trying to draw up the legislation.

"Jeno," he said, "we've got to lay it on the line with industry and tell them the production tax is not to be included in the amendment. That's the hang-up."

"Fred," I said, "we'll have to deal with the tax later. Right now we have to get the amendment passed. Don't say anything about the production tax in the legislation. The industry probably thinks it'll be frozen at five cents."

"Do you think they're stupid?"

"No, but they think we are. Don't bring it up."

The legislative process stumbled on. But the amendment finally did pass, three years later, thanks in large part to the intervention of the president of the United States. I met with Jack Kennedy during his stopover in Duluth on September 25, 1963. He agreed to speak with U.S. Steel's president, Roger Blough, who would try to get Chris Beukema, their local man, to agree to the provisions of the amendment.

That happened, and the amendment passed.

About a month later, John F. Kennedy—that great man—was assassinated in Dallas.

That was my first meeting with a president, but not my last. More about that later.

AFTER THE TACONITE AMENDMENT CAME TO PASS, the industry loved me. Soon they would come to hate me. That's because the time soon came to deal with the tax issue.

With construction of the taconite plants under way, we of NEMO—Lee Vann and myself—tackled that five cents a ton production tax. Even at full capacity (about 60 million tons a year), the tax would distribute a measly $3 million a year to the Iron Range towns—west to Aitkin and east to Aurora— that had to provide the additional staff and services to service the new plants.

First, we sent up a trial balloon to establish the principle that the production tax was *not* part of the amendment and that the tax *could* be raised. We went first for pennies—an increase from five cents to eleven cents a ton.

The industry didn't like that. And they hated what came next.

As president of NEMO, I personally commissioned and paid the renowned Stanford Research Institute of Menlo Park, California, to make a worldwide study to determine what the northeastern Minnesota taconite industry could afford to pay per ton in production tax, while remaining competitive with taconite from the rest of the world.

Their answer in June 1970: at least $1 a ton, equivalent to $4 in today's dollars.

The struggle went on for years. A former governor—and my friend—Rudy Perpich helped a lot. The strategy was to get the tax pegged to the price of steel. And that's what was finally done under what came to be known as the Paulucci Bill (M.S.298.223 and M.S.298.291.294), made law by the Minnesota Legislature in 1977.

The tax was increased to more than $3 a ton until the Iron Range Rehabilitation Board (IRRRB), encouraged by Governor Arne Carlson, cut it back to something over $2.

The result, on 60 million tons production capacity, is $120 million a year. Much of the proceeds under the Paulucci Bill were supposed to be set aside in trust for protection of the environment, diversification of employment as taconite processing declines over the years, and for distribution to the towns for development projects that create employment.

All this is under the management of the IRRRB commissioner, plus the governor.

Some of those trust funds have dissipated. Let's hope and pray that most of the money will be there for the benefit of our youth and the generations to follow.

A few years ago, Chris Beukema wrote to me from his retirement home in Florida: "Jeno, are you still chasing windmills?"

I answered: "Yes, Chis. And that production tax turned out to be a pretty expensive windmill for the industry, didn't it?"

But all that was in the past, and Chris and I became friends. When he became ill just before he died, I offered to fly him to the Mayo Clinic. A good man, he fought for his industry.

Later on I worked with the industry on a number of projects, notably trying to solve the problem of taconite tailings being dumped into Lake Superior. Sometimes they loved me; sometimes they hated me.

> *Jeno's Credo:*
> *Who in hell cares if I make enemies . . .*
> *as long as I serve the common cause.*

Part Three

Money In The Bank— Now What?

When I sold Chun King for $63 million, I suddenly became rich and fairly famous. At the time, the Dow Jones average was at 650, an amount that would equate to about a billion dollars now. The media loved it. One reporter joked that when I deposited my check with the little bank in Duluth, I broke the bank.

Amazing how my image suddenly changed, especially in the eyes of the elite of Duluth—those prominent citizens who had inherited some money, made some money, or wanted people to believe they had money. Until then, they had regarded me as a Dago ruffian from the Iron Range who should go back to the mines and dig.

But after the sale, I got telegrams of congratulations from them. I was the angel of northeastern Minnesota. I even received an invitation to join the Kitchi Gammi Club, the hallmark of distinction in Duluth for almost a century. But I wasn't prepared for that, so I politely declined.

But the big question was how to manage the money I'd earned, and make it grow. It was all new to me, and I needed advice. I talked to everybody from high-powered investment bankers to commodities masterminds to well-meaning friends. Their advice, as you'll see, ranged from good to bad to god-awful.

Jeno's Credo:

Look beyond the horizon. Today's is already old. The only new is tomorrow's . . . But don't be an expert too soon.

The Cornelius Company . . . getting involved to protect your investment.

Chapter 21

Making Money Is a Hassle—Investing It Is a Bitch

When you're a successful entrepreneur, the crucial question is what to do with all those liquid assets after your first big score.

For me, it was a struggle. I didn't know it, but I'd already made my first big mistake. When I sold Chun King to R. J. Reynolds for $63 million, some advisors said, "Jeno, take the money in stock, not cash. You'll do better in the long run."

I didn't listen. If I had taken that advice, I would have ended up as the largest shareholder of R. J. Reynolds Industries. Then, if I'd kept my shares through the subsequent merger with Nabisco Brands, and then held on when RJR Nabisco was sold in the famous power struggle with Kohlberg Kravis Roberts & Co. in 1988 (you might remember the book and TV movie, *Barbarians at the Gate*) . . .

. . . my stock would have been worth . . .

Hell, I don't want to even try to add it up.

With money in the bank, I proceeded to make poor investments in precious metals (a commodities genius was sure I'd make millions; it took a threatened lawsuit to get about half my money back), and a mutual fund company and other ventures that are too tedious to talk about. I'd made millions, but I was in danger of pissing away billions.

What sticks in my mind is my experience with investment advisors.

RIGHT OFF THE BAT, I began to get calls from brokers about investments they wanted to recommend. I chose Donaldson, Lufkin & Jenrette, a firm that had started just a few years earlier and was the darling of Wall Street.

DLJ said I should have a diversified portfolio, which sounded reasonable. First off, they suggested 25 percent ownership of two new companies, Sealed Air and U.S. Surgical. Sealed Air was the pioneer in making those blankets of trapped air bubbles as protective packaging for shipments, and U.S. Surgical had a new process for using staples instead of stitches in surgery. Both companies became very successful. But when I was a little ahead, I sold out of both—missing out on millions as the stocks continued to soar out of sight.

Another suggestion from DLJ was options. I wasn't sure what options were (I'm still not), but DLJ explained that there was no risk, because there was this timetable where if you sold an option that was going to lose, you could hedge on it by buying another option to cover yourself. Or something like that.

I invested $10 million. Before long, it was down to $5 million. I got Bill Donaldson, one of the partners, on the phone. I said they didn't appear to be following the procedure as outlined. Then I made an unheard-of demand. I wanted my $10 million back.

"Well, you lost it in the market. Give us a chance, and we'll try to earn it back for you."

"No, you don't hear me too well. I want the whole ten million back, now."

I guess he thought I was crazy. Nothing like that was ever done on Wall Street. But then I made a couple more phone calls and found that DLJ was vulnerable in two ways—first, one of the partners was about to go to work for the president; second, they were about to take the firm public. Those were two good reasons why they didn't want any unfavorable publicity—such as a lawsuit.

Going for the jugular, I called Bill Donaldson again and told him plainly that I was about to go to the Securities and Exchange Commission with my complaint. If he wanted to talk it over, I suggested he come up to Duluth to see me—and bring a check for $10 million.

He asked how to get to Duluth. I told him to take the plane to Chicago and head north by snowmobile. Then we compromised and agreed to meet in Minneapolis at the offices of my attorney, the always-reliable Peter Dorsey.

When we met, Bill gave me the same song-and-dance about options and the hedge system. Yes, it was unfortunate that the account had lost $5 million, and so on.

I lost my temper—or seemed to. Actually this was one of my strategic losses of temper.

Bill Donaldson stood up to it, to his credit. He said something like, "Don't take that attitude with me. I've seen irate people before."

"That may be true," I said, "but you've never had one goddamn mad Wop on your hands."

I finally looked him in the eye and said, "Listen, do you want to settle this thing now and see to it that we get the full ten million dollars, and we forget about doing business together but part friends? Or do you want me to go to the SEC tomorrow?"

That's really all I had to say. Bill realized that if I did go to the SEC, there was every possibility that their plans to offer stock would be screwed or delayed.

The $10 million was transferred to me within twenty-four hours.

Net, I took a loss. Sure, I got my money back. But my return on investment was zero.

Nice work, Jeno.

ON ANOTHER OCCASION, my friends at DLJ made a recommendation that eventually took me to a place I'd never been—the majority owner and CEO, for God's sake, of a publicly owned company. It was a marathon.

DLJ suggested that I take a serious look at the Cornelius Company, with headquarters in Anoka, Minnesota, about 150 miles southwest of Duluth. Their business was manufacturing soft drink dispensing units—for Coke and Pepsi—to be used in bars and restaurants.

"Jeno," the DLJ partner told me, "this is a fast-growing company in a good field of business, and they damn near have a monopoly because of Dick Cornelius' patents.

"He's an inventive genius. He has plants all over the world, including a joint venture in Japan. Why don't you visit with him?"

The DLJ people arranged a meeting with Dick Cornelius in Anoka. He met me in his small cubbyhole office. Dick was very personable and knowledgeable about all his equipment. He took me for a quick tour of the plant. It was only about 60,000 square feet, as I recall it.

Dick also told me about a new invention of his. He called it the Frosty Freeze. It was going to be an automatic coin-fed or manually operated semi-freeze-type drink machine, dispensing a frosty fruit drink in an eight- to twelve-ounce cup.

The way Dick described it, this machine was the greatest thing since sliced bread. It was nothing less than a revolution in the beverage industry.

I got so thirsty I asked for a sample.

Sorry, the machine wasn't perfected yet. A few bugs to be straightened out, then it would be ready for market.

Dick was so enthusiastic and full of promises about his worldwide company that I was convinced it was a good investment. It was selling over-the-counter at $30 a share, and I authorized DLJ to buy 100,000 shares.

Up to this point, I had never owned a share of publicly traded stock, being as I always owned 100 percent of my companies. But how could the darlings and geniuses of Wall Street be wrong?

Now here I am, a major shareholder in a worldwide public company. I start reading the *Wall Street Journal,* and every day I look for the Cornelius over-the-counter quotation. For a couple of weeks, it stayed around the high twenties and low thirties. Not making any money yet. The Frosty Freeze must still have bugs.

About three weeks later, the stock was down to $25. I got hold of Cornelius and asked, "Dick, I just lost half a million on your stock. What's wrong?"

"Oh nothing, just normal with the stock market."

I figured it was my inexperience. "Jeno," I said to myself, "if you're going to be a sophisticated investor, you've got to discipline yourself. Don't get excited about these small ups and downs." So I resolved not to read the *Wall Street Journal* for four weeks (which wasn't all that hard not to do, by the way).

After the four weeks, I turned to the tables again and . . . holy shit! Cornelius was down to $20. The next day $18, with a lot of "short-selling." Took me years to figure out what the hell that meant.

In any event, I now had a loss of $1.2 million.

The DLJ people said not to worry, it was just a "paper loss."

"Paper loss!" I hollered over the phone. "What the hell do you think money is printed on—cellophane?

"You told me to buy this. It's your mistake. I want my full three million dollars and *you* take this paper loss."

They hung up on me.

Nice people!

So I called Dick Cornelius again. All I got was more of the same. "Everything's fine. Just a slight delay. The stock is down due to profit-taking."

"What profit-taking?" I asked. "Hell, this is loss-taking. Dick, I want to visit with you at once. I'll be there tomorrow."

"Jeno, why don't you wait a few days. Our executive committee will be meeting at the Minneapolis Club [I think it was]. They'll better enlighten you as to how well we are doing. The stock market is not a reflection of that."

"Well, when it was thirty dollars a share, what was that a reflection of?"

Three days later I was at the fancy Minneapolis Club. The executive committee meeting began at nine A.M. Some lawyer was presiding—not a good sign. Also present were an investment banker from Piper Jaffray Company of Minneapolis; Clarence Frame, then president of First Bank of St. Paul and Minneapolis; several others whose names I don't remember; and of course, Dick Cornelius.

Dick introduced me to the group, stating that he had invited me because I was a new investor with some 5 percent of the company stock, and unfortunately I was unhappy with the stock performance.

Other than Clarence Frame, who knew me and was one of my bankers, the committee looked at me as if I were a peon greenhorn from the sticks of the Iron Range.

The lawyer chairman, in a condescending voice, said, "Mr. Paulucci, what is your problem? We have a busy agenda here today."

"Fine," I said. "I won't delay your agenda. Here is *your* problem, not *mine.* I was given rosy promises by the chairman and founder of your company. Based on those promises, I bought three million dollars worth of stock, worth only one-point-eight million today.

"My request is simple. Here's the hundred thousand shares," I went on, tossing the certificates on the table. "I want my money back—all three million—and you can proceed with your busy agenda."

The chairman smiled and said I didn't seem to realize how the stock market works. "You must be a very naive investor, indeed," he said. "As everyone knows, you can make money or lose money in the stock market."

"Hell," I said, "if I wanted to lose money, I could have gone to Nevada. Mr. Cornelius gave me a lot of promises, so now just give me my three million back."

"We can't favor one stockholder," he countered. "That would cause an avalanche of claims for refunds. Why don't you just leave well enough alone and let us build this company so you and others will not only get your original investment back but maybe a lot more?"

He continued, "Patience, my dear friend" . . . as if it were the blessing of the Pope.

"No," I answered. "I was given specific promises—not fulfilled. I want my three million dollars back or I'll sue your combined asses in court."

That's when my friend Clarence Frame entered the conversation.

"Jeno," he said, "I realize that you might prevail in court. But your lawsuit could also result in bankrupting this company and get you nothing but an empty judgment.

"I've got to be honest with you," he said, looking at me and shrugging off the worried glances of the other members of this august executive committee. "This company has some real problems that are just beginning to unfold. Instead of a lawsuit, I suggest you join this committee. We could use some good business advice and judgment."

The others didn't like it, but they didn't object.

I said I'd think it over and give them my decision by the next morning. My best cool judgment told me: Don't sue. See if you can get your money back by finding out what's wrong and seeing to it that corrections are made. How hard could that be?

So I became a member of the executive committee of a public company, something like I'd been with R. J. Reynolds.

Believe me, I dug in fast—and took charge, following one of my Jeno's Credos that had served me well:

> *Jeno's Credo:*
> *Always look for what's wrong—*
> *not for what's right*

Number one. I went to Europe, and found that Cornelius's European headquarters was on the island of Majorca in Spain. Nice place for the president of

Cornelius-Europe, a man named Ole Bach, to hide away with his mistress.

I arranged to close the Majorca headquarters and move it to Langenfeld, Germany, where we had a factory. Fired Ole Bach and replaced him with John Buyse, one of the Cornelius executives in the United States.

Number Two. I studied the contract Cornelius had with Joseph Blood, the president of U.S. operations, who I'd decided was not up to the position. Our directors wanted to buy out his contract. Screw that.

"Your new world headquarters," I told Joe Blood, "is Langenfeld, Germany. Start packing."

"You can't do that. I've got a contract."

"Read it. We can transfer you anywhere."

He tried Germany for two months. But his new wife didn't like it. He quit, and good riddance.

We consolidated our European plants and sales organizations so they all ran out of Germany.

Number Three. John Buyse, now president for Europe, wanted an upgrade. He wanted to be president of Cornelius-U.S.A. When we said no, he put together a petition of all European managers—sales, factory, and finance—saying they'd be very unhappy if their pal John wasn't promoted.

I flew to Frankfort overnight. My cousin, Celso Paulucci, came from Italy and drove me to a meeting of all the European management at a hotel in Dusseldorf.

They thought they were in for a pleasant exchange of views. They weren't. I told them that John Buyse was fired, and they also would be fired if they didn't get back to work at once.

"We understand," one manager said. "So let's at least have a nice lunch while we're here."

"Oh sure. Enjoy yourselves. Sorry I can't join you, but I've already chewed about twenty asses in the last twenty minutes, and I'm not hungry anymore."

Number Four. I went back to the United States and found a real talent, a man named Jerry Gobel, and promoted him to president of U.S. operations.

Dick Cornelius didn't like my high-handed measures. He resigned and put his shares on the market. Our family bought them all at $2.50 a share, and for the first time, I took over as chairman and CEO of a public company.

What we needed, I decided at once, was a strong board of directors instead of that collection of know-nothings I'd met at the Minneapolis Club. I arranged for a number of directors to resign with our sincere thanks—just leave. But Clarence Frame remained. He was an excellent businessman with good insight and financial knowledge and experience from the past. So did that representative from Piper Jaffray, a sound investment banker whose name still escapes me.

Jerry Gobel, who'd turned out to be a tough, smart president for the U.S. side of things, came to the board as worldwide president. We also brought in Carl Roepke, Jr. from San Francisco, one of the finest business minds I knew. He'd been my food broker for many years and, looking back, was the only broker in fifty years that I'd never had to fire.

Another newcomer was Lud Andolsek, who was chairman of the Civil Service Commission and had a world of knowledge about Washington circles.

Still another new board member was a bright young businessman named Mick Paulucci. I didn't want him aboard because he was my son, but because he is smart as hell and I knew his advice would be unsentimental and based on the bottom line. Mick did his homework.

About this time, the *Wall Street Journal* ran an article about the shares of Cornelius going from $30 to $2.50. They noted that one Jeno F. Paulucci had fired three presidents in nine months.

I got the editor on the phone and asked, "Why don't you get your facts straight? I didn't fire three presidents in nine months. I fired *four.*"

I also told him that Cornelius was all through being a nice place to vacation, complete with mistresses on the shores of Majorca, or dinners in London at Rothchilds Club, or the sandy beaches of Rio or Acapulco, with topless beauties parading around at company expense.

The honeymoon was over.

Not to go into too many details, but Jerry, Mick, and I had a lot of fun straightening out that company. In constant consultation with the other board members—and I thank them all—we looked closely at all the Cornelius Company facilities in the United States and Europe. We reallocated our resources—trim some here and add some there—and hammered out a viable structure.

We made some profitable acquistions. Jerry Gobel arranged to sell 50 percent of the European operations, which were still a can of worms, to a British company, IMI Corporation. We set up a new world headquarters in Anoka and consolidated all the U.S. offices.

Wall Street took notice. Cornelius shares were recovering nicely.

I decided it was time to bow out. We sold the remainder of Cornelius to IMI at a profit to my family of about $25 million.

Sometimes I wished I'd never listened to Donaldson, Lufkin & Jenrette and gotten into that mess in the first place. But as I said, it was fun.

Despite everything, I think DLJ were damn good investment people and still are today. They were acquired a few years ago by Credit Suisse First Boston, but some of the founders are still on the scene, and still doing good work.

In each case, they offered what they thought was sound advice, and it's not their fault that I followed it.

Pointer from the Peddler: Most often, the best use of your profits from selling a company is to plow them back into what you know best. As the old saying goes, "Shoemaker, stick to your last."

That's my philosophy. But it can be carried too far if it causes you to pass up golden opportunities that are sitting there right in front of your face . . . as will be seen in the next chapter.

ADDENDUM

For all its faults and management fat, the Cornelius Company did have some interesting technology in the works. One system that caught my attention during those years was called the Home Refresher.

The concept was simple. Consumers would install this small cabinet—maybe two feet wide and three feet tall—connect it to water and a power outlet, then put in cola or other soft drink syrups from the super-market. Then they could help themselves at home to soft drinks that cost about a nickel a drink, with no cans or bottles to throw away or recycle.

I worked with the Sanyo Company, our partners in Japan, to perfect the machine. Then, when we sold Cornelius to IMI, I didn't want to let go of it because I saw it as a revolution in the beverage industry.

Accordingly, I bought the rights to the Home Re-fresher from IMI on the basis of a 5 percent royalty to me on every machine they sold. I could see them being installed in millions of households throughout the world, wherever one had access to clean drinking water.

To date, the only one I know of is sitting in my R&D department in Duluth.

Turned out that IMI had no intention of selling Home Refreshers because they were afraid of going into competition with customers like Coke and Pepsi.

I could understand that. Still, they were screwing me out of a royalty I had coming.

So I sent them an invoice based on 5 percent of the units they could have sold, but didn't. When they balked, I suggested they read the fine print on the agreement we'd reached, which stated clearly that I was entitled to royalties whether they sold the ma-chines or not.

Net, I collected about $5 million or $6 million.

That was another little business venture that didn't quite work out as expected. But the Home Refresher is an idea that won't go away. One of these days . . .

Pointer from the Peddler: When you draw up a contract, pay close attention to the fine print. The devil is in the details. And make sure that fine print is yours.

Chapter 22

Jeno the Sports Mogul

*I*f you've got money to invest, what could be better than professional sports? With that industry about ready to take off, here was a way, I was told, to pile up profits and have fun doing it.

I had several chances to become a sports mogul. How did they work out? Well, is there a Jeno Paulucci Stadium in Miami, Florida?

No. But there could have been.

In 1967, not long after I sold Chun King, a Minneapolis lawyer named Joe Robbie contacted me. We had met through Hubert Humphrey and our mutual interest in Minnesota politics. Joe remembered that I had a home in Florida and wondered if I might be willing to invest in an expansion football team called, of all goofy things, the Miami Dolphins.

Joe, who never had money of his own, evidently convinced Hollywood entertainer Danny Thomas (they were both Lebanese, and old friends) to become the original buyer. Managing the team for Danny, Joe

Kid Paulucci, the sports mogul.

fell in love with what he was doing. Danny, on the other hand, discovered he didn't like owning a sports franchise all that much, and wanted out.

To hold onto his job, Joe decided to seek a new backer to buy out Danny Thomas and become the sole owner of the team.

We agreed to meet at the Diplomat Hotel in Miami Beach and talk it over. Sure enough, Danny Thomas showed up clearly anxious to sell, while Joe was just as eager to manage the team for me. The asking price was $4 million, and Thomas was more than happy to take terms rather than cash.

When I left, I told them I'd think about it.

But Joe was a good talker and had pretty well convinced me that we could make money at this and have fun at the same time.

"How did it go?" Lois asked, when I got back to the car.

We had driven down from Sanford with another couple, a friend of mine named Kay Shoemaker, a successful real estate developer, and his wife Sophia. They listened as I pulled the car back to the highway.

I hedged, "Well, I don't think much of the name. 'Dolphins' sounds pretty tame to me."

My wife looked at me knowingly.

"But you *are* interested?"

At that moment Kay Shoemaker piped up from the back seat. "Jeno, are you nuts? I've lived in Florida all my life, and take it from me, professional football will never be popular down here. Florida is a *college* football state. The University of Miami—the Hurricanes—own this town!"

Well, I thought about that for a few minutes as I drove out of the city. I knew the Minnesota Vikings were going great guns up north, but what did I know about south Florida? What did I know about professional football, for that matter?

Those doubts were enough for me.

I found a phone booth and called the hotel. Danny Thomas had already left, but I managed to catch Joe Robbie and told him, "Joe, do you think I'm nuts? Don't you know pro football will never be successful in Florida? This is a college football state."

He was enormously disappointed.

"Jeno," Joe Robbie said, "you are wrong. You're making a terrible mistake." How right he was.

But in the end Joe should have thanked me. He wanted to stay in football so badly that, after I turned him down, he found a union pension fund in Chicago, which belonged to the Railroad Brotherhood, willing to loan him the money to buy the team.

He became the owner of the Dolphins.

At first the Dolphins didn't do too well. The joke was: "Win one for the Flipper." But a few seasons later Don Shula's "Flippers" won seventeen games in a row, including the Super Bowl, with every home game played to sold-out crowds of screaming Floridian fans of pro football.

Not many years later, the franchise was so successful that Joe Robbie could build his own stadium and move out of the decrepit Orange Bowl. Today, no one would argue that the team is worth 100 times—conceivably 200 times–more than what I would have paid for it.

I recall tuning in a TV game at home and listening to the announcer proclaim: "Live from Joe Robbie Stadium." Lois remarked, in that quiet way of hers: "Shouldn't they be saying 'Live from Jeno Paulucci Stadium'?"

I reached for the remote.

OTHER OPPORTUNITIES came along in other sports.

When I worked with Minnesota businessman Bob Short during the 1968 Humphrey presidential campaign, he happened to be looking into buying the Washington Senators major league baseball team. Having already turned a quick profit by buying the original Minneapolis Lakers pro basketball team, moving the franchise to Los Angeles, and then selling it again, Bob apparently had a similar fate in mind for the Senators. They had been a losing proposition for some time and were put on the block with a price tag of $10 million.

One day at the Watergate offices, where we were working on the Humphrey campaign, he suggested we each take a half-interest in the team. At first I made my standard reply about not being much of a sports fan. Especially not for $5 million. (After all, I'd had the chance to buy *all* of the Dolphins for $4 million.)

Bob kept talking. When he said we only needed a million apiece and could use the franchise itself for the rest, my ears perked up.

I agreed to inspect the team's books and look over the stadium with him. Neither was very impressive, but Bob convinced me it didn't matter. The serious money would be made on the deal we struck to move the team elsewhere.

Where?

"Texas, maybe," he shrugged offhandedly.

I agreed to go fifty-fifty with him.

Negotiations for the sale got under way, and finally Bob reported back to me.

"Jeno, we're ready to go."

"Fine," I replied. "How do you want my million dollars?"

He became a little flustered.

"Well, in cash. But we're going to need a little more than that, as it turns out . . ."

"Like how much?"

"We have to personally guarantee the balance of eight million dollars."

"You mean now you're telling me that we both sign for the eight million dollars, and if one of us doesn't pay, the other has the entire obligation on his hands?"

"That's the deal," he confirmed.

Now I had no reason to doubt Bob's honesty or negotiating skills, but the unexpected change of signals was enough to spook me. All of a sudden I was risking $9 million instead of $1 million.

I backed out.

Well, Bob was upset, but he managed to come up with the financing anyway and bought the team.

Three years later, true to his word, they became the Texas Rangers, another profitable sports franchise owned, at one point, by one George W. Bush.

There weren't any hard feelings on Bob's part. Why should there be? He made another fortune.

After he sold the Rangers in 1974, he came back to me with another proposition: Now he wanted us to buy the *New York Yankees!* CBS was willing to part with them for $25 million, he said.

No way, I said. I'd lost all interest in being a sports mogul.

Looking back, you could say I missed out on the sports opportunity of a lifetime. George Steinbrenner, a Cleveland businessman, put together funds to buy a team that is now regarded as the most valuable sports franchise in the universe.

That wasn't quite the last opportunity for the Pauluccis to get into professional sports.

In the early 1980s, my son Mick came to me, seeking advice. He had a chance to buy Bernie Ridder's share of the Minnesota Vikings football team. Ridder was one of the owners of the Knight-Ridder newspaper publishing chain that included the St. Paul and Duluth newspapers.

Mick could pick up Bernie's 25 percent interest in the team for $8 million.

I told Mick to forget about it, giving him a lecture about soaring player salaries and unpredictable revenues. My son shrugged and decided to pass.

In 1998, the team sold for $250 million (plus the assumption of debt).

I'm sure Mick followed the developments and counted up the cash missing from the Paulucci family fortune. But he never mentioned it to me, not once.

Mick has a kind heart.

No sports moguls in the Paulucci family so far.

Chapter 23

The Call of the Wild

I don't want to leave the impression that these years of starting new businesses, making good and bad investments, were all work, work, work. It's true that I didn't have much time for recreation. But when I did take the time, I played almost harder than I worked.

Some people get up before dawn and go out running. Others play tennis or raquetball. I've never done that, and the only way I'll play golf is if everybody agrees not to keep score.

What I did was go way up north and fish.

Nearby northern Minnesota, where I kept a lodge for years, is known as a sportsman's paradise. But it's not quite perfect. For that you have to go farther up into the wilderness of Canada—and the more remote the better.

SOME THIRTY YEARS AGO, I had built for me a cluster of cabins in northern Ontario and called it

281

Relaxing in a sportsman's paradise.

Wilderness Village, though most people just called it Jeno's Outpost Camp.

If there's a true paradise on earth, this is it—set on the sandy shore of Brennan Lake, which is now a Canadian National Park, with adjoining lakes such as Windfall and Termite, with great fishing holes all around, some of them just above dangerous water-falls. When you get there, you immediately go into low gear. You relax. You eat well, sleep well, and when you're ready, you fish like hell.

All the log buildings were built by George Belmore, a Canadian who is part Norwegian, and his family. George's son Gordy is the manager. I am the mayor of Wilderness Village, because I own the place and there's only one vote, and it's mine.

I kept three airplanes on floats to transport me and my friends, Lois and the family, and other guests. Once a year, I would bring high-performance employees up to the camp—an incentive they fought for.

Yeah, I sometimes got into some kind of trouble at the Outpost, particularly when I was accompanied by that great old fishing buddy of mine, Ed Korkki.

When we would get out in the boat, Ed was stimulated by his Peppermint Schnapps (80 proof). Sometimes I'd try to keep up with him with a little too much of my health tonic, Fernet Branca (only 60 proof, but who's kidding who?).

To tell the truth, we could get pretty tipsy in a sixteen-foot boat with the sun beating down for some ten- or twelve-hour stretches.

I recall getting damn near drowned one day, when the boat went over the falls. And there was the occasion when the vice president of the United States, Fritz Mondale, came up to fish and spent most of his time trying to shake off his cadre of Secret Service agents. Those are a couple of stories I'll save for later.

My friends and I did a lot of fishing at the Outpost over many years, and those were glorious days. Sometimes we also hunted, but not often. In fact, after thinking it over, I decided not to allow hunting at all. If our guests wanted to take a camera to seek out moose or caribou or bear, fine. But no hunting. Let the animals breed and raise their young without any interference from us.

We also enforced the catch and release policy for fishing—and I don't mean catch and release the fish into the tub in the boat. We kept only what we would eat that day, plus the legal limit of walleye (six then, two now) and big Northern Pike (three).

For a while I didn't raise hell if some of our guests caught and kept more than they should. But then we had to cut other guests' quantity down, so we'd be equal and legal. So in my capacity as mayor of Wilderness Village, I finally decreed that everyone— no exceptions—gets only their individual legal limit of walleye and Northerns.

I've closed the Outpost for years at a time to give the fish a chance to live without a hook dangling in front of them.

THE LAST TIME I WAS AT THE OUTPOST (as this is written), I was determined to get one prize Northern Pike—a trophy fish to take home. This was late September, the final day there for the season, and I didn't want any small fish.

My pilot Rodney Dunn and I took the Cessna 206 on floats to fly into Four Skin Lake, where the big Northerns run up to thirty pounds. I was using a large red-and-white Daredevil metal spoon with treble hooks. It was about six inches long and an inch and a half wide at its widest part.

So I was casting this monster Daredevil lure some thirty feet into a bed of weeds where the big Northern usually lurk. I kept casting and reeling in, casting and reeling in for over an hour. Rod kept running the boat and trolling for walleyes.

All at once I felt a helluva yank as my lure settled in the weed bed. Suddenly excited, I knew I had a big one.

That Northern was a fighter. It ran, or should I say swam, for forty or fifty feet in one direction, then would turn around and come back to the boat at lightning speed. I had to keep playing out line, then reeling in as fast as I could to keep up with it.

This tug of war went on for about half an hour before the Northern surfaced so I could see it. Had to be at least thirty pounds. The fish looked exhausted. So was I. I decided to crank my reel as hard as I could and bring him in. But the fish was stubborn. He made one more spectacular leap out of the water, shook his massive head—and spit out the hooks.

Since I was pulling hard, the lure snapped back toward me like a bullet. It hit me square in the face and one of the treble hooks went into my mouth and out under my lower lip.

Damn, that hurt! I hadn't hooked the fish. He had hooked me!

Looking at that six-inch lure hanging out of my mouth, Rod got a little nervous. He said we had to rush back to camp.

"Hell, no," I said. "First, Rod, you unhook the damn lure from the line, please, so something worse doesn't happen. Then take your pliers and pull the hook out of my mouth."

Rod started wondering aloud whether I'd had a tetanus shot recently, to prevent lockjaw. I said I wasn't worried about that, just wanted to get the hook out, because it was kind of heavy and uncomfortable. I told him to give me the damn pliers and I'd pull it out, if he didn't want to be the surgeon.

Well, any kid who fishes knows that I should have had Rod file off the barbs and then pull the barbless hook through backwards. But I was in too big a hurry to get back after the Old Fighter, as I was beginning to think of that prize Northern Pike.

Finally Rod saw there was no use arguing with me, so in his new role as pilot/surgeon, he took the pliers and started gingerly pulling at the hook from inside my mouth.

"Am I hurting you?"

"You sure as hell are, but that's what's needed to pull out this damn hook—so pull!"

The hook came out, well baited with a chunk of my flesh. Well, now I know how the fish feel.

"We'd better get back to camp," Rod urged, "then fly to Duluth so a doctor can sew up that lip."

"Hell, no," I answered. "Give me that Peppermint Schnapps that Ed Korkki drinks." I soaked my handkerchief with the Schnapps and put it in my mouth, hanging part of it over my lip, not caring how it looked.

We started fishing again, taking after that same Old Fighter with the same metal spoon. But no luck.

By that point I could see Rod was nervous as a whore in church, so after a few more soakings of Schnapps, we went back to camp.

The next day I didn't have lockjaw, but I sure had a sore lip and also a helluva hangover from Ed Korkki's Peppermint Schnapps. I'd stick to Fernet in the future.

It didn't help that our guests, after looking me over and expressing sympathy, started calling me Chief Hook in Mouth.

AS I LOOK BACK OVER THESE OUTPOST adventures, which have been going on for three decades since we built the place, I want to express my thanks to the Belmore family, with George as the patriarch and Gordy as manager of Wilderness Village.

The Belmore family has its own cabins across the bay where they live in the summer while they do all the work at Outpost, in a most professional manner. Then in the winter, the Belmores return to Allenwater and Sioux Lookout, where the children go to school. Gordy has his own float plane and flies back and forth when needed.

Wilderness Village—or Outpost Camp—would never have been the paradise it is without the wonderful Belmore family.

My thanks also go out to our great pilots and hosts, Chief Pilot Don Anderson; Orville Dahl and Dean Brickson; Conrad Garthus, pilot of the Cessna Caravan or the twin-engine Beech; Jeff Flynn, our latest jet and float plane pilot; and Rodney Dunn, twin-engine Beech pilot and occasional surgeon with pliers ministering to Chief Hook in Mouth Paulucci.

If I ever got back up there again, I vowed, I'd get even with Old Fighter, reel him in and take him home as a trophy.

But I almost hoped I wouldn't.

Part Four

My Life as a "Lawyer"

Some people say I'm litigious. Now where did they get that idea? Well, maybe it has something to do with my being involved in about sixty lawsuits in sixty years.

No, I'm not a real lawyer. A year of pre-law at Hibbing Junior College left me quite a few credits short of a degree. But I learned, over the years, that going to court, or threatening to go to court, is just a normal part of being in business.

Sometimes you win; sometimes you lose; sometimes you compromise. But failing to stand up for your rights is the worst mistake you can make. Never hesitate to use the power of the law to back up your beliefs.

Looking back, I divide my lawsuits into two categories: PCs (proved correct) and PIAs (pains in the ass). Some of them were a combination of PC and PIA. But along the way, I developed some guidelines for myself.

First, get the best legal advice you can find.

Second, work closely with your advisors. Don't just turn it over to them and let them make the decisions for you.

Third, weigh the costs against the potential gain. If you see a good chance for a PC—go for it.

Lawsuits can be short and sweet, or long and tedious. They also can be fun . . . no kidding. I guess that friend of mine was right when he said, "Jeno, you're more litigious than religious."

Jeno's Credo:
The hands that help are
far greater than lips
that just pray.

Going to court is a normal part of being in business, but is often a PIA.

Chapter 24

Learning the Trade

*M*y initiation into the club of serious lawsuits came in 1936, when I was a teenage salesman for Hancock Nelson.

After a Saturday sales meeting in St. Paul, I was driving my 1929 Ford early Sunday on the way back to Hibbing. A friend of mine named Vic Plese was with me. On a slippery back road, the car rolled over. Vic thought his back was hurt, and this good friend of mine decided to sue.

He hired an attorney by the name of John Naughton—one of the best on the Iron Range—who brought suit against both Hancock Nelson and me. Being I was not an employee, only a commission salesman, the company said its insurance didn't cover me.

Yes it did, said Naughton. I had been attending their sales meeting, commission or not. In response, Hancock's insurance company hired a Duluth attorney named John Jenswold. His assignment was to clear both the insurance company and Hancock—and stick it to Jeno.

It didn't work out that way. When the trial came to Judge Hughes's court in Hibbing, I took the stand as an adverse witness. The result: John Naughton had enough evidence to nail the insurance company for a $10,000 settlement to Vic Plese. I was in the clear.

The owner of Hancock Nelson, a sharp Irishman named O'Brien, called me to St. Paul.

"You outsmarted us, you little Dago," he said. "Normally I'd tell you to get out. But you must be a helluva salesman, so forget it and keep selling."

Smart guy. I made him a lot of money after that.

John Jenswold wouldn't talk to me for three or four years. But later, when I'd formed Chun King, Inc., he became one of my attorneys.

This was my first major lawsuit, partly a PC but mostly a PIA.

Later came the suit against Hancock Nelson—which I've already recounted—when I sued for about $10,000 in lost commissions but had to settle for $500. Definitely a PIA.

And of course the dispute over the garlic machine, when that fellow Clark Johnston and I took turns trying to get each other thrown in jail.

After David Persha and I became business partners came the epic battle against Norman LaPole, which you may recall. He was the canner with the enamel-lined cans and the kangaroo court in Wisconsin. Another PIA, although I eventually got revenge against that bastard.

I WAS JUST GETTING WARMED UP. Several of the lawsuits that followed involved some of the people who packaged our products.

Back in the 1950s, when we were growing our own vegetables up at Wilderness Valley Farms, one of our best crops was mushrooms. Our agronomist would carefully mix the native sandy loam and peat with horse manure brought in from Chicago racing stables. We'd let it settle for a couple days, then spread mushroom spawn (seed) over it. Mushrooms would grow in a matter of weeks. When they were fully grown, we would harvest the mushrooms and clean out the beds, starting over with fresh compost.

But what to do with the old compost? It was still plenty active.

I had what I was sure was a great idea. I decided to market the still-fertile compost for gardens and lawn care. All we had to do was come up with a way to package it.

When the representative from the Milprint Company of Milwaukee visited us, I shared my vision of selling three-pound bags of compost for $1.49. Our own Ben Larsen designed the package and I came up with the name: Living Earth.

Did Milprint have a bag we could use?

"Well, not exactly," the rep hemmed. "But our chemists and packaging engineers can come up with something in no time. After all, that's our business."

Milprint developed plastic-lined bags for us and we began selling Living Earth to supermarkets and gardening centers all over the United States. Unfortunately,

Milprint had not taken into account the uric acid from the horse manure. Before long, "living earth" was coming out of the bags on grocers' shelves and garden shop floors.

Goodbye, Living Earth. Hello, lawsuit.

This one was especially juicy because of the presence of Ray Palmer, the elderly lawyer in Duluth who had passionately disliked me ever since our legal collision, years earlier, over the garlic machines.

Attorney Palmer, representing Milprint, had the gall to accost me in a courthouse hallway between sessions and warn, "Okay, Paulucci, now we're going to teach you some law. Watch what happens now!"

The trial lasted about a week before it went to the jury. One noon hour the jurors filed past us on their way to lunch. One juror winked at me, and Palmer caught it. I was sure I had never seen this guy before in my life, but Palmer dragged my attorney, the reliable Peter Dorsey, into the judge's chambers.

"I told you so" was written all over Palmer's face when they emerged. He had persuaded the judge to excuse the offending juror. (The poor fellow had been impressed by our case and evidently wanted to let me know he was on our side.)

Palmer's next trip into chambers wasn't so pleasant.

Peter Dorsey had been whacking the packaging company around, and I had taken the stand for a whole day. I countered Attorney Palmer on his cross-examination so effectively that he hyperventilated and passed out right into the judge's chambers.

His assistant, a lawyer half his age, took over. With Palmer indisposed, the jury came in with what they considered a generous hometown verdict.

I wasn't there for the verdict. Peter Dorsey called, full of pride, to tell me we'd won.

"How much?"

"A hundred and ninety-five thousand bucks."

"Bullshit," I shot back. "Appeal it."

"No, Jeno, you misunderstand. We won."

"Peter," I said, "we've got Palmer on the ropes. He's so worn out, you'll get more immediately. Just appeal the case."

Within a week after Peter Dorsey notified the court of the appeal, the judgment was increased, after negotiation, by about 20 percent.

Mr. Palmer may have tried to give me a lesson in the law, but instead we delivered a master's degree to Mr. Palmer . . . Iron Range style! We collected about a quarter-million dollars, as I remember it.

But that was small consolation. This lawsuit was a PC, but also a PIA when it came to the overall loss of a helluva profitable business.

Pointer from the Peddler: Don't settle a PC at the first opportunity. If you've got your opponent on the ropes, keep punching. Go for a knockout.

Chapter 25

Pissed Off at Packagers

When we entered the Chinese frozen food business with the Chun King brand, we had the highest quality products ready to go nationwide, but we wanted something to catch the consumer's eye. Our artist, Ben Larsen, came up with terrific packaging designs. Then we found a company in Indiana, called Shellmar Betner, that had a process for printing special inks directly on aluminum foil.

It was more expensive than printing on standard wax paper, but it gave us a quality look nobody else had. Our red-foil packages just screamed for attention in the supermarket frozen sections.

In only three months, we had nationwide distribution. But almost immediately we started getting complaints from everybody—the brokers, the supermarkets, and consumers themselves.

It was that special red ink. It was rubbing off the foil packaging and getting all over everything, including customers' clothes.

Page 32
Total $15,000,000.00

Puzzling through packing problems.

After a few meetings with the president of Shell-mar Betner, in person and then on the phone, he offered $30,000 to cover the faulty packaging and the dry-cleaning bills for consumers.

Bullshit.

"I've got three months of inventory out there," I said. "That's four hundred thousand cases of frozen-food packages selling at five dollars a case to the trade. My arithmetic tells me that's two million dollars worth of product that I may have to take back and make good on."

"That's all I can give you, I'm afraid," he said. "This came straight from New York. We're a division of Continental Can, and this comes from the office of the president, Lucius Clay himself. Surely you have heard of General Clay."

Well, I knew the man had something to do with getting the Russians to back down in Berlin. But I wasn't in the mood for a history lesson.

"Maybe I ought to talk to New York, too, to this General Clay."

"I don't think that would be possible. He's a pretty busy man."

"Well, I better talk to someone besides you. Otherwise you'll have a five- or ten-million dollar lawsuit on your hands."

"That's ridiculous," he responded.

"Try me," I said, and hung up.

I never got to meet General Lucius Clay, hero of the Berlin Airlift. When I flew to New York, I met with his executive assistant. He was also ex-military. He had served in Berlin and followed Clay in the front door at Continental. Let's call him Lt. General Wiseguy.

"Let's go to lunch," were the first words out of Lt. General Wiseguy's mouth, after we shook hands in his office. Tall, with a crew cut and a confident manner, he led me to a nearby five-star restaurant on top of the Chrysler Building, where everybody called him General, and a small army fell all over themselves clearing a path to our table, and bringing rolls and butter for the general and his guest.

"What do you think of this place?" the general asked, throwing out his arms once we were seated. "I call it being on top of the world.

"Over there," he pointed, "you can see Central Park. I like to take a morning run in the Park before going to the office. And over there," . . . pointing in a different direction, "Times Square. You really ought to catch a show or two while you're here. I could leave tickets at the box office . . ."

At that point, I sort of lost it.

"Hey," I said, throwing my napkin on the table, "I didn't come to New York to catch up on Broadway shows. I want to know what you're going to do about these faulty packages that are rubbing off red ink all over people's clothes."

"Well," he began, taking a bite of his dinner roll. "We've talked to the Shellmar Betner people, and we understand they've offered to pay for the packaging and any dry-cleaning claims.

"What would you say to a total of fifty thousand to cover all your contingencies?"

"I'd say, screw it. If that's your idea of a reasonable settlement, what I'd like to do is shove your military ass right off the roof of this penthouse clip joint."

Guess I was talking too loud. Genteel New Yorkers at nearby tables were beginning to look over with concern. They weren't accustomed to an Iron Range ruffian at the top of the world.

"Don't talk to me like that," he said.

"I just did."

There was a long pause while Lt. General Wiseguy regained his composure.

"Well, what is it you want?"

Finally, we were getting somewhere. I told him that my calculations of our losses, and what I wanted from Continental Can, was $900,000 (about $9 million in today's dollars).

His whole demeanor changed. "You know, I'd like to give you more than the fifty thousand dollars, Mr. Paulucci," he said, shaking his head sadly. "But my hands are tied on this one."

He leaned forward as if to give me the inside story.

"In case you didn't know, all of Continental Can is presently operating under this gosh-darned consent decree imposed by the U.S. Justice Department. I don't pretend to know all the ins and outs. But what I understand is that we've got to be extremely careful about favoring one valued customer over another."

"Go on."

"Well, you're a highly valued customer, but the Justice Department is going to come down on us if we make a deal with you that we can't offer to everyone else. We're under extremely tight restrictions here. We can engage in nothing even hinting of any kind of impropriety whatsoever . . ."

"Let me get this straight," I interrupted. "You're telling me you'd love to help me get out of the hole you put me in, but you can't pay me nine hundred thousand because the feds are going to accuse you of playing favorites and violating some consent decree?"

My host nodded gravely.

"I think you've finally got it, Mr. Paulucci."

"You know, I think I do," I said, making up my mind as I rose from the table. "If you'll excuse me, I've got a plane to catch."

I didn't even stop at the hotel. After leaving the general to eat his executive lunch alone on top of the world, I hopped a cab straight out to LaGuardia, where my Aero Commander was parked.

"Back to Duluth, boss?" asked my pilot, Virgil Koidahl, as I came aboard.

"Heck no, Virgil," I said. "File for Washington, D.C."

Virgil never even blinked.

By three in the afternoon, we had landed at Washington National, and I grabbed a cab.

"Where to?" the driver asked.

"Where do you find justice in this town?"

"I'm the last guy to tell you that, buddy."

"Let's try the United States Justice Department."

The cabby dropped me in front of the long steps of a monumental building with huge stone columns. I glanced at my watch. If I hurried, I just might make it.

Inside, an attendant directed me down the hall to a pay phone. I gave the long-distance operator the number for Continental Can headquarters in New York and began feeding coins into the slot.

When the operator on the switchboard answered, I asked to speak to Lt. General Wiseguy. I got his secretary instead.

"The general is tied up in a meeting, I'm afraid," was the not-unexpected answer.

"Well, I really do have to speak to him. Could you pass him a note, please?"

"I don't think that would be possible, sir. It's really a very important meeting."

"Well, I think the general will find this very important, too. Just say in this note that Jeno Paulucci is on the line, and he's calling from the Justice Department down in Washington, D.C. And tell him Jeno would like to know the name of the guy he should see about the consent decree the general happened to mention over lunch today. Tell him the name slipped my mind."

Less than a minute later, the general was on the line.

"Jeno," he greeted me. "My secretary said something about Washington. Are you really down there?"

"Right smack in the middle of the halls of the U.S. Justice Department," I confirmed. "But I'm running out of change here. You've got to tell me who to see in order to plead my case about this obstacle that has come between us."

There was a long pause.

"Jeno, I don't think that'll be necessary," the general sighed. "I've been giving the matter more thought. Why don't we meet in my office tomorrow morning?"

"I am only coming back there for one thing," I warned him.

"What's that?"

"My nine hundred thousand dollars."

There was another long pause.

"Why don't you come in at nine," the general said in surrender. "I think we can take care of you."

At nine-thirty the next morning, I walked out of the headquarters of Continental Can with a check for $900,000. I had also made it clear that I wasn't about to sign anything that released them from further liability.

"I don't know yet if this amount is going to cover everything," I said in parting. "If it does, you are off the hook. You've got Jeno's word on that, and that's all you are going to get."

Pointer from the Peddler: Sometimes the best lawsuits of all are those you don't have to file, just threaten to file—if you are right.

By eleven o'clock, I was back at LaGuardia.

"Where to this time, boss?" Virgil asked me.

"File for Duluth. We're back in the Chinese frozen food business."

NOT LONG AFTER THAT, we followed up on the initial frozen food product with a Cantonese TV dinner. No fancy foil this time, just a waxed paper box. But one of the ends didn't seal properly, and the dinner trays inside sometimes fell out of the package.

Unbelievably, the problem packager was, once again, the Shellmar Betner division of Continental Can, the pride of Indiana.

I called Frank Gill, a friend of mine with whom I'd long done business. He was head of Continental Can in Chicago. I explained the situation and asked him who I should talk to in order to get this mess straightened out.

"Bill Cameron," he said. "He's the new executive vice president in New York. He's from Chicago and he's a good guy."

No he wasn't. When I went to see him in New York, he damn near sneered, "Paulucci, they tell me you've been here before, sticking your nose in the trough."

"Not by choice."

"Well, I'm wise to your kind. Don't think you're going to buffalo me like you did my predecessor."

I assumed he was referring to Lt. General Wiseguy.

"All you're getting this time," he continued, "is the cost of the packaging. Sign here," he said, pushing a piece of paper across the desk, "and we'll be done with it."

"And if I don't?" I asked, pushing the paper back to him without reading it.

"I dare you to sue us."

I didn't take his dare. Instead, when I got back to Duluth, I called his competitors—American Can in St. Paul and National Can in Chicago. I asked both what kind of deal they could make if I bought my cans from them instead of Continental Can. They were eager for my business, ready to make concessions, and agreed to write me letters to that effect.

Then I sent copies of the letters to Frank Gill. He phoned back immediately.

"Jeno," he said, "what did I do wrong?"

"It's nothing you did. It's that asshole Cameron in your home office."

"He didn't have any suggestions?"

"Yeah, he did. He told me, more or less, to go screw myself."

Silence on the phone. Then, "Did you have any figures in mind?"

"Now that you mention it, I'll settle for somewhere between three and five hundred thousand." (That's $3 million to $5 million in today's dollars.)

Frank sucked in his breath. "Is that really what it's going to cost you to clean up the problem?"

"Hell no. Off the record, Frank, since we're old friends, I'll tell you straight. It's going to cost that much because that horse's ass Cameron tried to throw his weight around."

Frank sent my correspondence to headquarters, did what he had to do, and soon I got my check for $500,000. I stayed with Continental Can, and six months later heard that Mr. Bill Cameron had been demoted.

Damn, wasn't that too bad!

THEN IT WAS THE CHUN KING TV DINNERS. When people took the aluminum tray out of the oven, expecting the pleasant aroma of chow mein to fill the kitchen, they instead got what some called "a funny chemical smell."

We traced the problem back to the coating on the trays, supplied by a company called Revere Metals. They were willing to reimburse us for the faulty trays. But we had unsalable inventory out there, and I wanted restitution for the cost of dumping it and replacing it.

I got Revere Metals on the phone and said I wanted to come and see them.

"Where are you guys, anyway?" I asked.

"New York, sir."

"Give me the address. I'll be seeing you."

This time I took along my accountant, Les Carlson, and an assistant, Justin Schmidt. We checked into the Park Lane. I went over my papers that evening, preparing for the meeting next morning, while Les and Justin went out on the town. They blew in about three A.M., and were still a little hungover when a cab took us to the address we'd been given for our scheduled meeting.

It turned out to be somewhere in Brooklyn, a building that looked like a warehouse.

"Hey Justin," said Les, "this place looks worse than that bar you dragged me into last night."

But the sign on the door said *Revere.* We went upstairs to an office overlooking a dark storage bay. Two men were huddled at the end of a worn conference table. One of them was a Revere vice president and the other was a corporate attorney.

The lawyer had a long dissertation prepared concerning the limits of Revere's obligation under New York law. He went on and on.

"You know," I interrupted, "I keep hearing you say New York law this and New York that. I happen to do business in Minnesota, and I'm wondering what Minnesota law has to say about all this.

"Every day that goes by without this matter being settled costs me another fifty grand. This could wind up as a multimillion-dollar lawsuit.

"So maybe we should adjourn, do a little more legal research, and see what law does apply here."

Revere's lawyer didn't see why that would be necessary.

"Because if I give my honest legal opinion right now," I continued, "I'd say that contract of yours isn't worth the toilet paper you use in this crummy place."

"NO BAR HOPPING TONIGHT," I warned Les and Justin when we got back to the hotel. "We've got work to do. Get out a legal pad. No, not that one, Justin. Go out to some office supply store and get the longest damn legal pad you can find."

When Justin returned with this mammoth legal pad, I gave him his assignment. "Write out thirty pages. I don't care what you write down. Your life history, whatever."

When he'd finished, I didn't read a word of it. "And now," I said, "let's get together and write out a couple more pages with every damn claim we can throw at Revere if they don't settle this tomorrow morning."

We wrote down things like loss of business, consumer lawsuits, flushing bad product out of the market, health hazards involving the FDA, advertising to regain consumer confidence, and on and on. Then we attached a dollar amount to each item. Les did the accounting.

"What have we got?" I asked.

"Looks like a total claim between ten and fifteen million," Les said.

"Fine. Now let's get some sleep."

Next morning, the three of us were back in Brooklyn, at the crummy conference table with the Revere vice president and their lawyer, and another vice president they'd brought in to even up the sides. Three against three.

The attorney started in again about the precedence of New York over Minnesota law. I stopped him.

"It's time we talked a little common sense here," I said reasonably. "Mr. Schmidt has been kind enough to draw up a summary document of all the problems Chun King faces as a result of this unfortunate situation. How many pages do you have there, Justin?"

"Thirty-two."

I feigned surprise. "Hey, that's a lot. We don't want to take up too much of these gentlemen's time. Just read the claims you've come up with, and the dollar values associated with each claim."

Justin started thumbing through page after page of his life story until he got to the claims and the dollar amounts. He read them out, item by item. When he was finished, I summarized. "Gentlemen, do we all go back to our law books and see each other in court, or do we do something else?"

The two Revere vice presidents and their lawyer asked to be excused. They were out there in that dingy corridor for about forty-five minutes. When they returned, the chief vp asked what it would take to clear up the situation. I'd spent some time thinking about that.

"Six hundred fifty thousand dollars," I said.

After some quibbling, I came down to $550,000 (equivalent to $5.5 million in today's dollars). The check was made out that day and delivered to me at the Park Lane.

"Good work," I told Les and Justin. "It's your last night in New York. Go out and have a ball."

IT MAY SOUND AS IF packaging problems slowed the growth of the company. Not so. Despite these distractions, Chun King continued to gain market share and became the dominant brand in the Oriental foods industry.

At any rate, these three legal encounters were solidly in the PC column. We were Proved Correct each time.

I'm sure you've noticed another thing they had in common: None of them went to court. In fact, I acted as my own lawyer in each case.

Bring on the bar exam.

Chapter 26

Ridiculing the Ridiculous Media

If you're deeply involved in business and community affairs, sooner or later you're going to be attacked by the media. It could be vicious.

Make no mistake, over the years I've enjoyed good relations with a number of reporters and columnists—those who tried to be fair instead of "exposing" a non-existent scandal that would get their byline on the front page. It was usually their bosses who were the problem.

They feel all-powerful, these publishers of newspapers and owners of TV stations—and in a sense they are, because in most markets there's only one newspaper and a couple of local stations. They snort their own ink, and it goes to their heads.

They love to tell the public what to think. Most of all, they love to destroy the reputation of some high-profile target—like me—or try to.

Can you sue the media? Sure, the courts are open to all.

Lee Vann (left), Jeno, and Don Mason—Chun King public relations director—find the means to take on the media.

Can you win? Not likely. If you sue, odds are you're heading for a PIA. These Ink Snorters, as I call them, will take cover behind the First Amendment. But sometimes, it's worth the Pain in the Ass.

I've never won a suit against the media. But I've won in the court of public opinion by using a greater weapon—*ridicule.*

THE FIRST TIME I CHALLENGED THE INK SNORTERS was in 1947, when Chun King was just struggling to its feet. One Sunday the St. Paul *Pioneer Press* published a bold headline on the front page: STATE GOES INTO CHOP SUEY BUSINESS.

Evidently Mr. Ink Snorter didn't like the rather modest $250,000 loan from the Iron Range Resources and Rehabilitation Board that helped me expand Chun King facilities. It was a twenty-year loan that I repaid in seven years, and it helped create more than 1,000 year-round jobs in Duluth. It was the best investment the IRRRB had ever made in its sixty-year history since Governor Harold Stassen established the agency to help provide jobs in northeastern Minnesota. But that proof was still to come.

In response, I decided to take action against the *Pioneer Press.* I sued that lousy fish-wrapper for damages.

Getting nowhere, I tried another tactic. I contacted a state senator from Grand Rapids who was sympathetic to the IRRRB, and suggested that he write a letter to the paper, arguing against the newspaper's headline and the article. The senator demanded equal space on the front page: "Senator O'Brien responds . . ."

Actually my sales manager, Jim Lee; my attorney John Jenswold; and I wrote the letter for the senator's review.

I didn't recover any damages, but the public concluded that the claims of the *Pioneer Press* were ridiculous. We came out smelling like a rose, as we should have, thanks to the cooperation of Senator O'Brien.

YEARS LATER, DOWN IN FLORIDA, another influential newspaper stuck its nose into my business. The *Orlando Sentinel* is the largest paper in central Florida, the one everybody reads around our offices and home in Sanford.

I'd never had a problem with their business editor, Jack Snyder, whom I'd found to be fair and reasonable. But the publisher and his henchmen had been differing with me, off and on, for years.

Then, in 1985, the *Sentinel* went into shock over a real estate transaction of mine.

On the last day of 1984, I bought a tract of land as an investment. I paid $3.5 million for 2,658 acres. Frankly, I didn't even go to see it. Ever. My friend and real estate guru, E. Everette Huskey, known as "Mr. Real Estate" in central Florida, told me, "Jeno, buy it. You can't lose."

He was right. In a matter of months, both the City of Sanford and Seminole County wanted to buy the property. They needed large contiguous acreage for sewage aeration, because the area was growing so fast.

In fact, the city and the county got into a bidding war. The county came up with an offer of $7.5 million. I thanked Mr. Real Estate for his golden advice and signed the purchase contract. I ain't stupid.

The county formally accepted the contract at its regular board meeting. But they had lots of other business to consider that evening, and they didn't get around to the acceptance until about two A.M.—they tell me. I wasn't present, nor were any of my people.

I'd bought the property for about $1,320 an acre and sold it less than a year later, on November 21, 1985, for $2,820 an acre. In those booming times, real estate brokers might have sniffed at such a pittance—only $1,500 profit per acre. But I was more than satisfied.

All at once the *Orlando Sentinel* suspected skullduggery. How late was that meeting? Who was there? Why did the county bid that high price?

The *Sentinel* ran front-page articles about the transaction for three days in a row. They couldn't stand the fact that I'd made a few million in such a short time.

So I sued them, to get their attention. Then I prepared a full-page ad for their newspaper. I laid out the simple facts of the matter, said I'd welcome a grand jury investigation, and suggested that the self-important editor and his near-sighted dirt-diggers wouldn't know the truth if they got hit with a shovel full of it.

This was ridicule, and it got the public on my side. I dropped the suit. When the grand jury investigation was over—to which neither I nor any of my people were ever asked to attend—the transaction was declared a clean, arms-length deal.

A reporter for the *Orlando Sentinel* called me for a closing comment. My response was short and a wee bit profane.

LET'S JUMP AHEAD A FEW YEARS. I'd like to tell you about another slugfest with an Ink Snorter that was maybe the most fun of all. This one was started by the Minneapolis *Star-Tribune*...commonly known as the Red Star due to its ultra left-wing politics.

Not long ago, the *New York Times* identified the *Star-Tribune* as "perhaps the most ridiculed newspaper in the country" (August 21, 1995; you can look it up).

This is a rag that even rotten, stinking dead fish wouldn't want to be wrapped in.

The Red Star glories in picking out some public figure and then, through a so-called investigative reporter—the true scum of the earth—trying to ruin that person's career, family, and reputation.

They did quite a job on the world famous organ transplant surgeon at the University of Minnesota, Dr. John Najarian. He was declared absolutely clean as a bone on every charge, but his career was wrecked.

They tried to do a job on hard-headed Governor Arne Carlson, but they didn't succeed. He called the Star cowardly for hiding behind the First Amendment.

They took on the president of the University of Minnesota, Nils Hasselmo. Their unfounded charges based on lies and innuendo had a negative impact on his career, even though none of the charges were true.

That's what I call yellow-piss journalism at its worst!

I had long been filled with disgust for the Red Star when they decided it was time to bury Jeno. The reasoning of the owners and publisher must have been: "He's too successful, so he must be as crooked as we are."

They assigned a dirt-digger named Joe Rigert, their star "investigative reporter," to investigate Jeno.

Why did Jeno start in Duluth with his latest company in 1990 but employ only 300 in Duluth, then hire more than 1,200 in Jackson, Ohio? It was a simple matter of economics, but they didn't want to know about that.

When Joe Rigert got an assignment like that, he could take six months to a year; whatever it took to get his dirt-digging done. He had the help of the Red Star's Duluth correspondent who, in my opinion, stank just a little less . . . but only a little . . . as a character assassin. Together they conspired to try to prove that Jeno had manipulated funds and/or persuaded Duluth officials by promising more jobs than I produced.

If the *Duluth News Tribune* publisher had kept his nose out of my business, another 1,000 jobs would be in northeastern Minnesota. Never was there anything clandestine about me or my conduct of business.

Joe Rigert and his Red Star Mafia contacted city officials in Duluth and Jackson. They contacted the governors' offices in Minnesota and Ohio. They went to the attorney general of Minnesota. They searched out current and past employees, looking for the dark side of Jeno.

Meanwhile, Jeno wasn't sleeping. I hired my own researcher to take a look at the publisher, the editors, and especially Joe Rigert. Not the Duluth reporter; he was a worthless waste of time, I thought.

We didn't have to look far to find the dark side of Joe Rigert. Lo and behold, a few years back he had buried the family's pet cat *alive* because it wasn't feeling too good. Yow! He even bragged about it in a column he had at the time, syndicated to a few more rags. Evidently his odious article about "why I buried our family pet cat alive" was the demise of his column.

To all indications, his readers were outraged that anybody could be so monstrous. So this ethical and moral giant lost his column but hung on to his job as scandal-monger.

Shortly before Rigert's series of articles was to begin, I sued the paper over some stupid lie by the Duluth idiot. I needed to do that to let the rest of the state media know that Jeno was taking on the Red Star, rather than waiting for their flood of lies to get into print.

Then I beat them to the punch with a full-page ad ridiculing both the cat-burying super-sleuth and the rag itself. The headline: MEOW, MEOW.

Here it is. Read and chuckle with me, just like all the other media in the Twin Cities, Duluth, and the rest of the state—and the people—did. Note that I managed to get in a plug for our products.

The day after the ad ran, support came from an unexpected source. A contingent from that fierce animal rights organization called PETA (People for the Ethical Treatment of Animals) picketed the offices of the Red Star, there on the streets of Minneapolis. Talk

MEOW
MEOW

To Readers of this newspaper. Before long you will be seeing a series of articles concerning myself, Jeno F. Paulucci, and my latest food company, Luigino's, Inc.

The articles will be written mostly by Joe Rigert, the so-called "Character Assassin," who also has admitted to BURYING HIS OWN PET CAT ALIVE... believe it or not. But this is one "CAT" he isn't going to bury.

The Star-Tribune, in our opinion, has viciously tried to bury my friend, Curt Carlson. It tried to bury Governor Arne Carlson. It hasn't quite succeeded in burying University President Nils Hasselmo, and IT SURE IS NOT GOING TO BURY THIS "CAT."

So when you read the articles, bear in mind that this, above all, is retribution by the Minneapolis Star-Tribune and their fancy editors and management for my suing them, in Duluth, for defamation when they lied about me a few months ago. They hope to get even, I guess ... Lots of luck, Star!

You know, every one of us who gets in the public eye makes good reading copy. Stories like this sell papers and make lots of money for the FAT CAT publishers, including our paying $14,000 for this full page ad to let you know that, MEOW, MEOW, Mr. Rigert better FIND ANOTHER CAT TO BURY ALIVE ... it ain't going to be Jeno.

Thank you. I'll be looking forward to your comments.

Jeno

Jeno F. Paulucci

P.S. So the cost of this ad shouldn't be a total loss, please try Michelina's® and Yu Sing® Entrees, if you have not already. We pack them. We think they are very, very good. I think you will too.

Paid for by Jeno and Luigino's, Inc., on behalf of the good reputation of the Paulucci Family and Luigino's, Inc.

P.P.S. When the articles appear, save the newspapers. They make good fish wrapping.

about a media event! I was astonished, but grateful that these good people didn't like the idea of burying cats alive any more than I did.

The TV and radio stations and other newspapers throughout the state played the story big and often. It was the talk of Minnesota for weeks. Even the *Wall Street Journal* quoted me and my ad.

The Red Star went ahead and ran the articles by investigator Rigert, but their readers were laughing too loud or were too nauseated to give his words any credibility. Ridicule ruled.

The ad I placed cost $14,000. But as a result of the publicity (and the product mention I included in the ad), I got more than that back in direct increased sales of Michelina's and Yu Sing products.

Here was a first class PC. I'm sure that Mr. Joseph Rigert wished he'd never heard of Jeno.

Keep trying to bury me, Joe. At least I can defend myself, unlike your family's pet cat.

Another benefit from this farce was my getting to know the famous, flamboyant civil liberties attorney William Kunstler. I'd become acquainted with him earlier when we met and chatted about some civil rights matters. He was born on July 7, same day as me, but a year later in 1919.

Bill Kunstler had defended "radicals" from Lenny Bruce to Martin Luther King, Malcolm X and American Indian movement leaders. He was a show-boat in court, and was even sentenced to prison for contempt.

My kind of guy. I retained him to work with me on this media problem, behind the scenes. He had this advice:

Pointer from the Peddler: Only this time it's not from me, but from Bill Kunstler. He said, "Jeno, sue them only for attention. The only way you can win over the bastards is to get even. Ridicule those character assassins." You can't get any better legal counsel than that.

Bill phoned me the day before he died. He was in upstate New York. Had a home up there somewhere, but for some reason didn't have a phone. So he called me from a phone booth and we talked about some civil rights matters of mutual interest.

As we were finishing our conversation, Bill's voice rose a little. "Hey Jeno, there are two black bears outside this phone booth! What should I do?"

"Keep talking and keep the door closed," I answered. He did, and the bears went away.

The next day Bill dropped dead of a heart attack at age seventy-six. It seems he had a heart condition that those of us who were his friends never knew about.

A great loss.

Thanks, Bill. I'll never forget your advice, and I'll keep on using it.

IN FACT, I'VE DEVELOPED a system for ridiculing the media that you might want to try if you're a businessman or businesswoman who's been dealt with unjustly.

First, research the particular newspaper or TV or radio station that you're going to get even with. Find out what the mistakes of the writers or editors have been in the past.

Then reserve space for a full-page ad in the newspaper, even if that medium is not the culprit. Take page 3, the first page the reader sees when opening the paper. Make it on a Tuesday, the day the paper is thinnest, with the least number of ads.

Have fun when you write out the ad. Call them things like "ink snorter," "loudmouth," or "pinhead." Remember, it's all about ridicule. Also name the publisher or the owner of the station. They can't stand ridicule.

Send the copy for the ad at the last minute so they can't react at once. They'll most likely reply the next day through the editorial page.

For example, when I attacked the *Orlando Sentinel* some years ago, they said something like, "Normally, we don't make comments concerning advertising that's placed in this newspaper; however, in this case . . . blah blah blah, crap this, crap that . . ." A lame defense, adding to the ridicule.

Finally, I recommend sending copies of your ad to other media. There's nothing newspapers and radio and TV stations like to do more than use somebody else's words to ridicule their competitors.

By following this formula, you'll get even with the bastards who've besmirched your reputation. You'll come out smelling like a rose and if you're anything like me, you'll laugh all the way to the newstand.

LET'S BE CLEAR: I'm not condemning everyone in the media business. They're not all Ink Snorters. Many are decent people trying to do a decent job.

For instance, there was Bernie Ridder, now deceased, the former chairman of Knight Ridder Publications and one of the original members of that publishing family. He was the first publisher of the *Duluth News-Tribune.* His son is chairman and CEO of Knight-Ridder now.

Bernie was one hell of a guy with a great family, and their newspapers reflect it. Once in a while they do get a publisher who lets the ink go to his head. But it's the exception to the rule.

I also recall with affection media pros such as George Lazarus (also deceased), business columnist of the *Chicago Tribune;* Jack Snyder, business editor of the *Orlando Sentinel;* Al Rosenfield and Warren Thayer of *Frozen Food Age.*

And I can't forget my old pen pal, the late Jim Klobuchar, a columnist for the Red Star itself, and the author of a half-dozen books of humor and human interest stories. Jim got into the habit of phoning me once in a while just to get me started on some subject he knew I'd get excited about. The result was fodder for his column, because I always talked to him just like I talk in this book.

Great sparring sessions. Great fun, Jim. Bless you. I never even had to sue you.

Chapter 27

Bernie's Winter Vacation

*M*any of my lawsuits, important as they were at the time, were more or less incidental to my businesses. Others resulted in profound changes. I'm going to take a brief look at one of those in the next chapter.

Meanwhile, for the record—and I hope for your amusement—here are a few of the PCs and PIAs that took place in the '60s and '70s.

In 1961, I had to sue Minnesota Mining and Manufacturing (3M) and a competitor of mine, Jan U Wine Canned Chinese Foods, in Los Angeles, for infringing on my patented method of taping two cans together for sale as one item. It was a simple patent, but novel.

The 3M Company was supplying the tape. Their salespeople saw how the system worked and realized they could sell more tape by showing Jan U Wine how to use it, despite my patent. I sued. The Superior Court judge called 3M crooks—right to their faces—and found against them with a cease and desist order. But 3M appealed and won.

Bernie spent his winter vacation snowbound in Duluth, Minnesota.

Result: a PIA. But 3M has been *persona non grata* with me ever since. They remain on my shit list.

In 1967, as a resident of Sanford, Florida, I organized legal proceedings *by* the City of Sanford *against* the United States Department of Defense and the General Accounting Office. They had closed the Sanford Naval Air Station and then wanted to charge the town more than a million dollars for the property. After we got through with them, they turned over that 865–acre property to Sanford for one dollar.

Result: a PC. Today it's called the Orlando-Sanford Airport and Industrial Park and is worth millions upon millions.

In 1972, I took on Kellogg's, the cereal powerhouse, when they started using my secret formulas for making pizza rolls in competition with me. I found out that Kellogg's had hired two former employees of mine who, in turn, paid off two of my research people for the formulas. When confronted with the threat of a lawsuit as well as a grand jury investigation being organized by St. Louis County Attorney Keith Brownell, Kellogg's sent their top counsel to negotiate with me at our attorneys' office in Minneapolis. I raised hell, chewed him up, and spit him out.

Kellogg's immediately fired the two former employees and got out of the pizza roll business . . . pronto!

Result: Sure as hell a PC.

ALONG ABOUT THAT TIME, I happened to notice a $67,000 write-off on the books at Jeno's, Inc.

"What's this for?" I asked Don Wirtanen, the Jeno's president.

"Oh, John Carlson said we might as well write this one off. That machine we got from Solbern never worked. It got to be more trouble than it was worth to keep fooling with it. So we decided to scrap it."

John was our company engineer. The piece of equipment was supposed to automatically pack pizza rolls twelve to a box. But the machine didn't count so good. Sometimes it put in twelve. Others times more, other times a lot less.

Why didn't Solbern just take the machine back? Don replied, "Well, they thought the machine was doing what it was supposed to do, only we weren't running it properly."

"And?"

"We kept adjusting it according to their instructions, but we couldn't make it work no matter what we did. Like I said, John finally gave up."

"Did the machine, in John's opinion, ever do what it was supposed to do?"

"No, I guess not," Don admitted.

Taking matters in my own hands, I called the Solbern Company in New Jersey.

The owner came on the line. He was a talkative fellow named Bernie Eisenberg.

"Oh, I've heard a lot about you, Mr. Paulucci," he began. "We're both entrepreneurs, I understand. Sorry I've never had the pleasure of meeting you.

"I'm told you spend a lot of time in Florida," he rambled. "I go down there every winter myself. Yes, sir. Wouldn't miss it for the world. I'm there January and February every year. I don't know how anybody takes the winters out where you are, in Minnesota. They're bad enough here in Jersey . . ."

I interrupted. "I'm calling about that machine you sold us."

"Oh, that," he continued cheerfully. "I know our people did everything they possibly could to get you started. How's it working these days?"

"It's not. That's the problem."

"Really?"

I let the silence stretch out between us. Bernie spoke up at last.

"Well, maybe they did mention something about your people not seeming to understand how to . . ."

"If that's the case," I interrupted again, "why don't you send somebody out here to show us how to do it right?"

"I suppose we could do that," he mumbled.

"You'd better do something," I growled.

A man from Solbern showed up and worked with our people on how to run the "foolproof" packing machine they sold us. It didn't help. In fact, it turned into a worse headache than ever.

I called Bernie back.

"What did your man tell you about his trip out here?" I asked.

"I'm afraid he said your people weren't very co-operative," he replied distantly.

"He's wrong. I know damn well we bent over backward and then some. Look, why don't I just send the damn thing back, and you refund what I paid?"

"Why should I do that?" Bernie argued. "The machine works."

"Then sell it to someone else. I don't care what you do with it. Just get it out of here and give me back my money."

"It works, I tell you."

"In that case, I'll see you in court."

My attorney Peter Dorsey filed suit. In addition to the $67,000 cost of the machine, we tacked on another $100,000 for loss of business plus the aggravation and trouble it had caused us.

"I'll have the papers ready to serve in a couple of weeks," Peter advised. This was the middle of July.

Then an idea struck me.

"Wait a minute, Peter. Is there any statute of limitations on what we're dealing with here?"

"Nothing to worry about. We've got time."

"Then let's wait on this one."

"How long?"

"Well, you tell me. But I want to make sure we get the case on the Duluth court calendar for next January."

That's what happened. For four weeks in the dead of a northern Minnesota winter, the trial of our lawsuit against the Solbern Company dragged on. We brought in a parade of witnesses while Bernie Eisenberg, required to be present, sat there shivering.

Unlike Bernie, the sun-lover from Jersey, I was in Florida. When the jury brought in its verdict, Peter called me.

"Congratulations, Jeno," Peter greeted me. "They found in our favor."

"How much?"

"Forty-five thousand dollars."

"Don't take it," I said. "I want the full sixty-seven thousand at least."

"Have a heart, Jeno," Peter pleaded. "You should have seen that poor Eisenberg fellow by the end of the trial."

"A little pale, was he?

"He had to be helped out of the courtroom."

"Gee, maybe I better give him a call and see how he's doing," I said.

Eisenberg was back in New Jersey, but not in his office. His secretary gave me the home number.

Bernie answered the phone himself. "Oh, it's you," he said in a thin voice. "I hope this won't take too long. I'm not feeling so hot. That trial ruined my whole vacation. Never saw weather like that in my whole life. Nothing like Miami Beach, I'll tell you.

"Well, you won your money, Paulucci. What do you want now? You can keep the machine for all I care."

"I don't want the damn machine," I cut in. "I want my other twenty-two thousand dollars."

"You mean you want *more* money?"

"I want a full refund, Eisenberg. I'm going to appeal this case until I get it. I'll have you back in Duluth so fast it'll make your head spin."

The other end of the line went dead. I waited.

Finally, a woman's voice came on the line. She sounded terribly upset.

"This is Mrs. Eisenberg. My husband just collapsed. I'm going to have to call an ambulance. To whom am I speaking, please?"

I told her.

"Oh, it's you! Haven't you done enough to us already? Do you want to give poor Bernie a heart attack?"

And she hung up.

Now my conscience began to bother me.

Okay, Bernie could have been acting. But if he wasn't, nobody deserved to die just because I wanted a refund for a machine that didn't work. I didn't send him tickets for a Florida vacation, but I didn't pursue the lawsuit any further.

I never did hear what became of Bernie.

Result: a PIA. With extenuating circumstances.

Chapter 28

After a Long, Lawsuit, a New Company Is Born

*T*he lawsuits and countersuits between Pillsbury and me lasted more than four years. When they were finally over, Pillsbury and I had paid enough legal fees—more than $5 million each—to put the children and grandchildren of all our distinguished counselors through graduate school.

Most of the time, nothing much happened, except for the lawyers sending bills. So I won't go into the tedious details. The only reason I'm discussing it at all is the result: the sale of one primary business and the very unorthodox start of another.

This costly and confusing hodgepodge of a legal struggle began when Pillsbury acquired the Totino Company of Minneapolis, a competitor of mine in the frozen pizza business. Rose and Jim Totino were also friends and I congratulated them on their success.

A long, long lawsuit leads to the birth of a new company.
(Duluth News-Tribune illustration)

Then we began to lose market share to Pillsbury/Totino because they had a new way of frying pizza crust instead of baking it. They called it Crisp Crust. Rose was going around the country promoting this revolutionary new crust as "a recipe handed down from her mother, Armita Cruciani."

I knew better. Crisp Crust was actually a knock-off of a patent I owned as a result of acquiring a small bakery company some years earlier. So in 1984, I decided to sue Pillsbury for patent infringement.

I LOOKED AROUND AND FOUND what seemed to be the best legal soldiers for this war—a Washington, D.C., firm praised by *Fortune* magazine as "the last word" in patent infringement. The top partner agreed to be my lead counsel at an hourly rate of $300. However, he'd need to hire a second-string man in Minneapolis at $275 an hour. Plus 14 percent of any settlement.

We sued Pillsbury. They sued back, claiming that we were violating *their* patent with the new fried crust process we had begun to use.

My lawyers assured me that the whole thing shouldn't take more than a year.

Four years later, the case had yet to go to court. Jeno's was still losing market share. My lawyers wanted more money. My family just wanted out. Pillsbury, hog-tied by the legal maneuvering (about six different "causes of action" that you don't want to hear about), seemed ready to call it quits.

I set up a meeting with my Washington attorneys and John French, the lead attorney for Pillsbury.

I told them I'd had a change of heart. I'd decided to get out and sell my company—*to Pillsbury.*

IT WAS AS IF I'D DROPPED a grenade in that room. Nobody knew how to react.

"It's a great deal for Pillsbury," I finally said to John. "Together Pillsbury and Jeno's will own half the frozen pizza business in the country."

"But that would be a monopoly," John said, recovering from the shock. "The Justice Department would never allow that."

"No, John, you're looking at this all wrong. Sure, you'll have half the frozen pizza business. But when you look at the total pizza universe, you have to include not just frozen pizzas from the grocer but home delivery and pizzerias in malls all over the country. That's a market worth billions, and you'll be lucky to have five percent of it. The Justice Department isn't going to complain about that."

They didn't, as Pillsbury learned after putting out some feelers. After a while, they agreed to acquire Jeno's, which occurred in 1985.

For $135 million in cash, Pillsbury took the name "Jeno's Inc." and the pizza plants and equipment in Ohio. Our family kept the remaining assets, worth around $50 million.

But the story wasn't quite over. After the sale, I continued to study the details and found out that Pillsbury had understated the appraisal value of some of our assets. They owed us more money, and I was prepared to sue.

Meanwhile, Pillsbury had been acquired by Grand Metropolitan, the big British conglomerate. So I brought suit against Grand Met. I had lunch with their Supreme Commander or whatever he was called—the most British Brit you can imagine.

He had a rich, juicy accent and a look-down-his-nose attitude. Looking at him over the table, I thought he really ought to be wearing a monocle, to make the picture complete. He said they owed me nothing and in fact I might owe them if I sued.

"Thank you," I said. "Let's try it."

Jerry Jenko, their general counsel, saw the merits of my lawsuit. Grand Met finally settled for another $13 million and at the same time, asked me to pack their pizza rolls for about five years. Which I did . . . some 20 or 25 million cases at a profit of about $2 a case.

So after all those years of PIA—Pains in the Ass—the battle of Pillsbury ended up as a solid PC—Proved Correct. I just wish the commander had been wearing a monocle to drop into his lunch when I told him he was being sued. That would have been perfect.

On the downside, I'd had to sign an agreement not to go into competition with them for five years. With the ideas I had to start a new foods company, it was like five years in jail.

I had other enterprises—real estate, banks, restaurants, and so forth—but they didn't take up my day. I was itching to get back in the food business as soon as the five-year non-compete period was over.

But in what form? What niche could I fill?

THE OPPORTUNITY I SETTLED ON was microwavable frozen entrees. Consumers wanted convenience, and the microwave oven was it. Instead of cooking on the stove or waiting for a conventional oven to heat up, they could enjoy their lunch or dinner in three to five minutes.

We experimented with frozen rice dishes—Chinese fried rice and risottos (or Italian rice). In the end I chose pasta.

The company was to be called Luigino's. That's me, before I changed my name to Jeno at age seven. The brand name would be Michelina's. That's my mother, whose long-remembered recipes were the basis of the business.

As the non-compete sentence was drawing to a close, I called up former associates—the "Gang that Wouldn't Retire" that I've told you about—and invited them to be part of this new enterprise.

I also called buyers at four of the largest supermarket chains in the country–Winn Dixie, Publix, Food Lion, and Super Valu. I told them I was about to take a gamble. Maybe they'd like to get in on the action. All four buyers agreed to a cutting, a tasting of my new products.

I showed up at each buyer's office with white boxes (our labeling wasn't ready). I opened the boxes. They tasted; they liked; they said they'd buy. But now came the gamble.

First, they'd have to take entire shipments directly from us. No local warehousing. No less-than-truckload shipments.

Second, no "slotting" payments, the charge commonly paid by suppliers to get their products on the shelf.

Third, most radical of all, I wasn't going to advertise in the media, though I'd cooperate for in-store promotions. And I'd pass along to them the savings from not advertising.

If they met my unheard-of conditions, they could retail Michelina's for 99 cents and make a lot of money while enticing people into the stores.

They knew me and trusted me, and bought into my proposal. So did the other chains soon after.

The five years of non-compete with Pillsbury expired in November 1990. That month we made our first shipment of a line of eight Michelina's microwavable entrees from Duluth. Two years later we entered the international market with shipments to England and Canada.

I re-acquired the old Jeno's, Inc. plant in Jackson, Ohio, that Pillsbury had closed. It now services customers from Europe to Australia and New Zealand.

A vibrant new company was born.

BEFORE WE LEAVE THIS SUBJECT, I have to point out another unusual aspect of the startup of Luigino's. If my dealings with grocery chains were unorthodox, my source of capital was moreso.

It worked this way: I didn't invest one penny of my own money in the company. Instead, I used jobs as a commodity in my negotiations with government bodies that would benefit from them.

I got a loan from the City of Duluth, promptly repaid; another of $500,000 from St. Louis County, repaid out of profits; another of more than $20 million from the State of Ohio, promptly repaid. The State of

Minnesota put up $5 million in bonding, also repaid out of profits. Then I went out and leased equipment, also paid for out of profits.

One of my lawyers asked me, "Jeno, what's your return on investment to date?"

"Are you out of your mind?" I responded. "I never invested a dime!" Thus illustrating a thesis of mine that has been proven true time and again: Jobs are the most valuable commodity on earth, to be traded just as if they were money.

Too bad most of the jobs eventually went to Ohio, as a result of a conflict I will recount in the next chapter. But none of the loans cost the city, county, or state anything, because they were all repaid.

BY ANY MEASURE, Luigino's, now combined with my Yu Sing Chinese brand, is a major success, worth hundreds of millions of dollars today without any investment on my part. But as I've said, I build companies to sell them, not to go to bed with them. One of these days this company will go the way of Chun King and Jeno's, sold at considerable profit to the Paulucci family.

My wife Lois dreads the day.

"What will you do with yourself?" she asks. "You hate television."

What I'll do, my love, is see what comes next.

Chapter 29

Debacle in Duluth: The Rape of the Taxpayer

While all those suits and countersuits were going on between Pillsbury and me, leading to the creation of a new company, another ugly, long-term dispute was also taking place. This one ended up with me suing the City of Duluth—the most depressing court battle of my life.

I'd loved Duluth since my days as a kid barker on First Street, selling strawberries, watermelons, tomatoes, and "Argentine" bananas. Suing my adopted hometown, believe me, was a hard decision.

Was it a PC or a PIA? It was both. In the end, I was Proved Correct. But when I consider the emotional cost to me and my family, and the financial cost to the taxpayers of Duluth, it was a Pain in the Ass, start to finish.

A little background: For years and years, Duluth and I had this strange love-hate relationship.

The love part began in the 1960s with passage of the Taconite Amendment to the Minnesota constitution

Message chalked on a wall of the Duluth plant. Illustration of Jeno taking the cities of Duluth and Superior to task for questioning gift facilities, job offers.
*(Published in the **Duluth News-Tribune**)*

and the "Paulucci Bill" that put the taconite industry on a sound footing. It continued when I pushed through the building of the Arena-Auditorium, helped to create the Duluth International Air Terminal, invested in the Spirit Mountain Recreation Area south of town, and promoted the skywalk and other projects to modernize the center city.

At one point, a national magazine called Duluth "Jeno's town." But it wasn't, and it isn't. The old-line Kitchi Gammi crowd wanted no part of me, nor I of them. While the taxpaying public was in the middle, waiting to see which way the wind shifted.

The hate part rose to the surface in 1981, and it was all about jobs.

Jobs, as I've said, are the world's number one commodity. Bring in jobs, you're a hero. Take away jobs, you're scum. Take away jobs and try to bring them back, you're still scum.

WITH JENO'S, INC., IN A PRICE WAR with the Pillsbury Company and its Totino's brand of frozen pizza, and shipping costs going through the roof, we suffered a net loss of more than $16 million in 1981. If I wanted to save the company that I'd given outright to our three children, plus trusts for our four grandchildren, I had to find a more economical way to operate the company.

I had to close four food processing plants, three in Duluth and one across the bay in Superior, Wisconsin—with a loss of 1,500 jobs—and move the pizza roll and frozen pizza operations to a consolidated operation in Wellston, Ohio.

When I made the announcement to our employees, they didn't rise up in rebellion. I offered to move them to Ohio, anyone who wanted to relocate. Most couldn't do that, but they understood.

The media didn't understand. Neither did the public. Not even when I opened our books to show our losses and, more important, promised in full-page newspaper ads to return jobs to Duluth with the new food business I planned to start.

We were pariahs, me and my family, subject to hate editorials and hate mail you can't imagine. The only friends I had in town, it seemed, were old fishing buddies like Frank Befera and Ed Korkki.

All the same, I made plans to re-open operations in Duluth, and restore jobs. All I needed was time.

Unknown to the public, I was in the process of selling Jeno's to Pillsbury, as I've related, and I was going to be under non-compete restrictions for five years. But after that, I could start a new foods business—Chinese food under the Yu Sing brand—right in Duluth, a magnet to restore jobs.

But it was not to be.

And about seven years later, the hate part grew all out of proportion.

IN THE LATE '80s, still concerned about bringing jobs to Duluth, I got involved in a plan to bring another industry into the city—paper manufacturing. I worked with Mayor John Fedo in negotiations with Blandin Paper out of Grand Rapids. That failed. Then it developed that Minnesota Power and a company called Pentair had combined to form a company called

Lake Superior Paper that would establish a plant out in West Duluth. They said they'd employ some 1,200 people in high-paying jobs to begin with, then double employment within a couple or three years.

The hitch was that they needed ninety-two acres. And they didn't want a chop suey plant anywhere near them. So the ninety-two acres included my nineteen acres and my 150,000 square-foot, United States Department of Agriculture approved plant, with lots of room for expansion, along with parking space and access east and west—all that to be taken over through eminent domain.

I'd bought the plant years earlier and invested about $5 million to expand it. Then sold it to R. J. Reynolds as part of the Chun King deal. They invested another couple of million for more expansion. Then I bought it back and put it in mothballs, preoccupied with the Jeno's Inc. operations in Ohio, but planning to use it as the cornerstone of my new business.

Now it was about to be taken away.

THE LAKE SUPERIOR PROPOSAL was complicated, and as it played out, a nightmare for the taxpayers of Duluth. I have trouble recalling all the details. But with the kind assistance of our current mayor, the excellent Herb Bergson, who looked back into the city archives, I've pieced together this strange story of municipal misdeeds.

Minnesota Power had a delapidated, coal burning steam plant called the Hibbard Plant, closed down for a number of years. Minnesota Power agreed to give the plant to the City of Duluth, no doubt for a tax credit. In turn, the city agreed to invest approximately $50 million, largely in bonds at taxpayer expense, to convert Hibbard from coal to wood-burning, including such items as acquisition and relocation costs and the addition of steam lines and sewers. After all was complete, Hibbard could take the wood waste from the Lake Superior Paper, burn it, and turn it into energy—thus cutting the cost of fuel.

But was Minnesota Power going to run the plant at cost? No, it was going to charge the City of Duluth for managing it, while selling the steam that came from that $50 million in city funds to Lake Superior at a profit!

The deal was going to cost the City of Duluth some $75 million total when all the interest was paid and all the bonds paid off.

Add another $4 to $5 million that the City of Duluth would invest in eminent domain and all the other costs to get Lake Superior Paper established, and you have nothing less than the rape of the taxpayers.

Mayor John Fedo, with whom I'd worked, had his appraisers look over the plant. They concluded that it was closed and not worth much. The city offered me about $500,000.

That was a pittance. To replace a plant like that, USDA-approved, with cement blocks and whatever, would cost around $12 million.

A half million to take away that plant I'd worked so hard to build and practically lived in for years— and more important, take away my opportunity to go back in business there and re-employ 1,000 or more people? That was beyond ridiculous.

I told the city that I didn't want their half million. I wanted to operate my plant.

I marked off seven acres that the City of Duluth and Lake Superior Paper could have for nothing. But I wanted to keep twelve acres and the plant.

The answer: Absolutely not. We cannot have a chop suey plant next to a paper plant.

You'd think the people of Duluth would say, "Hey, wait. Why not keep both plants, and both sets of jobs?" They didn't because the hate-Jeno syndrome had exploded. All around town the perception was that Jeno was holding out for more money. Jeno, our former hero, was just a greedy Dago.

Once again, my family was the object of scorn, and my supporters were fewer and fewer by the day.

One of my best friends gave me this advice: "Jeno, you're seventy years of age. You know you're not going to get into business again. Why don't you give the plant and property to Minnesota Power?"

"Are you out of your mind?" I said. "I should give up the opportunity to re-employ people just because you think I'm too old?"

"Well," he said, "it would really help you and give you a great name in Duluth."

Fuck the great name. I already deserved what I deserved. I was so disgusted I went to Italy for a month. Upon my return, I went to court. I first tried to get an injunction against the city's eminent domain. My friend Judge Jack Litman, who'd gone fishing with me in the Northwest Territories, turned down the injunction.

The eminent domain went through, and they tore down my plant. I went out there, looked around at the ruins that had been so much a part of my life, and cried. I picked up some of the discarded bricks, which I still have.

SO I SUED THE CITY OF DULUTH on the basis that eminent domain is only to be used for a public purpose. My plan to create a new company and 1,000 jobs was every bit as much a public purpose as Lake Superior's plan to build a paper plant and supposedly bring in jobs that were largely guesswork. All I wanted was enough money to rebuild my plant.

We went to court with Judge Barnes, a good judge. But when I looked at the jury, I could see that they were against me.

Fortunately for me, some idiot wrote a letter to the *Duluth News-Tribune,* going on about my greed and everything else, and the ink-snorter publisher, Jim Gels, was dumb enough to print it. I had my attorneys go to Judge Barnes and ask for a mistrial. He declined, so I told our attorneys to go back and poll the jury. How many of them had read the article?

Believe it or not, five of them had read the article. That was enough for the judge to call a mistrial.

I then went to Minnesota Power and said I was going to sue them separately for violating the eminent domain in a conspiracy with Pentair.

We finally settled out of court. I got a lot more than the $500,000 pittance, but not quite the $12 million it would cost to replace the plant.

With the cash in hand, I went out and bought the old Elliott meat packing plant for a lousy $40,000, just to keep a base in Duluth. At the same time, I re-bought a plant in Jackson, Ohio, that I'd sold to Pillsbury as part of Jeno's Inc., which they had closed. I started operations there and expanded it to some 750,000 square feet employing some 1,500 to 2,000 people, all unionized and many of them the disadvantaged "unemployables" that no one else would hire.

LET'S DO SOME ACCOUNTING. If the City of Duluth had allowed me to keep my acreage and proceed with my new company, Luigino's Inc, all those jobs with a payroll of $40 to $50 million a year—and all that community wealth—could have been in Duluth at no cost to the city, not one dollar.

Contrast that with the cost of the Lake Superior Paper plant project of some $75 million including the bonds and the cost of upgrading the broken-down Hibbard steam plant that never worked and, as Mayor Herb Bergson told me in our recent correspondence, never returned any profit to the city.

The paper plant has changed hands a couple of times and today employs about 300 people. I predict it will close soon when the wood pulp runs out. Do the math—it works out to about $250,000 per employee.

So far I've rescued about 300 jobs, 200 of them in the reconverted Elliott meat packing plant and 100 in our headquarters on Lake Avenue South.

Who got screwed?

Not Minnesota Power nor Pentair, who sold out early. Not Jeno. I escaped without damage. But the people of Duluth—they were screwed royally.

In the end, it wasn't Jeno who was greedy, but my dear Duluthian elite.

JENO'S CREDO:
Greed is like a jackal. Sometimes it eats its own guts!

I still love Duluth, just as I did a lifetime ago when I was selling those fragrant "Argentine" bananas on the sidewalk of First Street.

Lois and I stay here in our comfortable Pike Lake home a few months each year. Today, in December 2004, as another winter storm blows in, I'm in my office on Lake Avenue South dictating the remainder of this book . . . as the love-hate relationship between Duluth and me melts away like the snows of yesteryear.

Maybe I'm mellowing. But after all those years of angry conflict with the Duluth elite and their Kitchi Gammi Club, I've decided they aren't all bad. Far from it. Incorporated in 1883, taking its name from the Objibwe term for Lake Superior, Kitchi Gammi has by and large tried to promote the best interests of the city we all love.

Sure, there are still a few phony elites among them, some rotten apples who sometimes undermine the club's good name. But overall, Kitchi Gammi is a fine institution.

Peace.

Chapter 30

A Lake, a Lodge, and a Lawsuit

*F*or me, eminent domain has usually been bad news. As I've just recounted, it cost me a food processing plant in Duluth, and it cost the city more than a thousand jobs. Many years earlier, when I was too young to know what was going on, it cost my family our home in North Hibbing. Being renters, we received no compensation when the state government seized the property to make room for an iron mine.

Here's another eminent domain story that turned out a little better.

In the late 1970s, my old friend Elmer L. Andersen, former governor of Minnesota, spearheaded a movement to create Voyageurs National Park out of the lakes, streams, and woodlands along the Canadian border. In case you don't know, *voyageurs* were the early French adventurers who went by canoe into the wilderness to bring valuable fur back to fashion-conscious civilization.

JENO'S WILDERNESS LODGE   LAKE KABETOGAMA, MINN.

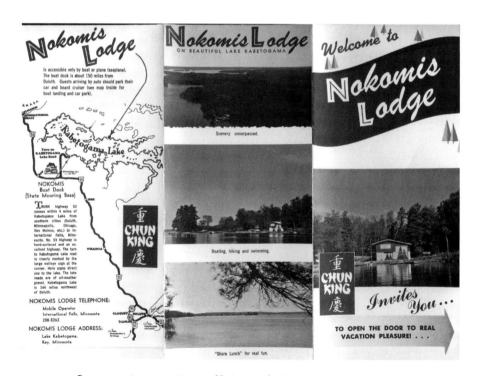

*Eminent domain claims Nokomis Lodge within boundaries
of proposed national park.*

I thought Elmer had a good idea. For better than twenty years, I'd been enjoying the view from the front porch of our summer lodge at a scenic point on Lake Kabetogama. History like this was well worth preserving.

However, I'd spent close to $1 million to renovate what had been a rundown lodge, modernize the main building that slept twenty, and add a caretaker's cabin, power generators, and so forth. If this was going to be an eminent domain takeover, I expected decent compensation. So did the other property owners on the lake.

That's not what we were offered. Most of the owners received offers of one-third to one-half what it would cost to duplicate their homes elsewhere. My offer was $223,000, "take it or leave it." I left it.

With my attorney Henry Cashen, I went to Washington to try to negotiate with the Department of the Interior, which runs the National Park Service. They advised us to deed the property to the government as a gift, so we could get favorable tax credit.

Going on to the Internal Revenue Service, we were told we could only claim market value, not replacement value. But market value, with the government about to take over the property, was zero.

I hired American Appraisal out of Milwaukee to assess the property for me. Their figure was $600,000. Unfortunately, American Appraisal wasn't on the IRS list of approved appraisers. Their list contained a half-dozen names, all employees of the federal government.

Eventually the matter was turned over to the Justice Department, which would formally execute the law of eminent domain and take over the property. By this time it was 1981. President Ronald Reagan took office and promptly cut back government spending. Elmer Andersen's Voyageurs National Park was among the projects put on hold.

Now what? Unable to sell, and expecting federal restrictions on access and land use at any time, our family decided to close the place up.

The other owners on the lake were also in limbo. They agreed to band together, hire a lawyer, and file a class-action suit to force the government to buy our property at a fair price.

A judge came out from Washington. After hearing testimony from all parties, he recommended that each owner meet with the Parks Service on his own to negotiate a price. So much for the class action.

The attorney for the now-splintered owners group, Bill Essling, advised me to meet with the Parks Service. "Get what you can right now," he said. "They're making new offers to the other owners and have come up in price. Your neighbors all seem glad to take the offers."

Bill was young and, it struck me, a bit eager to settle. After all, he was entitled to a 10 percent commission no matter what the owners took home. But I met with the Parks Service at Fort Snelling in St. Paul, bringing along Essling and my former general counsel, Bob Heller.

The Parks Service had two representatives present, one local and the other a big brusque guy from the regional office in Omaha, who wanted to make it clear that he was taking no nonsense.

"Mr. Paulucci, I understand we originally offered you $223,000 for your property," Mr. No-Nonsense began, squaring off the papers in front of him. "Is that correct?"

"It is."

"Well, we've thought it over and you'll be happy to learn that we've raised the figure considerably. We've also made new proposals to the other landowners, and . . ."

"So I've been told," I interrupted, glancing at the grinning Bill Essling on our side of the table.

"Now you must understand, Mr. Paulucci, that we're lucky to be having this conversation. The Parks Service has very limited funds available at this time. Your offered appraisal was . . . let's see . . . $600,000. But as a taxpayer, I'm sure you can appreciate our need to be prudent."

"How prudent?" I asked.

"We can give you $330,000."

Bill looked at me, his grin widening.

"Do we have a deal then, Mr. Paulucci?" asked Mr. No-Nonsense.

I took my time in replying, ignoring the expectant faces around the table.

"Gentlemen, I'm afraid not." I answered at last, bringing out some papers I'd brought along. "You see, I've changed my mind about selling. Here are the court records from your testimony to the judge who came out here. There aren't any restrictions at all on how to operate the new park."

As I suspected, I was the only one who had read the records.

"Until the government says otherwise, I can do what I want with this property. Take a look at this."

I unrolled a large map showing in detail my fifteen-acre parcel on Lake Kabetogama.

"An engineer in Duluth drew this up for me," I said. "He divided my property into half-acre plots that I plan to sell for individual cabins. Some year-round, some just for the summer. Keeping the main lodge for a commercial center, of course.

"Hell, I'm very excited about this. You guys are stuck with your limited budget, so while I thought I was going to be a seller, now I'm a developer.

"Could I interest any of you in buying a lake cottage?"

That was a joke, but nobody laughed. The man from Omaha and his local negotiator went outside for five minutes, and returned with an offer to match my appraisal of $600,000. I said no thanks. They went outside again and came back with an offer of $750,000.

"If you don't mind going outside one more time," I said, "I'd like to talk this over with my folks."

Unwillingly, the Parks Service folks went out one more time.

My lawyers, Bob Heller and the youthful Essling, were all over me.

"What are you waiting for? Take their offer quick before they come to their senses."

I listened to their advice, but I'd made up my mind. I told Essling to invite them in again, and before they were back in the chairs, said, "Here's the deal. I'll take $900,000 cash, and I take everything on the property—generators, stoves, boats, furnishing, the whole works. I've got a great idea here and I'll find another lake to set up the same development I had in mind."

They accepted. As we were adjourning, I pulled Bill Essling aside and said, "Get back to your office and write the Parks Service a letter nailing down the terms we just agreed to. And don't forget to spell out the stuff we're taking from the lodge."

"I won't forget. I'll get right on it."

The young lawyer was humbly grateful. As well he might be, since he'd just been handed $57,000 more—10 percent of an additional $570,000—than he would have earned if I'd taken his advice.

The deal went through, and I sent a truck up to the lodge to strip it clean.

Then I got a call from Omaha. Not from Mr. No-Nonsense, but from the regional boss of the Parks Service.

"What the hell did you do to that lodge we just bought from you?" the boss demanded. "You must have taken $300,000 worth of property out of it!"

"That was part of the deal," I answered. "Don't you read your mail?"

Well, it turned out he had, and I hadn't.

"If you mean that letter from your attorney, I've got it right here in front of me. All it says is you're taking furnishings. That doesn't mean stripping the sauna down to the bare walls and taking the toilet seats. We're going to hold up payment."

Bill Essling, you jerk.

I finally agreed to deduct $25,000 from the sale price.

So this episode of eminent domain turned out to be a solid PC.

Just the same, my family's Lake Kabetogama lodge had disappeared just as surely as had my family's little house in North Hibbing.

Chapter 31

The PCs Kept Rolling Along . . . But So Did the PIAs

What's this—more lawsuits? How litigious can Jeno get?

Well, bear in mind that I averaged at least a case a year for more than sixty years. So I'm leaving out a helluva lot more than I'm including in this book. I'm relating only those that I recall as significant or kind of amusing—or both.

Here are a few more to close out this section on my life as a would-be lawyer.

THE FRACTURED FALCON

In October or November 1982, we had one helluva rainstorm in Sanford, Florida. The sky erupted with lightning, thunder, then hail the size of golf

PC or PIA, they just kept coming!

balls. Although we have our own hangar at the Sanford airport, our Falcon 20 jet was outside being prepared for refueling.

In less than ten minutes of this monster storm,
the Falcon was a mess. The hail left big dents in the
fuselage and wings. Our pilots rushed out and looked
it over with the maintenance people. Their conclusion: "Total loss. Can't fly without a new fuselage and
wing skins of aluminum."

No real problem. I'd had the foresight to insure
all our aircraft for the *new* replacement cost. Not replacement cost of the same year and model, but
new, as in off-the-line right now. The insurance
company was one of the largest aircraft insurers in
America, whose name I won't mention because I
hate to remind them of all the money they had to
cough up.

As is usual practice with any insurance company . . . whether for aircraft or general property . . .
the first thing that happens is a visit from an adjuster
whose job it is to try to settle as fast as possible for
as low a cost as possible. He arrived the day after the
hailstorm, examined the jet, then came to my office.

He was a young fellow, still wet behind the ears.
He said, "I calculate your damage at about
$300,000." That was the cost of bonding the fuse-
lage and filling dents, a quarter-inch to one inch in
diameter, with a plastic compound.

Big deal, I thought. Well, this kid thinks it's his
duty to shaft me if he can.

Rather than get into a long conversation, I said,
"Okay, that's just fine. You take the Falcon. Patch it

up with your bonding plastic. Keep it or sell it. But send me a check for $5,000,000 so I can buy a new Falcon, as my insurance coverage provides."

The kid turned blue. Then he turned white.

He stuttered, cleared his throat, and said, "Mr. Paulucci, you are so wrong! All we're obligated to do is fix the jet so it can fly safely."

"No, it's *you* who are so wrong," I said. I told him to go home; I would take care of it.

I hired a Miami lawyer who specialized in insurance cases, mostly representing the insurance companies. I figured he'd be perfect for me, being he had no conflict in representing me against this particular insurance company.

We sued and collected enough for me to buy not only another Falcon 20 that was practically new, but also a Falcon 10. Both planes had been owned by an oil sheik who had used them for a couple of months and then bought a Gulfstream.

That was a real PC, believe me.

But somehow, since that day, I've never been able to get insurance coverage on my aircraft on a new replacement basis. Guess they got smart. Now they'll only replace a damaged aircraft with one of the same model and condition or the appraised value, whichever is greater.

I think they learned a valuable lesson. Hey, what if I'd owned a 747!

I also learned a valuable lesson, which I'm happy to pass along.

Pointer from the Peddler: Insure your property on a worst-case scenario. Then settle for nothing less than the contract calls for. That will take care of at least one worst-case. And then, of course, get your plane the hell inside when a hailstorm is coming up.

SUING MICKEY MOUSE

This was another lawsuit I never filed that had an interesting conclusion. It wasn't a PC, but it wasn't a PIA either.

Now it's 1985. In developing a new city that I'll describe later—Heathrow, Florida, adjoining Sanford and near Orlando—I was one of many civic-minded people promoting high-speed rail transportation for central Florida. Consideration was given to fast rail transit from the Orlando International Airport to Walt Disney World to Orlando and eventually to Heathrow, with a terminus in Sanford or Daytona Beach, and it would even run all the way to Tampa in the future. Each phase would be developed along a certain time line.

The first proposed leg was from the airport to Disney to Orlando. So we had meetings with civic leaders from Orlando and surrounding communities, including an executive from Disney. Most of the meetings were held at the Heathrow Country Club.

The Disney executive who attended our meetings said our plan was too revolutionary, and Disney was against it.

No Disney meant no fast transit. No amount of talk or logic would sway the Disney executive, whose name I won't mention because he unfortunately passed away at an early age a few years after we locked horns.

I puzzled over this for a while, figuring that we'd have to make an end run to convince Disney to be less dictatorial and dogmatic.

I never could stomach all the concessions that the State of Florida gave Disney when they first announced plans for Disney World. Hell, Florida gave Disney, among other unusual powers, the right of eminent domain.

There had to be a constitutional question on the state level with the State of Florida transferring such power to a private corporation. So I hired Fletcher N. Baldwin, Jr., a professor of constitutional law at the University of Florida. His task was to determine whether any part of the Florida Constitution was violated in the deal given Disney.

About two months later I got a report about a hundred pages thick; a study of every concession made by the State of Florida to Disney. There were two important violations of the constitution, as I recall it. I believe one of them dealt with the eminent domain concession.

Once I got the report, I asked for ten extra copies. Then I asked the Disney executive for a private meeting. When he joined me, I had all ten copies on my desk, a pile of paper about ten inches high.

I gave him a copy, and asked him to study it and then call me to say whether he would cooperate before I distributed copies to the other members of the committee.

In a few days he called back. Their position had not changed. They preferred to stonewall the constitutional questions and challenge.

So be it.

I brought together the entire committee, complete with TV, radio, and newspaper people present. I distributed copies of the report and said it looked like we were going to have to seek judicial relief on the matter by asking the court to set aside some of the original agreement between the State of Florida and Disney. I then turned the matter over to our attorneys.

That evening, as Lois and I were settling in to watch the news on television, I was just a little apprehensive about what might be reported. I didn't want to disturb her, knowing how she hated . . . and still hates today . . . the public controversy I often create. She knows I do it for the general good, but that doesn't make it pleasant.

So I started to switch channels, very casually. But before I could do it, the announcement comes blasting through:

"Listen to Channel 2 at six o'clock. Jeno Paulucci is suing Disney!"

Lois was aghast. She gave me that cold stare that could sever steel in a second.

"Jeno Paulucci," she exclaimed, "you've been suing everyone. The Interior Department, the Defense Department, Kellogg's, and God knows who else . . . and now *Jeno Paulucci is going to sue Mickey Mouse! Are you out of your mind?"*

I could fight Disney, but not Lois. End of lawsuit. And the end of the fast rail transit talks.

But a little later, Florida appropriated money to study the possibility of a fast rail transit system from Orlando Airport to Disney to Tampa to Miami. Sanford and Heathrow would be in the system.

Disney and its new CEO, Michael Eisner, were among the promoters. Michael is a friend of mine and, in my opinion, one of the most visionary CEOs who ever existed, up to his resignation in 2005.

FUN IN NEW YORK

My son Mick and I were looking for condominiums in New York to use for occasional business and/or fun trips to the city. We chose a place called the Essex House, on Central Park South overlooking the park. Mick's five-bedroom condo was number 1730; Lois and I were one flight up at 1830.

The pleasant views cost us about $600,000 apiece.

Originally the Marriott hotel chain owned the building, which had regular hotel rooms on some floors and condos on the others. Somewhere along the line Marriott sold out to the Nikko Hotel Corporation, a subsidiary of Japan Air Lines. One day in 1991, Mick and I got letters from the new Japanese management, who told us they were planning extensive repairs and renovations to the premises.

The hotel would be closing in ninety days and would remain closed for approximately one year. We—the owners of the condos—were further informed that not only did we have to move out and forego the use of our property for twelve months, but also each of us was going to have to pay for the privilege, since the hotel would be assessing us a proprotionate share of the renovation expenses based on the square footage we owned.

Mick's bill alone came to more than $350,000. Lois and I were being asked to pay an equally preposterous amount.

In practice, Mick used his place much more than we did. But after reading over our "eviction notices," I winked at my son. "Let me handle this."

My real fun in New York was about to begin.

The first stop was a visit to the hotel management. I was looking forward to it, because I just love telling someone who's wrong to go to hell.

"Oh, Mr. Paulucci, so sorry you are upset, but this situation is the same for all our residents. As much as we would like to, we can't make special consideration for you."

An ingratiating smile and final offer: "Would Mr. Paulucci like a nice dinner tonight as our guest?"

"Guest, nothing. I'm going to sue your ass."

Within a week, our New York attorney served papers declaring that Mick and I would not pay one penny tribute to the refurbishing of the Essex House. In fact, the suit directed Nikko Corporation instead to reimburse us for the cost of renting comparable apartments in the city during the interim, plus damages to cover our inconvenience.

Well, somebody at Nikko must have realized that if the case ever went to court, other condo owners might follow my lead. So instead of handing over small fortunes for the redecorating, Mick and I returned home with checks in our pockets for $300,000 each.

But in Nikko's haste to quiet us, their officials made a second blunder.

Before signing the settlement letter, I asked them to provide a firm date when we could move back in. They chose—without any prompting whatsoever—*exactly one year from the start of construction.*

I immediately marked on my calendar yet another trip to the Big Apple I knew I was going to enjoy.

When I showed up at the hotel twelve months later, the lobby was full of carpenters, electricians, and plumbers. The place was still torn apart from top to bottom.

I nodded to the head of the construction crew.

"How are you coming today?" I asked in a neighborly way.

"Fine," he replied.

"When are you going to be done? It's been a year now, hasn't it?"

"Ran into some asbestos problems," he shrugged. "Looks like three or four months, at least."

"I see."

End of pleasant conversation.

Another stopover at our New York attorneys' office.

"Sue them again," I directed.

Soon after the papers were served, I received a call in my Florida office from the head honcho at Nikko. He wanted me to make one more trip to New York. Two days later, Mick and I sold our two condos, minus the furniture, to Nikko for $1.3 million each.

One more giant corporation that wasn't minding the store in Fun City.

MICHELINA'S VS. MICHELIN

As Michelina's frozen foods expanded into Europe, Michelin Tires contended in court that our brand name conflicted with the brand name for their tires. Somehow the public was going to get frozen foods confused with tires.

They sued us in France and Denmark and some other countries. We pointed out that we used the pronunciation key (say Mick-ah-LEE-nahs) on all international packages just to make sure people knew they were buying food, not tires or anything else.

The court in France threw out their claims and the dominos fell the same way in the other countries.

The Michelin matter was settled after we threatened a countersuit claiming deceptive trade practices and RICO (Racketeer Influenced Corrupt Organizations) violations. Threatened, not filed.

The damn arrogance of large corporations of any nationality, as well as their stupidity, continues to amaze me.

Another PC. We didn't make any money off it. But it was fun to turn the tire-maker's suit into roadkill.

THE UNLUCKY ELEVEN

In a land deal in Florida, I had to sue my fifty percent general partner. We didn't appreciate the commingling of that project money with other interests of the general partner, so I sued for payment of my fifty percent, and goodbye commingler.

In a mediation meeting to settle the lawsuit, they brought eleven executives; I brought one, plus my attorney. We started at nine A.M. The mediator was doing his best. I wanted $2.5 million; the general partner offered a lousy piece of land worth maybe a half million.

By three P.M., we were getting nowhere, so I decided to play a little chess with this group of attorneys that I was already beginning to think of as the Unlucky Eleven. We retired to our room; they retired to theirs. I told the mediator to go in and tell them I'd drop the lawsuit and become a *very active partner,* rather than just a financial one.

My attorney and the president of Paulucci International who were with me couldn't believe it. "Jeno, are you crazy? You don't want to be in business with them again!"

"Watch what happens."

The mediator conveyed my offer to the Unlucky Eleven and in about fifteen minutes he came back with a dour face and a discouraged look.

"Mr. Paulucci," he said, "I told them you wanted to be an active fifty percent partner, and I'm very embarrassed to tell you they all said absolutely not. In fact, one of them said he would rather have AIDS than you for a partner."

See. My chess move paid off.

By five P.M. that day I went home $2.3 million richer; pre-tax, of course.

> *Pointer from the Peddler: "It pays to be ignorant," goes one of my favorite Credos. The corollary: "It pays to be known as a son of a bitch." If they don't want any part of you, make them pay for the privilege.*

LEAN VS. LIGHT

The worldwide Nestle Corporation and its Stouffer's Food Division had a problem with our Michelina's line of Lean 'n Tasty low-fat entrees. They claimed they owned the word *lean.*

A patent on the word *lean?* What were they, nuts? I brought a Declaratory Judgment lawsuit against them.

I told their president to put $5 million on the table and I'd switch our brand to Light 'n Tasty rather than lean. If not, we'd sue their ass for abuse of power.

We won in court and we protected and retained the right to use the Lean 'n Tasty brand. Having made our point, we later merged that line into our regular Michelina's entrees, designated simply Low Fat.

AS WE SPEAK, I'm still in litigation on various matters. If something develops of interest before the book is published, maybe I'll write a postscript.

Part Five

The Many Faces
of Activism

*During my long career, I've worn a lot of hats
. . . Jeno the Peddler . . . Jeno the Entrepreneur
. . . Jeno the SOB and others. All true, and I can
change hats in two seconds flat. But the hat I
wear most proudly is that of Jeno the Activist.*

*What the hell is an activist? Just somebody who's
willing to devote time and energy and ideas—and
money—to get things done that you know damn
well should be done. My activism roamed from
Alaska and Canada to Italy and elsewhere, but it
started in my own backyard in Duluth.*

*Philanthropy? Hell, no. If it's going to be
effective, activism is a business, and there's
nothing soft about it.*

Jeno's Credo:
Man benefits in many ways
by his actions . . . not only
for profit, but for good.

Statement Into The Record

On April 14, 1945, Jeno F. Paulucci, age 26,
Duluth, MN lockup accused

On April 14, 1945, Jeno F. Paulucci, age 26, was sitting in the Duluth, MN lockup accused of chasing a man down the street with two butcher knives while drunk. "What if I caught him?" I thought. The stark realization that I could have killed someone changed my life forever. My life, and the life of hundreds of others – for the better.

tainted by drunkenness, age or passion of a moment – those who could rehabilitated. After 57 years, I'm still keeping my promise.

First you should know that, strictly because of employment practices I established in the 1940s and continue to this day in all of the more than 50 companies I've created or developed, my Jeno's, Inc., was selected United States Employer of the Year (1972) among all major corporations by the President's Council on Employment of the Handicapped and the National Association of Manufacturers. Jeno's had been named Employer of the Year by the City of Duluth and the State of Minnesota to qualify. The award recognized the fact that 61% of the approximately 2,000 Jeno's employees, all working under union contracts for the same wages and benefits as everyone else, were handicapped, disadvantaged, ex-convicts, recovering alcoholics or addicts – all considered "unemployable" by others. The loyalty and productivity of those to whom we gave a chance or a second chance is legend.

The policy continued and continues. The Wisconsin Rehabilitation Association rated Jeno's Employer of the Year 1979. I was

Becoming an advocate for the disadvantaged, the handicapped, convicts, reformed addicts, and others in need of a helping hand.

Chapter 32

A Statement for the Record

*T*hey say charity begins at home. So does activism, but it sure as hell ain't charity.

At the very beginning of my businesses—even before my community activism on behalf of the Taconite Amendment and so on—I laid down a policy to employ the "unemployables."

These so-called unemployables might be physically or mentally handicapped or people who needed a new start in life while recovering from addiction. This policy continued with the strong support of Bill Olson, my personnel manager for many years, and remains in effect.

It was and is good business. These folks, who get the same union wages and benefits and chance for advancement as anyone else, are a good investment. They work hard; they're low on absenteeism and high on loyalty. In fact, they often set an example for the "normal" people working alongside them.

I think of one young woman who joined us through a training program in cooperation with Goodwill Industries. I knew her father and mother in the days when they had to hold her hands and her head for the simplest activity like eating.

One morning, as I was backing my car into the garage below my Duluth office at about a quarter to six, I happened to see her walking jauntily by herself with her lunch pail—head held high, a sparkle in her eyes—going on the job before her shift even started.

She didn't need her parents to hold her hand any more. She'd just gotten off the bus on the corner and was proudly coming to work.

THERE'S ANOTHER TYPE OF DISADVANTAGED individual for whom I have a special feeling. These are convicts, people who have run afoul of the law in one way or another, whether it was due to a lapse of judgment or just being drunk as hell at the wrong time.

My empathy for them is easy to explain: I could have been one of them. There but for the grace of God . . .

Over the years I've read about, heard about, or been told about people who've been imprisoned. If I see anything unjust about the trial or the circumstances, I'll quietly launch an investigation. Not always, but sometimes I've found to my own satisfaction that the person was unduly convicted. Other times, it was just someone who needed another chance.

They get that chance from me in the form of legal support, intervention in the courts—and in many cases, a job.

But they've got to make good on that job. They're told, very bluntly, that they'll get no special privileges. Counseling, yes; pampering, no. I'm meaner than the meanest turnkey they ever met. That's the only way to get people to pick themselves up by their own bootstraps and learn to walk on their own.

Over the years, I've secured paroles, new trials, or the release of some hundred convicts and addicts. Only two ever returned to prison.

A FEW YEARS AGO, I INTERVENED in the case of HS, a young man who was facing forty years in prison without parole as an accomplice to a Molotov cocktail firebombing of a district attorney's home. Yes, he made a big mistake. He drove the car. He pleaded guilty under fear of his family being threatened. And he was convicted.

I looked into it and concluded that HS probably deserved a few years in jail, but not that life sentence.

When his appeal came to court, I asked the judge to put a personal Statement for the Record into the proceedings of the trial, which I quote here in part:

> *On April 14, 1945, Jeno F. Paulucci, age 26, was sitting in the Duluth, Minnesota, lockup accused of chasing a man down the street with two butcher knives while drunk. What if I had caught him? I thought. The stark realization that I could have killed someone changed my life forever.*

On that day I promised God to do all I could to help others in trouble for crimes committed—not those brought about by character traits but those caught up in unfortunate singular situations where the crime may have been tainted by drunkenness, addiction, ignorance, rage or the passion of a moment—those who could be rehabilitated. I'm still keeping my promise . . .

I continue to get involved directly in individual cases, referred to me by individuals or agencies that I've worked with in the past—and those that I feel I can help rehabilitate are often released to my care.

Here are just a few examples:

HS is the brother of a high school classmate, convicted of breaking and entering and of robbery. Released from prison into my custody, he became a long-term employee until his untimely death of natural causes.

TW was convicted of murder in the deaths of two persons in a shootout during a drunken rage bar fight in Michigan. He escaped from prison and was re-captured in Minnesota. After I learned of his case, I worked for more than a year for his release. I still have a painting I bought from him while he was in prison. Upon our investigation and appeal, TW's sentence was commuted to time served and he was put under very strict supervision on a work project. When we decided that the time was right, he moved back to Michigan and started a successful business of buying and remodeling homes.

RB was jailed for embezzlement and forgery. I pleaded for his release with the promise of a job. He has since been elected to the School Board and the City Council in his community, has pursued his education and has become a professor and a computer expert.

EK robbed a bank. I gained his release and custody and got him a job in a responsible position. He is now a marketing executive for a company in Florida.

JS's mother pleaded with me to help her son, who had committed armed robbery. I gained his release and he became a productive employee in one of my enterprises in Minnesota. In turn, his son is now one of my senior executives.

DD was a popular waiter in one of my restaurants who fell victim to drugs and liquor. I am presently financing his treatment in a rehabilitation facility and expect him back in six to eight weeks.

JH is serving two consecutive life sentences in Pennsylvania for murder, without parole. His sworn innocence has prompted me to hire an attorney who has arranged to visit with JH in the Pennsylvania prison and now is considering polygraph and DNA tests . . .

BD was a muscular boxer who worked side-by-side with me in the 1940s in a plant, where we cut 100–pound blocks of frozen meat. We often challenged one another in feats of strength required for the job. I tried to keep him straight, but admit I lost this one when drugs and other tragedies intervened.

Of late, JM, a person very close to me, was violating his probation. I felt that the only remedy would be putting JM back in jail for a month or more, so I insisted that the authorities do so; a heart-rending experience for me. Thankfully, JM's rehabilitation has been outstanding . . .

I'd had two decades of experience working with felons and convicts before I met Chuck Colson in the

Nixon White House. He later went to jail himself as a Watergate participant. After his release, he became a minister who now heads the Prison Fellowship organization. He and I have worked together on several criminal cases—some successfully, some not.

The foregoing is a short summary to identify Jeno F. Paulucci's experience, dedication and commitment to the successful rehabilitation of every person possible, when I deem that the person deserves it. My dedication continues to this day, and that's why I am here.

October 17, 2000 Signed
Jeno F. Paulucci
525 Lake Avenue South
Duluth MN 55802

I continue to work on cases like these all the time. A few turn out badly. But most result in solid, successful citizens. Those who work for me have earned my trust, which I return in full.

Chapter 33

When Eskimos Dined on Caviar

*A*t one time or another, I've feuded with the alphabet soup of federal agencies from the IRS to the FBI. But the one agency that has never been anything but helpful is the EDA, the Economic Development Administration.

It was headed for years by George Karras, a tough former union negotiator who got in your face and challenged you to prove your project was worth government funding.

We got along just fine. It was George who arranged for grants and loans that made possible the Arena-Auditorium complex, the regional library, the water treatment plant, the medical school at the University of Minnesota-Duluth, and the Spirit Mountain ski area south of the city.

One day in the early 1970s, I stopped by George's office in Washington to talk about some other projects I had in mind. But this time, he was the one who had a problem.

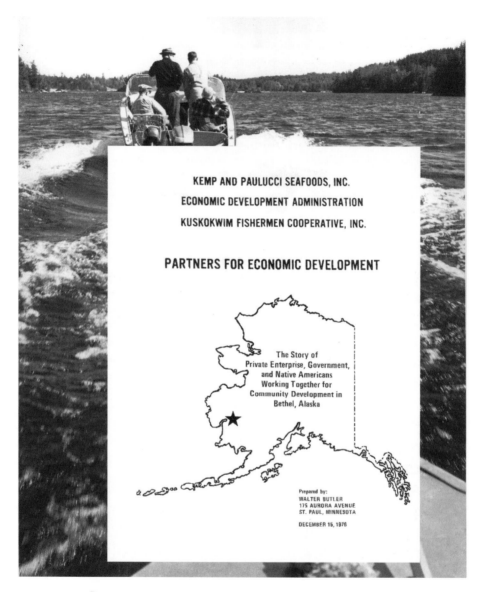

KEMP AND PAULUCCI SEAFOODS, INC.

ECONOMIC DEVELOPMENT ADMINISTRATION

KUSKOKWIM FISHERMEN COOPERATIVE, INC.

PARTNERS FOR ECONOMIC DEVELOPMENT

The Story of
Private Enterprise, Government,
and Native Americans
Working Together for
Community Development in
Bethel, Alaska

Prepared by:
WALTER BUTLER
175 AURORA AVENUE
ST. PAUL, MINNESOTA

DECEMBER 15, 1976

Forging a partnership to help a struggling community.

"Know anybody in the fishing business, Jeno?" he wanted to know.

"Maybe," I said. "What's up?"

"It's this way. We've sunk two million bucks into this fishing barge up in Alaska, trying to save the salmon fishing industry. Now it's all gone sour on me."

To explain, he pulled out a map and pointed to western Alaska, where the mouth of the Kuskokwim River empties into the Bering Sea. During the six- to eight-week spawning season each year, the salmon swim up this river to the town of Bethel, where the Native American population has the right to net them, subject to quotas. To help these Yu'pik Eskimos market their catch, the government had outfitted a special barge.

"It's not a fishing barge, but a processing barge," George clarified. "The fishermen bring the salmon in their own boats to be cleaned and stored on board in freezers."

From there the fish were flown to Seattle or picked up directly by foreign ships. Japan was a huge market for salmon caviar.

"We got involved because unemployment among these people is the highest in the United States," George said. "And when there's no work, they drink.

"Now the barge is falling apart. I don't know where we'll get the money to fix it. But the worst thing is nobody up there seems to know how to run this operation."

"And now you need somebody who can run this barge as a business," I said, catching on.

"Somebody like you, Jeno. Warm heart—hard head."

Hard enough to know this time it wasn't me. But I had an idea.

"I might have your man," I replied. "I'll let you know."

MY FRIEND LOUIS KEMP came by his Duluth fishing business from his father Abe, who started out buying up licenses to catch Lake Superior herring from down-on-their-luck North Shore fishermen. The Kemp family processed lake trout and also imported lutefisk from the Scandinavian countries.

When I called him about the barge, Louie was interested and immediately flew up to Bethel. He determined that another $500,000 was needed to replace rusted-out equipment and retrofit the barge.

"If we can come up with that," he reported, "we're in business."

I contacted George Karras and proposed a deal.

If the EDA put up the additional money, we would form the Paulucci-Kemp company to run the barge. My son Mick, who was beginning to be interested in offbeat business ventures, would own my 50 percent.

"I don't care who takes the 50 percent," George said, "as long as you're involved, Jeno."

"I'll keep an eye on things," I promised.

Millions of dollars in income came into the hands of those depressed Native Americans, and Louie himself became an active part of the local community. Eventually he bought a larger, more modern barge, which proved a wise decision when the old one sank shortly thereafter in a storm.

However, it turned out the real money to be made in salmon fishing was not in marketing the fish. Because of the way the price fluctuated, that proved to be more or less a break-even proposition.

The salmon eggs were something else entirely. Known as red caviar, the roe from these spawning fish disappeared as fast as Louie could lay his hands on it. This coveted delicacy sold to the Japanese for $4 to $7 a pound, a huge number back then.

But Louie was frustrated.

Each local fisherman, limited by his government quota, could sell him only so much salmon and so many eggs. This might not have been so bad, but each Eskimo also had the right to catch as many additional fish as he could consume and store at home between fishing seasons.

"Hell, Jeno," Louie complained over the phone, "these Eskimos don't like red caviar any better than I do. They just throw the stuff away."

"So?"

"They'd love to sell it to me, and I'd love to pay up to $1.50 a pound for the privilege."

Louie normally bought each fisherman's quota of salmon for 20 to 50 cents a pound, with nothing extra for the salmon roe. "Sounds like a helluva deal for everybody," I had to agree. "What's the catch?"

"It's illegal."

Louie explained the special law that forbade the sale of any part of this subsistence salmon. Because each fish contained a half-pound to a pound of eggs, we both saw thousands of dollars of valuable caviar going to waste each year.

"That's crazy."

"But what can I do, Jeno?"

Well, I had never been near Bethel, Alaska, and I didn't know salmon processing from harp tuning.

But I did know how to make a fuss.

First, I contacted George Karras, who told me it was a state, not a federal law that stood in our way. Next I talked to my friend and fishing buddy, then-Senator Fritz Mondale of Minnesota. He put me in touch with a fellow senator, Ted Stevens of Alaska.

"If it's a state law," Stevens said, "my hands are tied."

"Who *can* help us?"

"Well, you might start with the governor of Alaska, I suppose."

"What's his number?"

Senator Mondale put through the call to make sure I didn't get a long-distance brush-off.

I explained to the governor what a shame it was all those Native Americans in his state were being deprived of hundreds of dollars of additional income every year because of a silly law.

"The caviar's just being thrown away," I concluded. "Something should be done."

"I'll look into it, Jeno," he promised.

When the governor got back to me, however, he sounded discouraged.

"I talked to Mr. Alexander, our commissioner of natural resources," he began. "I'm afraid he's dead set against changing the law. Without it, he feels the fishermen will go after more fish than they could possibly use, just to sell the eggs."

"A very good point," I agreed, keeping my foot in the door. "But you folks are already tightly regulating the commercial fishing quotas, aren't you?"

"I guess you could say that . . ."

"Why can't you do the same thing with the subsistence side of it? You don't need this arbitrary law to keep those poor fishermen in line."

The governor was persuaded enough to offer himself an out. "Why don't you talk to Commissioner Alexander yourself?"

"I'll be glad to," I said. "Please tell him I'll be calling, *right away.*"

Commissioner Alexander was not too happy to hear a stranger from Duluth, Minnesota, tell him how to run the Alaska Department of Natural Resources.

We went round and round.

"I don't want to offend anyone here," I said at last, "but do you realize that before the Paulucci-Kemp operation began, the average annual income among all those fishermen up there was about five hundred dollars and they were all on welfare?" (A little homework comes in handy.) "And now, two years later, the unemployment and alcohol problems are way down?"

He couldn't argue with that.

"But the difference between staying in business or folding could well be that red caviar that's going back out to sea right now."

Commissioner Alexander was convinced. He pushed an amendment through the next session of the Alaskan legislature permitting the Native American Eskimos to sell the caviar to Paulucci-Kemp.

I was out of the business now, Mick having sold his half to Louie Kemp. But I remembered my promise to George Karras; I'd still keep an eye on things. What that meant, mostly, was reminding Louis on occasion to pay more attention to business in Alaska, and not spend so much of his time in California with his Hollywood friends such as Bobby Dylan . . . who probably enjoyed Beluga caviar but didn't give a damn how much it cost or where it came from.

I also published a booklet called *The Kemp-Paulucci-EDA Story* to tell anybody who might be interested how the private sector could work in partnership with government.

All in all, I was proud of being able to chalk up one success with Native Americans, even though it involved workers I never saw and a processing barge I never set foot on.

Chapter 34

Tribes and Tribulations

*I*t's a mistake to lump all Native North Americans into one category called "Indians." These people have as many different cultures and languages as Europeans. But they do have a couple of things in common.

First, they've all been screwed by the white man throughout history.

Second, they're a lot smarter than you might think. More than a few times, they proved to be a helluva lot sharper than me.

My efforts to help out these fine people in the United States and Canada were based, like all my activism, on business. The great goal was to create some kind of financial base they could operate on their own. Today many Indians know all about that. Their casinos are a growing industry. They're soaking up money from the gullible gamblers from the suburbs.

Call it the Red Man's Revenge.

But in the 1950s, all this success was far in the future. At that time, I tried to set up a partnership

*While searching for wild rice in Minnesota and Canada,
this Business Week photo of the harvest cost Jeno a truck.*

with the Bois Forte Band of Chippewa at the Nett Lake Reservation, about forty miles south of the Canadian border and about 120 miles north of Duluth.

THEY WERE GOING TO SUPPLY wild rice for my food business—to their profit and mine.

I had added a separate line of canned and frozen wild rice dishes under the Nokomis brand. I was getting national distribution, so I decided to standardize my source of roasted wild rice. We were buying it in hundred-pound bags from dealers who bought green rice from the Indians, then roasted it in a process similar to roasting green coffee beans.

But the source was unreliable. You would sometimes pay for Grade A at $2 to $4 a pound and end up with broken pieces and a bunch of twigs and crap in the bottom of the gunnysacks.

So I bought an airplane; a single-engine piston-driven Canadian workhorse called a Norseman. It was like a flying boxcar.

My brother-in-law, Leo Trepanier, would fly with a pilot named Kirby into Canada to bring back green, as well as roasted, wild rice during the short harvest season. Wild rice grows like wheat, except that it grows in lakes. Indians went through the rice fields in canoes and hit the stalks with a stick. The green rice would drop into the canoe to be brought to shore and sold for roasting.

Being the season is short; you had to be ready to buy before speculators bought it up, stored it, and forced the price up.

The Indians got maybe a quarter or a half-dollar a pound for the green rice brought in from the lake. They'd be lucky to harvest 2,000 to 5,000 pounds in a season, earning maybe $500 to $1,250 a year per family.

Speculators would pay no more than 50 cents a pound. They would get a 50 percent yield when roasting the rice, so their cost was a dollar a pound. After storing it for a while, they'd sell it for $4 per pound, or a $3 per pound profit.

I decided I could build a helluva business with my canned, packaged, and frozen wild rice products if I could standardize the cost and quality of my supply. And I could do it to the benefit of the Chippewa. So I set up an operation on Nett Lake Reservation and equipped it with all the cleaning and roasting equipment.

The plant and equipment was a gift from me to the Indians, and I was to have exclusive use of the plant for the rice we bought for ten years. After that, they could use the plant any way they wanted, not just for me.

This was around 1955, and my cost was about $50,000 . . . more like $500,000 today.

But the Chippewa just didn't like to be out there harvesting for more than a day or two a week, even though harvest time was only about six weeks.

To encourage them, we offered incentives. We had coupons to hand out for every hundred-pound bag of green rice we bought, redeemable for various prizes. A new Ford car was the grand prize for the Chippewa who harvested the most rice.

The American news media were fascinated. *Business Week* ran a feature article complete with a full-page photo of a charming Chippewa maiden in a canoe harvesting wild rice.

One Sunday we had a spaghetti dinner at the lake to build up enthusiasm and give out prizes (the Chippewa hadn't developed a taste for Chun King Chinese, but they did like spaghetti).

As I was seated at this long bench with the Indians, acting as the jovial host, this young Indian girl about sixteen years old came up to me.

"Do you recognize me?" she asked.

"Oh sure. You're the lovely young person in the picture in *Business Week.*"

"Yes I am," she said. "And Mr. Paulucci, don't you know that it's illegal to take photos of people and then publish them in a national magazine?"

This gal is pretty smart, I thought. I asked her name and she told me, but I've forgotten it. I'll call her Dawn.

"Well, Dawn," I said, "you knew that was a commercial photographer for *Business Week,* didn't you?"

"Oh yes, and I like the picture, but they didn't get permission for the photograph. That's illegal."

Oh boy. "Well, Dawn. What's done is done. What do you want from me?"

"I want one of your Orient Express trucks," she said.

Holy cow! This gal is *really* smart. She's asking me to give her one of my $30,000 semi-trailer units that I'd sent out to haul the wild rice out of the plant. I had a fleet of about twenty of them, and it looked like I was going to end up with nineteen.

"That's asking a lot, Dawn, don't you think?"

"No," she replied, very matter-of-factly. "I don't think that's a lot. Just give me that one there."

She pointed to a miniature tractor-trailer on a display we had set up. It was a promotional toy with my Orient Express marking signs on it, one of the prizes to be given away at the dinner. It cost about $100.

I wrote out, longhand, a photo release. She signed it, and I gave her the minature tractor-trailer and told our people to get another one for the prize drawings.

Then I gave her another $100 in ten-dollar bills and kissed her on the cheek. She left smiling and happy . . . and so did I.

Well, we finally gave up the project and let the Chippewa operate the plant any way they wanted. It was theirs, and God bless them.

MY BUSINESS DEALINGS with the Eskimos around Stark Lake, south of Yellowknife and the Great Slave Lake, were a mixed bag.

A group of us went up there to fish for big lake trout—thirty or forty pounds and even larger. We weren't having much luck, but one night we did come in with a tub loaded with lake trout—six of us, using three boats. The three Eskimo guides were supposed to clean them.

But our camp was on top of a big flat rock. You had to climb about 300 feet uphill to get to it. I decided to pay the men when we got off the boats so I wouldn't have to trudge down the hill to pay them when they were through cleaning the trout.

My brother-in-law, Leo Trepanier, thought it might be better to wait until they were done. He'd been all over Canada buying wild rice, and knew the territory. I wasn't even listening as I pulled out $30 for the guides to split.

Before we got to the top of the hill, we heard the sound of motorboats. The guides were putt-putting away, leaving all the ungutted trout in the tubs.

Okay, they put one over on me. But what the hell, it didn't hurt me to clean my own trout.

Those Eskimos in the Northwest Territories are good people. They live off the land in the most severe weather. They work as guides for people like us, and have their own nets for commercial fishing, which is allowed in the Territories. They trap in the winter for mink and other fur. With their dog teams, they follow their trap lines throughout the winter, sometimes getting lost due to snow blindness.

Above all, they wait each year for the caribou migration and their annual meat supply.

In all the years of I went to Stark Lake in July and August, I never heard one of them complain.

ON ANOTHER TRIP to Stark Lake in late July, I learned that the natives in a settlement called Snowdrift hadn't received their annual provisions yet . . . goods normally received when the ice would open up on the Great Slave Lake.

It had been a very cold season and by this point the natives were without sugar, coffee, soap, flour, and all the other staples they needed to survive.

The barge wouldn't be coming for two or three weeks, I was told.

On this trip I had a Royal Gull two-engine amphibian aircraft; the body was made in Italy by Piago and the engines were Lycoming. It was a flying boat. Don Anderson was my pilot.

I had Don fly me and my friend Frank Befera to Yellowknife, about an hour away. We went to a grocery store and we loaded two taxicabs with a list of provisions I was told the Snowdrift people needed.

We loaded our flying boat baggage chamber to the legal weight limit, and Don flew us back to Snowdrift. By the time we got there, Frank and I had consumed a bottle of champagne each, so we weren't in the best shape when we arrived.

Don taxied the Gull up to the little dock at Snowdrift and the residents started congregating. There must have been a hundred of them in a matter of minutes. I guess word had reached them that their friend "Cheno," as they called me, had something for them.

Men, women, children, and finally the head honcho, my friend the chief, came up to me as I got out of the aircraft. I asked Frank Befera, who was a little less stoned than me, to tell them we had a whole airplane full of provisions. They should come help us unload.

Frank did so, at length. He did all the talking and, damn it, Don Anderson and I did all the unloading.

Why the natives didn't help us I don't know, but when we had their dock loaded with flour, sugar, soap, cheese, and everything else, they all looked at us and started to clap and chant: "Cheno! Cheno! Cheno!"

I tell you, tears come to my eyes as I recall that night at Snowdrift. But I never went back to see how they were faring, and for that I feel guilty.

ANOTHER FAVORITE FISHING HOLE was Fort Reliance, north of Stark Lake. It was right next to the Canadian weather station. We'd come in on the Falcon to Yellowknife, then have one of my Beeches pick us up for the hour flight to Fort Reliance, where we rented a cabin accommodating about twelve people.

Those were great days in the 1960s. We took stupid chances and had great fun.

It was there that I met Edward Drybones, Jr., one of the greatest salesmen I've ever known.

I knew his family, who lived across the bay from our cabin. Edward Sr. and his daughter Esther had often guided for me. I called on them one afternoon, wanting to make the most of what was going to be the last day of the season. Edward and his daughter Esther were away at Yellowknife, but the grandmother was at home and so was her grandson, Edward Jr., who had just come back from months of traveling.

He was a fit, capable-looking young man, wellspoken with hardly a trace of an accent. Could he meet me at five o'clock the next morning? Sure.

He was there and ready to go at four forty-five. This kid is okay, I decided.

We put two outboard motors on my boat so we could travel in a hurry. But by noon, no keepers.

"Hey Edward, where in hell are the good spots?"

He stopped one motor and lowered the sound on the other. "Not around here," he said. "Jeno, I have to be honest with you. There are no big trophy trout on this lake anymore. You should try Artillery Lake."

"Where's that?"

"Up in the barrens—no trees. Our family owns land there. Green grass and a sandy beach. Lots of trout, fifty or sixty pounds. We've got a boat you could use. But there are no cabins."

After a couple more hours of no keepers, Edward brought up the subject that was on his mind. His family could build me a cabin on a grassy knoll above the lake, where the sixty-pound trout were waiting to be caught, only a half-hour away by plane from where we currently were at Fort Reliance.

By late afternoon, the tub still empty, we were in negotiations. I asked Edward what it would cost to build a cabin with a sitting room, kitchen, couple of bedrooms—maybe three—and two outside toilets. He estimated $2,500 or maybe $3,000 if I wanted it real nice with the extra bedroom. It would be built over the winter and spring and would be ready the next season.

Hesitantly, he asked for a few hundred up front. He could get credit from the lumber store for the rest, and I could pay him when I returned—and use their boat any time I wanted.

Fair enough. I peeled off $400 and said I'd see him in July.

Seven months later, the winter over and the weather getting a little warmer in Duluth, I started thinking about that cabin on Artillery Lake that was soon to be mine.

My secretary rang me in the office from her desk. "Jeno, do you know a fellow by the name of Drybones? He's calling collect from Yellowknife."

"Sure. He's building my cabin. Put him on."

"Hello Edward," I said. "How are you? How's my cabin coming along?"

Half finished, he said, and it was only March. His father and sister were out there working on it, even though it was still pretty cold, but he'd had to go to Yellowknife with his wife, who was having a baby. Could I send him another $700 in care of Nova Scotia Bank at Yellowknife to take care of expenses, so he could get back to Artillery Lake to help finish the cabin?

I hadn't heard anything about any wife or baby, but what the hell? I told Gail to wire the money. So far I'd only spent $1,100, and would have a balance of $1,900 when I took possession. I also asked Edward to send me a picture of the cabin.

Four weeks later, the picture hadn't arrived. Gail stepped into my office to say, "Your contractor, Mr. Drybones, is on the line . . . collect again."

"Put him on."

Edward couldn't understand why I hadn't received the picture. He'd send it again.

"But your cabin is completed," he said. "It's so beautiful. In fact, I have a big surprise for you when you open the door!"

And . . . he hated to mention it . . . but could I send perhaps half the balance to pay for some of the lumber he'd bought?

I didn't know what to do. Edward sounded so warm and friendly. I agreed and rang Gail to have her wire another $950 to the same bank.

"Before you do that," she said, "you may want to take this other call that just came in. It's from the Royal Canadian Mounted Police. They want to know if you've been doing business with one Edward Drybones."

"Tell them yes. He just built my cabin on Artillery Lake."

"That's what they want to talk to you about," she said, hiding a smirk.

The officer on the phone was calm and collected. He just wanted me to know that Edward Drybones, Jr., had been arrested on a charge he couldn't discuss. The prisoner must have made the collect call a few minutes earlier from jail.

"What about his wife and baby?" I asked.

No wife. No baby.

Believe it or not, when we went up to Fort Reliance the following July, I had Don Anderson fly me and Ed Korkki over to Artillery Lake. I looked down for my dream cabin on that green knoll. Nothing there. After about eight hours of fishing in that area, I found out there weren't many lake trout either.

On my return to Fort Reliance, Edward's father sent word that he and his daughter Esther would guide us for free until my $1,100 was credited. I thanked him and said that wouldn't be necessary.

I wasn't angry. It was an interesting experience, after all. But I still wondered what that great surprise would have been, if I'd ever opened the door of the cabin that wasn't there.

Chapter 35

Lessons from the Indian Nations

*T*his time, my attention was drawn to the plight of the Oglala Sioux on their Pine Ridge Reservation in the Badlands of South Dakota.

There's a lot of history around there. In 1890, it was the site of what came to be known as the Wounded Knee Massacre, the last-pitched battle in the Indian wars. More than 300 Sioux were shot down or died in snowdrifts.

Seventy-five years later, the American Indian Movement had a shoot-out with the FBI in the town of Oglala. One Indian was killed, and two FBI agents. One of the Oglala, Leonard Peltier, was sent to prison for life. He's still there. But did he get a fair trial?

That was one of the topics that I was discussing with my friend William Kunstler, the renowned advocate attorney who had represented the American Indian Movement, just before he died suddenly in 1995.

Indians and Eskimos have much to teach us.

MY INVOLVEMENT with the Oglala Sioux took place in the early 1970s, a couple of years after that infamous gunbattle.

I got a call from my old friend John Phillips, the president of R. J. Reynolds Foods when I was chairman, and the man who'd shepherded the sale of Chun King to Reynolds. He had become head of a New York City organization that recruited volunteer executives to help small firms by providing consulting services.

Knowing of my interest in causes like these, particularly when they involved Indians, John wanted to tell me about a little business the Oglala were trying to start in South Dakota. They were trying to sell fine handmade moccasins by catalog. And they were struggling.

Could I find time to go to South Dakota, maybe offer some advice?

I could. I flew into Pine Ridge. Two of the Oglala people picked me up and drove me to the reservation. I never in my life saw a more depressing sight.

There were buildings for people to live in, one or two stories high, but the windows were all boarded up.

"Did you have a hail storm here?" I asked my escorts.

"No. Our residents sold the windows for drugs and liquor."

I noticed the young people just sitting around the streets, glassy eyed, there by the storefronts with their metal barricades so no one could break in.

So this is what we had done to these Native Americans, we foreigners, we barbarians who stole their land, broke their spirit, and took away their self-respect.

I sure was ready to do whatever I could to help them.

My hosts took me to a small, one-story frame building, barricaded of course. They showed me what they were trying to sell—about eighty to a hundred different styles of moccasins.

Not very impressive, I thought. But over to the side they had another display of little Indian dolls dressed in deerskin clothing—cute as hell with black hair, I suppose from a horse's tail. Sort of an Indian Barbie doll.

I asked a few questions. All the moccasins, and the dolls, were crafted by the reservation people back in their tents and houses on a piecework basis. They were trying to sell them via a couple of wholesalers who sent out catalogs of all kinds of Indian crafts, including those of the Oglala.

It was clear that they had good things to sell, but lacked business skills. I asked which of the items were selling the most. Usually in a business like this, you find that just a few of the items account for the majority of sales. Those are the ones to concentrate on, if you want to build a successful business.

The Oglala agreed to look into their records. A couple of weeks later I returned with my accounting assistant, Ron Scinocca, Sr.

We found that just 10 percent of the items comprised 80 percent of the sales volume, and most of them were the dolls. Concentrate on them, I suggested, and eliminate most of the other items, thus reducing inventory and obsolescence. More than that, I said I would have a brochure made up for buyers, and mailing lists to distribute the brochure and thus broaden their market.

The dolls were moderately priced, and I felt it wouldn't hurt to raise the price a little, because these dolls were treasures.

Working with the Oglala, we developed better systems. I also funded some new computers as well as store equipment, and other necessities.

Ron and I, along with representatives of the Oglala tribe, flew to Washington, D.C., to try to get the Bureau of Indian Affairs to be more cooperative and to make some money grants. This was a much-needed enterprise, we told them, which provided income and kept those living on the reservation occupied. We went to Washington twice, and got nowhere.

No, the Bureau was rife with its own political infighting and cliques that made me want to vomit.

I wish I could have had those almighty Bureau of Indian Affairs high muckity-mucks spend just one day and night on that reservation. Then they might have come to their senses. They were just a bunch of disgusting self-serving bureaucrats who forgot what in hell they were supposed to be doing, which was to help those Native Americans help themselves.

I spent about $100,000 to help with the project before I finally gave up, I'm sorry to say. I couldn't think of anything else to do. My consolation is that I know they are a little better off than when I started to help . . . and I hope they're doing okay now.

Given the way those poor natives were being treated and governed, no damn wonder they fought with the FBI, not far away from the site of the Wounded Knee Massacre.

> *Pointer from the Peddler: Not all, or even most, projects with the disadvantaged are going to be a complete success. That's no reason to stop trying.*

THOSE WERE JUST A FEW HIGHLIGHTS of my association with Native Americans. Obviously, not all were successful. But I tried as hard as I could, and I just wish to God I'd been able to do more.

These people have much to teach us.

I'm reminded of an Eskimo guide we had one year in the Arctic, north of Cambridge Bay. I'd aborted a previous trip up there when one of our Beechcraft engines blew out over the ocean.

But we went again, several times, to stand on the shore and cast for lake trout or those beautiful red char.

Our guide on this occasion was named Eddie. He had a wife, a nine-year-old son, and a baby about a year old. I still cherish a photo of Eddie, his family, and me. I've often thought that if I had a choice of being in a picture with Native Americans or with the president of the United States, the president would have to wait.

About five years before I knew him, both of Eddie's legs had been amputated, I suppose because of some accident. He walked on two wooden stumps, but he could get in and out of boats, carry fish, climb ladders. He walked stiff-legged, of course, as if he were on stilts.

What amazed me was that his nine-year-old son, Eddie Jr., walked the same stiff way as his dad, although there was nothing wrong with his legs. Up hills, down hills, getting into boats, he emulated his father.

It wasn't my place, but once I asked Eddie, "How come your son walks that way? Shouldn't he walk normally?"

He just looked at me as if to ask, "What's normal?"

Good question. In that isolated environment, the son thought that the way his father walked must be the way *he* should walk. I'm no psychologist, but I think there's a profound lesson here.

At an early age, sons do want to be like their fathers. If the father is honest and upright and courageous, chances are the son will be the same.

I'm sure that young man, who must be in his thirties or forties by now, walks like anybody else. But I'm also sure that he has a story to tell the world about his father's courage, up there in the desolate Arctic, where anyone else in his condition couldn't walk at all.

Chapter 36

Buongiorno, Italian-Americans

*O*f all my efforts as an activist, the one I'm most proud of is the creation of an organization called the National Italian American Foundation.

It grew out of some deeply held convictions that took hold over the years.

THE WORST FORM OF CANCER on the planet, I feel, is one that nobody seems able to cure. Call it discrimination, call it prejudice, call it bigotry. I call it sad, sickening, and stupid.

Anyone in his right mind knows we're all equal under God. But try to find anyone in his right mind.

Around the world, wars continue to be fought, or threaten to break out, because one group feels superior to another group, and vice versa. In Africa, it's blacks versus other blacks. In the Balkans, it's Serbs versus Croats versus Christians versus Muslims. In South Asia, it's Pakistanis versus Hindus. In the

To Jeno Paulucci
With best wishes, Ronald Reagan Nancy Reagan

From frustrated barker to spokesman for 25 million citizens.
The NIAF celebrates achievement.

Middle East, it's Muslims versus other Muslims, and of course Palestinians versus Jews.

All too often, the root of the warfare is religion. Despite all the good that religion has done for individual souls, religious dogma, in my opinion, has been a plague since the Middle Ages.

In this country, we haven't had any Civil Wars lately, but blacks and Hispanics and Jews and others are still subject to discrimination—subtle or not so subtle.

I know a lot about discrimination. At a very early age, I found myself sitting in the back row of the classroom—when my grades should have put me on the front row—because I was a dirty little Wop whose hair smelled of kerosene—my mother's home treatment for lice. It didn't matter that I never got lice in our fastidious home, but probably from some of the teacher's pets in the front row.

I was a Wop, so it must be my fault.

In later years, I couldn't get rich enough to escape the stigma of being this Italian upstart who must have some connection to the Mafia.

When my son Mick was ten years old, he came home one evening and told me he'd been hearing comments about the Mafia from the other kids at school.

It didn't bother him much; it was kind of exciting. So he asked me, "Dad, what syndicate do you belong to?"

Mick and I had a long talk. I told him about all the reasons that Italian-Americans had to be proud of their heritage, and assured him I wasn't a gangster. I think he was a little disappointed.

THAT CONVERSATION STAYED IN MY MIND for many years, but it wasn't until 1976 that I decided it was time for Italian-Americans to speak up, and speak out. I formed this organization that I named the National Italian American Foundation—the NIAF—to celebrate our heritage and our achievements, and put an end to the subtle discrimination.

In all modesty, I was an unlikely choice to be the godfather.

I had never joined political parties or clubs or social or sports groups (Lois and I weren't antisocial; we just weren't joiners). Never accepted state or federal appointments. Didn't have any academic credentials except a high school diploma, if I could even find it.

Still, nobody else had tried to bring together the 25 million Italian-Americans to speak with one voice, so I assigned that job to myself.

First off, I decided that the NIAF should be located in our nation's capital, Washington, D.C., where we could access the Italian-American Congressional delegation, about thirty members of Congress at that time. That would be the core of our support.

Thankfully, I found the greatest supporters one could ever hope for. Congressman Frank Annunzio—in my opinion, the dean of the Italian-American Congressional delegation—Congressman Peter Rodino, Senator Pete Domenici, and others joined in. Former Massachusetts Governor and Secretary of Transportation John Volpe, then ambassador to Italy, became one of our first NIAF presidents.

Another great supporter in those formative days was Jack Valenti, president of the Motion Picture Association of America and former administrative assistant to President Lyndon Johnson. Our West Coast base was also strengthened by Joseph Alioto, former mayor of San Francisco.

So I was able to get the "big guns" in the Italian-American community to give their blessing.

But I didn't ask for money, just influence. I was fully prepared to fund the start of the organization—by myself.

First, I covered all the expenses of the Washington office and its staff, travel, and the luncheons and dinners coast to coast as we spread our gospel.

Second, I set up a Council of 1,000, styled after Florida's Governor's Council of 100, of which I was a member. It was the Council's job to be our voice in every part of America. If a member wanted to contribute $100 to $1,000, fine, but that was secondary.

Eventually, the Council provided financial help, so that all the money didn't have to come out of my pocket; and still later, funds were generated by our annual banquets.

Third, we put together a prestigious group of Italian-Americans as our first board of directors.

Fourth, we decided to host a black-tie Gala Dinner in September 1976, in the largest banquet hall at the Washington Hilton—which offered space for some 2,800 people. This was the do-or-die way for us to launch NIAF from nothing to an international success, overnight.

If it was to be successful, I realized, we needed a full house. The Italian-American Congressional delegation sold about 500 tickets to lobbying groups and others at a price of $100 a plate (it's $300 now). We needed about 2,000 more. Otherwise the press, who of course were also invited, would call it a failure.

The solution was something they do in show business when they're not selling enough tickets— "paper the house." In other words, give away tickets to people whose presence you want and need.

That was going to require an additional investment from me. So I contributed $200,000 to the non-profit Foundation for 2,000 tickets to be given to every prestigious Italian-American we could think of, plus all the members of Congress.

Hell, we papered the house so well that even President Gerald Ford accepted our invitation. When he accepted, so did Jimmy Carter, the Democratic presidential nominee, and my friend Fritz Mondale, the nominee for vice president.

We had them all in their black ties—a crowded two-tier dais plus a full house in the banquet hall. Several even came from Italy to be there.

Jack Valenti was master of ceremonies. As founding chairman, I gave the welcoming remarks and told the audience—which wasn't just the 2,500 people there in person, but also the millions we reached through reports of the event on TV and the radio, and in newspapers and magazines—who we were, why we were there, and what we were going to do in the future.

It was one of the most exhilarating and successful *sales* of my life, and this peddler was damn proud!

For only $200,000 plus whatever I had spent before that—maybe another $250,000—the world was listening to us. As it does today. It was cheap, and so was the additional $500,000 plus what I spent to cover expenses as our newborn began to walk—and run—and above all talk, talk, talk to the world about the positive past and present accomplishments and contributions of Italian-Americans.

The media coverage of the first Gala Dinner was nothing short of miraculous. Most of the reporters loved the idea. One didn't, but she gave us even more ammunition. I refer to the negative damn near full-page story in the Washington Post written by a so-called social reporter named Sally Quinn.

That reporter broad (that's about as courteous as I can get) wrote that long Sunday feature saying that the 2,500 people attending were a mixture of Congressional freeloaders and Catholic hierarchy in flowing robes.

Sure, we had a cardinal and a monsignor there. We might even have had the Pope if we had thought of it.

She likened us to a high-class gathering of the syndicate. It was insulting and emphasized the stereotyping of Italian-Americans.

And it was just great!

That article gave us an even more powerful springboard to get support from the Italian-American community at all levels. We used the article as a message to tell our community throughout the United States that it was time to speak up.

We'd been struggling uphill, but from then on it was downhill, so to speak, in building the organization.

I wasn't the star of the show. The ambassadors, senators, congressmen, governors, and other distinguished people I'd brought together—they were the stars. However, behind the scenes, I made it clear that I was going to run the Foundation until it was a true success, the same as I would run any business of mine that I owned 100 percent.

I let everyone know—including our officers and board members and executive directors (of which there were quite a few, because I did fire some of them now and then)—that there was to be no political infighting and no personal elbowing to gain from their association with the Foundation. In other words, I was the same so-called son of a bitch that I was in my business life.

Good move. Otherwise, the Foundation would not have grown as it did for the seventeen unforgettable years I was its chairman and CEO.

When I did retire, I left an executive director in Dr. Fred Rotondaro, who was dedicated and selfless in his work—and effective.

The Foundation claimed about a million dollars and seventeen years of my life, and it was worth every penny and every hour.

The Foundation also served a secondary purpose. It has become the catalyst for other organizations representing Native Americans, African-Americans, Asian-Americans, and others who want to emulate what the NIAF has done.

Looking back at those annual Gala Dinners, we never had one dinner that wasn't attended by a president of the United States, along with the presidential candidate of the opposing party in election years, and illustrious guests from abroad.

Giulio Andreotti, then Prime Minister of the Republic of Italy, recalls coming directly from a NATO meeting in Brussels, changing his clothes on the plane, and arriving just in time for the dinner.

"In the speeches one issue was always present—the contributions of the immigrants to the prestige of the New World," he wrote me recently. "This was a new type of relationship with the country of origin. I experienced this emotion and I cannot forget it."

Neither can I.

Discrimination against Italian-Americans isn't dead. That TV show *The Sopranos* is very popular, but it still ties us into the Mafia as surely as the kids did in Mick's schoolyard. The work of the NIAF continues.

I'm proud of this organization and the time, money, and effort I expended to bring it to life, then leave it in the capable hands of those who have carried on, such as Chairman Frank Stella.

That's why I say *Buongiorno*—Good morning, Italian-Americans. God bless us, and God bless America.

Chapter 37

New Town for a New Time

*T*his episode didn't start out as activism. Merely the purchase of a home and some land in Florida.

But before it was over, I found myself building a new town and championing the economic development of the whole area. And that called for the most active kind of activism . . . such as running across a busy freeway and scaling a ten-foot fence with barbed wire at the top.

IN THE 1950s, LOIS AND I bought a second home in Sanford, Florida. I'd liked the looks of the place when I first flew in to buy celery . . . lakes and rolling hills, a southern version of northern Minnesota. We've spent many happy half-years there.

At the same time, Lois and her brother, Leo Trepanier, purchased 150 acres of former orange groves nearby, land that became known as L&L Acres.

Leo was thinking ahead about his investment. One day he asked me, "Jeno, why don't you ask that

I found myself building a new town.

congressman friend from back home to help us get an interchange at Lake Mary?"

"What's an interchange?"

Leo looked at me as though I had been hibernating in one of my bean sprout incubators in Duluth.

"That's the exit–entrance ramps. An interchange lets cars get on and off these limited-access highways, such as I-4."

Interstate 4 is the major artery connecting both coasts of central Florida. It slices southwest from Daytona Beach on the Atlantic to Tampa on the Gulf. L&L Acres happened to be located along the west edge of I-4 about fifteen miles north of Orlando, about five miles from our house. On the east side of I-4 was a small town called Lake Mary.

It was just sleepy, rolling countryside at the time.

Now that I knew what an interchange was, I asked Leo, "Why do I need to call a congressman?"

Leo had the whole thing worked out. "Your friend John Blatnik in Washington is chairman of the Public Works Committee that appropriates funding for highways, bridges, and . . . interchanges."

I was beginning to see his point.

"There's great potential for growth around Lake Mary," Leo continued. "It's a natural spot for an interchange. Tell John Blatnik that."

Leo was not alone, of course, in realizing that President Eisenhower's publicly financed system of interstate highways was going to do for the country what railroads had done in the nineteenth century. Wherever the Iron Horse went, the immigrants settled. And wherever Florida's runaway population got off those freeways in the middle of the twentieth century, people were going to live and shop.

"Okay, I got it," I said. "But before I talk to John about an interchange, I want to do one thing."

"What's that?"

"Buy more land."

Lois and I and the family bought an additional 3,000 acres of orange grove and cattle pasture, adjoining L&L Acres, for about $3 million or $1,000 an acre.

When John Blatnik stopped by our house on his next Florida vacation, I suggested, "John, how about taking a drive over to the town of Lake Mary."

"What for?"

I outlined Leo's proposal.

"I'll have it checked out at once," he said, without leaving our living room.

Ten days later he called me from Washington.

"We're presenting a bill to the committee in our next budget, Jeno," John informed me. "You'll get that Lake Mary interchange."

And we did.

Years later, in 1985, when Bob Graham was Florida's governor, I was in Tallahassee visiting the secretary of transportation with a new proposal. He was a man named George Pappas, who had held the job forever.

"You know, Mr. Paulucci," Pappas reflected, "I remember when they asked me to go out and cut the ribbon for that interchange on Interstate 4. When I got out there, along with all these other federal, state, and county officials, I wondered what all the fuss was about. This interchange was out in the country, a long way from anything."

"You didn't think it was needed," I prompted.

"No," he said, "at the time I thought the Lake Mary Boulevard interchange was one of the worst pork-barrel boondoggles I'd ever seen.

"Well, thank God somebody had the nerve and the foresight to get us to move when we did. "

I told him I was glad he felt that way. But I wasn't the one with the nerve and foresight. It was Leo Trepanier . . . and Lois.

But then we needed more help with that interchange. We needed it *tripled* in size.

SOMETHING ELSE HAD HAPPENED to that acreage my family had bought in Florida. My family had started a new town there, a new town for a new time, a town that looked ahead to the way Americans were going to live in the future.

My son Mick came up with the name Heathrow— a prestigious destination, like the London airport.

Very fitting, I thought, since my dear wife Lois is of English heritage with some French. Much better than giving it some Italian name I might have suggested like, maybe, Appian Way.

I won't go into the details of bringing this new town into being from the day of groundbreaking, November 12, 1982. Suffice it to say that today it is a secured planned community with its own federal post office, and with state-of-the-art telecommunications and fiber-optics throughout; fine parks, trees, and lakes; plus elegant golf and tennis clubs, restaurants, and ornamental street lighting. Every home and office is protected with twenty-four-hour closed circuit monitors and personal security systems.

Homes and townhouses and condos range in value from $125,000 to $10 million. Some of them are owned by famous sports and entertainment figures. But it's an open community. We never even thought of trying to exclude anyone, like the Bal Harbor Club used to do in Miami Beach.

And yes, the Lake Mary interchange was eventually expanded, and today it's one of the largest in Florida, serving not just Heathrow but all the towns around there—in one of the fastest-growing areas in the country.

But there is more to Heathrow than the beautiful homes. We also established an office complex, well-planned and restricted to three stories. Early on, I realized that these offices were the key to the future. For Heathrow to stand on its own, we needed to attract corporations.

HERE'S WHERE THE SKILLS of the Peddler from the Iron Range came into play.

The greatest resource any peddler has is his own conviction that what he's peddling will deliver the ultimate promise, no matter what puffery may be needed in making the pitch.

It was that conviction that caused me to set my sights on the American Automobile Association, which was looking around for a place to build its new world headquarters.

Early one morning, I think it was in 1984, I read in the *Orlando Sentinel* that AAA was going to move its headquarters from Falls Church, Virginia, to some other city not yet chosen. They had retained a consulting firm to study possible locations and make a recommendation.

I knew that if I got the American Automobile Association to make their headquarters in Heathrow— to be one of the first major corporations to locate there—others would follow.

The AAA is the world's largest mapmaker and distributor. Their headquarters location is on every map they distribute. So they could literally put Heathrow on the map.

They had the list down to twenty cities, the article said, and one of them was Orlando.

I dialed information, got the phone number of AAA headquarters, and dialed them. A woman answered. Thank God a live person, not some robot asking me to press buttons, because then I might have said to hell with the whole thing.

I asked her for the name of the person in charge of the relocation study. She checked, came back to me with the name, and rang his office.

His name was John Allerton. I remember it because he was so courteous to this person calling out of the blue, so to speak, asking if I could come in to see him to discuss why Heathrow was the best site for their headquarters.

He said, "Why don't you send me some written information on Heathrow, Mr. Paulucci, and we'll forward it to our consultants. However, it will take another six months before we have reduced the number of possible sites from twenty to a targeted three."

I thanked him and hung up. Then I pondered the situation for a couple hours.

Hell, I thought, if I wait six months, AAA may well have convinced themselves to go to another city. I just couldn't take that chance.

So I picked up the phone and called AAA again. I asked that nice operator for John Allerton as if I'd known him forever.

"John," I began, "this is Jeno again. Your six months is up. Can I come in to see you tomorrow? Because what I have is too good to wait any longer."

He chuckled and said, "Isn't that being a little hasty, Mr. Paulucci?"

"It would be," I answered, "if I didn't have such a golden opportunity for you. Besides, I'd like to meet you; you're such a nice guy. Please call me Jeno, and would ten A.M. tomorrow at your office be okay?"

Polite as he was, he must have felt the only way to get rid of this Jeno person was to see him.

"Okay, tomorrow, ten A.M. But I won't have very much time, so you'll have to be brief."

"Don't worry. I'm always brief. Thanks, and I'll see you tomorrow."

Six months was condensed into one day!

To get ready for the meeting, I had my secretary in Duluth, Gail Bukowski, call the limo service we use in the Washington, D.C., area. She asked for the driver I used most, a fellow by the name of Larry Williams. She told Larry that I would be arriving at Dulles the following morning, and Larry was to meet me at the Butler fixed base operation at nine-fifteen so I could make my ten A.M. appointment with AAA in Falls Church.

Leaving nothing to chance, as usual, Gail asked Larry to make a dry run, so he would know exactly where the building was and how much time would be needed to drive there from Dulles at that time of day.

Next morning, Larry met me at nine-fifteen and we were at AAA headquarters by nine thirty-five. I got a chance to chat with the receptionist near the first floor entrance, right off the parking lot. Who knows, she might have been the wife of the president. You never know nowadays, so I was especially charming, which I can be if I practice smiling for at least five minutes ahead of time.

In any event, she saw to it that my AAA contact saw me early. I showed John Allerton all our Heathrow literature, including aerial maps of the area and the I-4 interchange, and where Heathrow was in relation to the Orlando Airport and the closer Sanford Airport.

We talked for about a half-hour. Then he said, regretfully, that he didn't think we had a chance because Heathrow was too far from the Orlando Airport. I told him that by the time they were ready to build, there would be a beltline expressway from the airport, and Lake Mary Boulevard would be four lanes wide, reducing the time from the airport to only twenty-five minutes, based on our research.

All well and good, he said. It was true that AAA was just about down to three cities, now, with Orlando one of them.

He did console me by saying, "Jeno, give us at least two months. I promise you no decision will be made before you are so advised."

So I returned to Florida to run my businesses while stewing over this stalemate with the AAA.

In about a month, I learned that they had retained a respected architectural firm—Spillis, Candella and Partners, Inc., of Coral Gables, Florida, with offices in Orlando—to plan their new headquarters. That sounded like the other two cities were out of the picture.

Now it was either Orlando—or Heathrow.

Chapter 38

Climb Every Mountain, Scale Every Fence . . . Even if You Have to Tie Up Every Highway

*H*aving appointed myself Peddler-in-Chief of Heathrow and this booming slice of central Florida around it, I was just getting warmed up.

First I called the architect, Hilario Candella. He advised me that, yes, AAA had retained his firm to design an office building for its 500 headquarters employees, serving a worldwide membership of some 30 million.

What was the thinking on Orlando versus Heathrow? He told me that AAA was close to choosing the Orlando complex called Central Park.

"As architects," he said, "we would much prefer the site in Heathrow that you've offered, but our

How AAA came to put Heathrow on its maps.

client is concerned about the time it would take to get there from the Orlando Airport."

Central Park was just twenty-five minutes from the airport, supposedly, while Heathrow was maybe forty-five minutes away. That was the hang-up.

"But Mr. Candella," I said, "I told them about the new beltline expressway and the widening of Lake Mary Boulevard. Didn't they take that into consideration?"

"I don't know," he said. "But I suspect they don't give any credence to what might happen in the future, so they most likely will have us design a building to suit an area of about forty acres they will buy at Orlando Central Park."

He knew and I knew that the traffic around there was a nightmare. It would be easier and just as fast to drive to Heathrow with the highway improvements that were planned.

But his hands were tied. He suggested I get back to AAA, but please to leave his name out of it.

I thanked him and picked up the phone again. I called my phone pal, the receptionist at AAA, and asked her who was president. "His name is James Creal," she said.

"Tell me a little about him."

"He's a very nice man," she said, "but very, very busy."

"Well, I'm a nice guy too. Also busy. Could you transfer me to his secretary?"

When I got the secretary on the line, I introduced myself and told her that I had to see Mr. Creal at once on a matter of great importance to AAA.

"Oh Mr. Paulucci, he's tied up for the next few weeks."

"All I need is five minutes of his time. How about early, when he gets to work . . . like tomorrow?"

She called me back in about an hour and said, "Can you be here at eight forty-five A.M.? Mr. Creal will see you for no more than fifteen minutes."

"Thank you so much."

I called my secretary, Gail, and asked her to line up our Falcon for a trip to Dulles in the morning for arrival at eight A.M., and to ask Larry, my driver, who knew the way to AAA, to be there at eight sharp. I gathered a bunch of literature and maps and was ready for takeoff early the next morning.

We arrived at Butler fixed base on schedule. I looked around for the reliable Larry, but didn't see him.

Where the hell was Larry?

A uniformed driver came up to me and said, "Mr. Paulucci, I'm Bill, your driver today. Larry is sick. Where to?"

"Do you know where AAA headquarters is?" I asked, beginning to be a little sick myself.

"Isn't it somewhere in Falls Church?"

Now I *was* sick.

"It's not *in* Falls Church. It's *outside* Falls Church. We can see it from the highway. Let's go. I've got to be there by eight forty-five at the latest."

So Bill drove me into Falls Church.

"Where in hell are we going?" I demanded. "I told you *outside* Falls Church."

"Okay, I think I know," Bill said. So on we drove.

We went past one interchange, and I could see the building alongside it. But by that time, Bill had got us on another interchange about 1,000 feet farther along. Hell, there were interchanges all over the damn place.

I looked at my watch. It was eight-twenty.

Damn it! I had only twenty-five minutes left, so I told Bill to hurry up and turn around and get over to the other interchange that had an exit to the building.

When I get nervous, it has the unfortunate effect of making others more nervous than I am.

Bill drove like hell, sweating on the steering wheel, and before I knew it, we were back on the same second interchange again, not the correct one.

Now it was eight-thirty.

"Bill," I said, very calmly. "This ain't it. Stop the car."

"What did you say, Mr. Paulucci?"

"Stop the fucking car!"

"Right here on the road?"

"Isn't that what I said?"

He pulled over on the grass. I jumped out, taking only my clipboard, leaving all the other Heathrow material in the limo.

So here's this sixty-eight-year-old man in a well-tailored suit and tie, carrying a clipboard, running across the pavement, stopping cars going this way, then waving his arms to stop cars going that way . . . running, running, running. And cussing.

I sprinted across the grass and across a ditch before I got to the right interchange. Again I started waving at cars going at both directions.

But I made it across the pavement and saw the AAA headquarters, sitting on top of the hill. All I had to do was climb up about thirty feet and I'd be there.

I grabbed one tree branch, then another to get up the hill without destroying my suit. At the top . . . holy God! . . . there was one of the tallest fences I'd ever seen!

It was one of those chain-link fences about twelve feet high—with barbed wire along the top.

They had more security than the White House.

By this time it was eight-forty. Five minutes left.

Well, at sixty-eight I wasn't too feeble to let a fence stand in my way. So I threw my clipboard over it and said to myself: *"Jeno! Fetch!"*

And I climbed over that sucker, making sure the barbed wire didn't damage my crown jewels. I hit the ground inside, collected the clipboard, and ran into the building.

My friend the receptionist smiled and said, "Oh hello, Mr. Paulucci. You went for a walk, did you?"

"Yes," I said, wiping sweat off my forehead. "Had a very nice stroll. I'd like to wash up a bit. Where's the restroom?"

"There it is. But hurry. It's eight forty-five and Mr. Creal is waiting."

WHEN I GOT TO PRESIDENT CREAL'S OFFICE on the fourth floor, he had two of his executives with him. He looked at me as a president should—kind of officious—and said, "Well, Mr. Paulucci, why did you ask for this meeting?"

"Before I tell you about Heathrow," I began, "may I take you over to the window? I want to show you something."

All three came with me. "Gentlemen," I said, "do you see that interchange way down there? Well, I got out of my limo and ran across that damn thing . . . across the grass . . . across this other interchange, stopping traffic both ways. I climbed your hill. I scaled your fence . . . all so I could be here on time.

"Now, do you think I would endanger my life if I didn't believe you'd be making a mistake if you don't come to Heathrow?"

Jim Creal had to laugh. "You did all that? Where were the dogs?"

I didn't know if he was joking or not, but said I was really glad I didn't run into any dogs.

"Well sit down," Jim Creal invited, "and tell us about Heathrow."

So I did, without benefit of the material I'd left in the car. They were impressed. And I felt I'd sold them on coming to Heathrow until one of the executives said, "Yes, everything you say may be true, but we must take into account that it takes fifteen to twenty minutes longer to get from the airport to Heathrow than to Orlando Central Park."

Here it was again. They were hung up on those few minutes, just as the architect Candella had said. And they politely dismissed my promises that by the time their new building was up, three or four years in the future, the beltline would be finished and Lake Mary Boulevard expanded to four lanes.

So, as I've often said, a peddler has to stick to his convictions as long as he's sure he can deliver the promise.

Even if he has to be a little devious to help someone from making a serious mistake.

A PLAN WAS FORMING in my mind as we sat there in President Creal's office.

I knew I'd been honest with them, but they weren't convinced. So I countered with this offer: "Gentlemen, you've been misinformed about these comparisons of driving times. I know you don't quite believe me, so I'll pay for a traffic study by any engineering firm you choose.

"Let's have them start a car at Heathrow, and at the exact same time start a car from Orlando Central Park, both going at the speed of the flow of traffic. Let's see which gets to the airport first."

Jim Creal agreed. "Well, I guess that will settle the matter once and for all," he said, probably thinking that this was the only way to get rid of this pest from Heathrow.

"Fine. You make the arrangements. Tell me when the test will take place. Have the engineers send me the bill."

I went out, found my limo and Bill, who had finally located the building, and was on my way back to Florida.

In the Sanford office, I explained the test to my people. They were less than enthusiastic. What the hell was Jeno up to now?

Tom Stevenson, who'd been studying the traffic situation for weeks, spoke up. "Jeno, you're going to lose. It will be fifteen to twenty minutes longer from here."

"Tom, is Lake Mary Boulevard going to be a four-lane road?"

"Yes."

"Is the new beltline going to connect with Lake Mary Boulevard, so you can go from Heathrow across the I-4 interchange on Lake Mary, connect with the beltline, and get to the airport in twenty-five to thirty minutes?"

"Yes, but not for three or four years."

"Well, then, is the AAA building going to be built overnight? Won't that also take three or four years? So let's help AAA make the right decision.

"When this engineering firm makes its test, Tom, suppose you see to it that two cars have flat tires on the highway from Orlando Central Park heading toward the airport. Space them about a mile apart."

"Jeno, that will stop traffic."

"Think so? Maybe you're right. Yeah, I'd say the flow of traffic that day is going to be *real* slow."

Sure enough, it was.

The engineer's written report of the two-car test, based on the flow of traffic, indicated that Heathrow was only three minutes longer to the aiport than Orlando Central Park.

Pointer from the Peddler: When people are too stubborn to believe the facts, use your imagination to save them from themselves.

It wasn't more than a couple of weeks before I got a call from AAA, saying they would like me to come see them.

The traffic flow study wasn't even discussed. All they wanted to know was the price per acre and the zoning and any other requirements if they built in Heathrow.

The American Automobile Association ended up purchasing thirty-nine acres for approximately $6 million. Their world headquarters in Heathrow, committed in December 1986 and occupied in November 1989, costing some $70 million, is a landmark in this new town for a new time.

Other corporations flocked around them.

Lake Mary Boulevard now is four lanes and connects with the Orlando beltline. You can drive from the Orlando Airport to Heathrow, or back to the airport, in . . . yes, twenty-five to thirty minutes.

TEN YEARS LATER, IN 1996, I happened to see some familiar faces at Luigino's Pasta and Steak House, my restaurant in Heathrow. Yes, these were AAA executives, having dinner a stone's throw away from their headquarters.

We re-introduced ourselves. One of them said they'd heard about my legendary run across the highway and my climb over the fence.

"Yeah, I did that," I said, "but what closed the deal was the flow of traffic study." And I told them, finally, the full story—how they got conned for their own good.

While they were scratching their heads, I told them dinner was on the house.

Today the Heathrow office park where AAA is located has been ranked by a Washington economic group as the second hottest business district in the country. I forget which district was first. I'm sure it wasn't Orlando Central Park. Traffic is too slow there, with all those flat-tire breakdowns.

Well, that's how Heathrow got on the map—all those AAA maps that say, "This map published annually by the American Automobile Association, Heathrow, FL, 32746."

At one point, the rumor went around that the Paulucci family had dropped some fifty million bucks at Heathrow. We'd unwisely invested, it was said, in the boom-and-bust Florida real estate market.

That's not quite how it worked out. We eventually sold most of Heathrow for $50 million, with the Paulucci family retaining 20 percent of the residential area, plus thousands of surrounding acres that appreciate every year.

Another interchange on I-4 was started in January of 1998, connecting with Highway 46A about a mile from the Lake Mary interchange, at the northern Heathrow boundary. I brought in about $11 million for that project from the federal government with the help of John Blatnik's successor, Congressman Jim Oberstar, who also served on the Public Works Committee.

Time has increased the cost of this interchange to $25 million, but I did my part. We saw the need for it thirteen years earlier and now it's here, opening a vast new stretch of acreage along Interstate 4.

In Heathrow, the Palulucci family created one of the finest new towns in the world. While we were at it, we helped lead the whole area of central Florida to a brighter and more secure future.

Do the math. Economic Sense + Common Sense + Activism = Progress for All.

Part Six

Presidents Are Just People . . . Who Want to Be Re-Elected

It's been my good fortune to meet with and advise seven presidents of the United States . . . along with a couple of other almost presidents. All of them were strong, forceful figures. You don't get into the history books, or get serenaded with Hail to the Chief *when you walk into the room,* by being modest.

All the same, they're just people, these leaders of the free world. Good people, most of them, who really, really want to get re-elected. They had their agenda—but I had mine.

Jeno's Credo:
It isn't easy to change society.
But if we speak out, if we become
involved at the highest levels,
we will find no greater joy or satisfaction
than knowing that we are working
to make a contribution to our fellow man.

President John F. Kennedy is welcomed to Duluth.

Chapter 39

John F. Kennedy

1961–1963

I never had the opportunity to get to know President Jack Kennedy, or have extended conversations with him as I did with later presidents. I met him only once, on September 25, 1963, when he was in Duluth on a campaign swing.

But that short meeting was one I'll never forget.

I came to ask him for a favor, and his response was swift and sure.

When I heard the president was coming to Duluth, I asked John Blatnik, my friend and esteemed congressman, to arrange a short visit.

"Well, Jeno, what's it about?" he asked.

"You'll know when I see the president."

True to form, John got us on the schedule for the next morning at the Hotel Duluth, where the president was staying overnight in a small suite. It was around seven-thirty A.M. when a Secret Service man escorted us into the parlor.

"I'm dressing," the president called out from the bedroom. "Come on in."

He was putting on his shirt and tying his tie. John introduced me.

I liked the way he looked me straight in the eye and said, "Hello, Jeno. Glad to know you. Any friend of a congressman is a friend of mine. What can I do for you?"

"Frankly, Mr. President, I need your help, which is very, very vital to the economic revival of this northeastern Minnesota country."

I was talking about the Taconite Amendment, of course, which I've discussed in an earlier chapter of this book. I explained that a number of us civic leaders, so to speak, had been working to get the steel industry and the people together to agree on this proposed amendment to the Minnesota Constitution that would ensure fair taxation to the mining industry if they invested billions of dollars in taconite processing plants on the Iron Range.

We'd been working on it for a long time, I said, and I felt personally responsible because it all started in my Chun King Chinese food offices on December 31, 1960.

He might have had an amused look in his eye, but he followed what I said, every word.

"Well, what can I do about it?"

I told him we had a problem with U.S. Steel's decision-maker here at the head of the lakes, a fellow by the name of Chris Beukema, who was in on the original meeting I'd headed but was holding out now.

He wanted a better deal for U.S. Steel, which we couldn't give because it would be singling out that company for favoritism over other processors.

"Well, what would you like to have me do about it?"

"What I'd like, Mr. President, is for you to get ahold of Roger Blough and tell him that his man, Chris Beukema, is standing in the way of thousands of jobs and the whole revitalization of this depressed area."

Roger Blough, of course, was the CEO of U.S. Steel back in Pittsburgh.

"Sounds reasonable, doesn't it, John?" the president asked, looking at the congressman.

"But you know, our relations with Roger Blough aren't so good right now."

I knew. The president's brother, Attorney General Bobby Kennedy, had recently served a legal notice on U.S. Steel and the conflict was all over the headlines.

The president shrugged. "But I'll try."

That was the end of my first meeting with a president.

Less than a week later, John Blatnik called to tell me that he'd had a call from the White House. The president had said, "Tell Jeno that we've talked to Roger Blough, and Chris Beukema is going to behave."

Sure enough, Beukema withdrew his objections at our next meeting a couple of days later, and therefore we had solidarity between the industry and unions. We went back into negotiations with the legislature and in time the Taconite Amendment was passed.

Two months after our conversation in the Hotel Duluth, the president went to Dallas on another campaign swing and that horrible thing happened on November 22, 1963.

I'm forever grateful to Jack Kennedy. I will never forget him or fail to say a prayer of thanks for his favor to the Iron Range, and for all he tried to do for our country.

ADDENDUM

As a result of my meeting with President Kennedy, I became acquainted with his brothers, both Bobby Kennedy, who fell victim to another assassin in another national tragedy on June 6, 1968, and Senator Edward Kennedy.

I was never too crazy about what I considered Ted Kennedy's radical policies, but he's well-meaning and it's hard not to like him.

Once I asked him about the accident he'd just had in an Aero Commander that someone else was piloting. He wasn't hurt—another Kennedy tragedy barely avoided. I happened to own an Aero Commander at the time so we had a mutual interest there in keeping those planes from crashing. I got to know him pretty well.

About ten or twelve years ago, Minnesota saw a close race for the Senate seat between Wendell Anderson, running for re-election, and Rudy Boschwitz on the Republican ticket. I ran into Ted Kennedy in the Halls of Congress.

"Jeno," he said, "I plan to be up in your Iron Range country to help Wendell. Is it safe up there?"

"Well certainly, Ted. It's very safe. We'll be glad to have you. Tell me when you're coming. I'll join you."

Sure enough, I met him in Duluth and drove up to the Range with him and Wendell in a private car.

Wendell sat up front with the driver and Ted and I were in the back seat.

The first stop on the schedule was the town of Eveleth, where there was going to be a rally for Wendell at the Holiday Inn. But the hot issue around there was a proposal to create something called the Boundary Waters Canoe Area. Wendell Anderson was in favor of the Boundary Waters. The local people weren't, and they were up in arms.

Just before we got to Eveleth, as we were going up a hill, a mob of protesters came out and stopped the car. They started shaking it up and down, up and down. They knew Wendell was in the car. I don't know whether they knew Ted Kennedy was also on board.

The senator was getting pale.

"Jeno, what's going on here? I thought you told me it was safe."

"Oh Ted, this is just a nice Iron Range welcome. Settle down and forget it."

But he didn't. Next time I saw him he gave me that whimsical, critical, cynical look and said, "Safe up there, huh?"

Chapter 40
Lyndon B. Johnson
1963–1969

I must say that of all the presidents I have been exposed to, worked with, listened to, advised, argued with, had dinner at the White House with, went to Europe with . . . this was the only one who gave me a pain in the ass.

Lyndon B. Johnson was about as cold a fish as I ever met.

But I supported him when he ran against Goldwater in 1964, having inherited the Presidency from the slain Kennedy. He named Hubert Humphrey of Minnesota as his running mate, and I got involved in that campaign because I wanted to help my friend Hubert become vice president, and eventually president.

I loved and respected that man. His vision of what was right for the country was years ahead of his time. But he wasn't the world's greatest politician.

As chairman of Independents for Johnson and Kennedy in the State of Minnesota, I was one of four major financial supporters for the national ticket

LBJ has his way.

(there was no limit to contributions in those days). The others were Dwayne Andreas of Archer-Daniels-Midland, Hollywood mogul Lou Wasserman, and the president of Occidental Petroleum, whose name escapes me at the moment.

I worked my butt off . . . for Hubert . . . and took a lot of personal satisfaction when the Johnson/Humphrey ticket won in a landslide.

Now it was time to work on my own agenda. I went to the White House with Hubert a few times, and then he'd take me in to see the president. What I wanted out of President Johnson was a new, more liberalized immigration law that wasn't so restrictive to those of ethnic origin, who usually found the doors closed unless they went through Canada.

Lyndon Johnson was building what he called a Great Society with his civil rights legislation. But he still had, in my opinion, a prejudice against ethnics, which of course included Italian-Americans.

There were quite a few pros and cons and visits and letters between myself and others, and lobbying. When I met with President Johnson, it took a long time to argue with him, but at least he would listen. When I started losing my temper, Hubert would sort of kick me under the desk, and I'd cool down.

Finally, we got an immigration bill that made sense, or at least was a hell of a lot better than what we'd had.

The last time I saw Lyndon Johnson was at the foot of the Statue of Liberty, where he signed the bill. I was there with Hubert, the governor of New York, and the mayor of New York City . . . whoever they were at the time.

The signing of that bill meant a lot to me. To Johnson, I'm pretty sure it was just another photo opportunity.

One day, Hubert asked me if I'd be interested in being ambassador to Italy. I told him I'd be a terrible diplomat. What I didn't tell him was that I wasn't interested in running a hotel at the American embassy for visiting VIPs. No thank you, Hubert.

But our friendship continued, and I watched the next four years take their toll on him. He never believed in the Vietnam War, but he was muzzled by his loyalty to Johnson.

Then came that stunning announcement one evening in the summer of 1968. Lois and I were at home in Sanford, watching the news, when Lyndon Johnson came on the screen and tugged his ear, reportedly a signal to his wife Lady Bird. He said he would not seek or accept re-nomination as President.

"Self-serving," I told Lois. "He knows he can't win either the election or the war."

I grabbed the phone and called Hubert. It took a while to get through to him.

"Jeno, I was surprised, too," he told me. The SOB had kept him in the dark to the end.

"Well Hubert," I said, "let's get to work."

Chapter 41

Hubert H. Humphrey— The President Who Might Have Been

*E*ven though he was vice president and heir apparent to Johnson, Hubert's nomination was no cinch. He had a formidable, popular opponent in Robert Kennedy, the late president's brother, until Bobby was shot down by that crazed Palestinian in California on the same night that he won the California Democratic primary.

Hubert also had to fight a rear-guard action against Senator Eugene McCarthy, also of Minnesota, who was stirring up the anti-war protesters.

Eventually it was clear that Hubert would in fact be nominated at the Democratic convention. It should have been a triumph for him. Instead it was a hollow victory . . . damn near a fiasco.

On the sweltering streets of Chicago in August 1968, we found demonstrations, riots, shouting kids

To Jeno Paulucci – a distinguished leader in business and civic affairs – my friend and advisor – with warm regards

Hubert H Humphrey

Hubert Humphrey might have been president.

being carted away by the cops. Mob scenes outside the hotel where I was huddled with Hubert and his closest supporters such as Dwayne Andreas and Bob Short. It was like a revolution in some banana republic.

I urged Hubert to speak out against the Vietnam War in his acceptance speech. With a few words, he could have turned off all that turmoil. But he refused to go against Johnson.

After his nomination, Hubert was wilted, just beaten down. Now he had to campaign against one of the most resourceful politicians in history.

Richard M. Nixon had been counted out after losing the presidential election in 1960 and the California gubernatorial race in 1962, after which he held a press conference and said, "You won't have Dick Nixon to kick around anymore." But he had made an amazing comeback and had won the Republican nomination at Miami Beach in early August, just a couple of weeks before Hubert's nomination by the Democrats.

Hubert also had to contend with George Wallace, running on a third party racist ticket, and Eugene McCarthy, who refused to withdraw and throw his support to Hubert.

McCarthy had been a good friend of mine. But I never forgave him for that.

So Hubert faced demons to the left and demons to the right, both siphoning off votes that could have gone to him.

To make it worse, Hubert's choice of key supporters was questionable, beginning with his selection of a running mate. I'd suggested Joseph Alioto of

California, someone who could pull in some votes. But he went with Edmund Muskie of Maine, a nice man whose power at the polls was zero.

Among his campaign leaders, I thought Bob Short as treasurer, and Dwayne Andreas as chief fund raiser, were sound men. I didn't know much about Joe Napolitan, who was supposed to be handling advertising.

What really worried me was Hubert's choice of Larry O'Brien as national campaign manager.

O'Brien had been in the Kennedy inner circle. Good for him. But everyone knew he was keeping his day job working for Howard Hughes. As the campaign began, I suspected that O'Brien didn't have his heart in it.

Hubert also had an unseen enemy named Lyndon Johnson. He was still the president, but he did nothing to rally support for Hubert or help with the vital job of fund-raising.

At one point, Lee Vann and I visited Hubert at his home in Waverly, Minnesota, where he was packing his bags to go to Washington. I told him frankly that the people he trusted, starting with Johnson, were letting him down.

"Hell, don't bother to pack your bags," I said. "We might as well all go home now."

"If I'm in that bad shape, Jeno," he said with his infectious grin, "I certainly can't have you deserting me."

He had an idea. "How about you and Lee become my eyes and ears in the campaign? Get involved in everything, and let me know what you think at all times."

We agreed, and a week later Lee and I set up our own suite of offices at the Watergate Hotel, overlooking the Potomac in Washington. We were next door to the Watergate building, where the Democratic National Committee had its headquarters.

Hubert invited us to a meeting with O'Brien and all his top advisors. He told them he wanted me as part of his team.

"Does he have a title?" someone asked.

"Title?" Hubert asked, with that familiar twinkle in his eye. "Why yes . . . he's my Director Without Portfolio."

After Hubert left the room, this committee, of which I was now a member, did some work that should have been done earlier. Exact assignments were laid out as to advertising, fund-raising, running the phone bank, overseeing the people in the field, and so on.

Lee and I stayed in the room after the others had gone out, presumably to get the campaign off the ground at last. Somehow I was still depressed.

"I don't trust O'Brien," I muttered. "I've yet to see him do anything but sit in a conference room and light cigars. Tell me, Lee, how he can run a decent campaign when he spends most of his time running back and forth to Las Vegas to work for Howard Hughes?"

"I couldn't say," Lee said, while picking up a wastebasket and emptying it on the table.

"What are you doing with that?"

"Looking for a note."

A word about Lee Vann. He was my most trusted assistant, damn near my shadow, for years and years

. . . a big chunky Minnesotan who always had a way of calming me down. He met an untimely death in 1993. I think about him to this day.

Lee Vann never missed much.

"Remember those notes that Larry and Joe kept passing to each other during the meeting?" he asked. "Joe threw one into the trash when he left. Ah, here it is."

Larry had written to Joe: "All this campaign needs now is a candidate. "

That was the kind of support Hubert was getting from his so-called campaign manager.

AS THE SUMMER ENDED and we moved into the last couple of months of the campaign, I kept checking with Bob and Dwayne to see how the fund raising was going. Not good. The usual Democratic contributors just weren't responding.

Lee and I went around the country trying to get cash. When normally you'd expect $100,000, we were lucky to get $50,000 or less.

Why? Because the undercurrent was that Lyndon Johnson didn't really want to see Hubert Humphrey take his place.

Advertising was another soft spot. Joe Napolitan, supposedly an advertising genius, had hired some other geniuses at Doyle, Dane and Bernbach, the agency famous for "creative" ads like the ones for the Volkswagen Beetle with the theme "Think small."

Lee and I went to the DD&B offices with Joe Napolitan to see some previews of commercials. On the way up in the elevator, I noticed a group of people wearing McCarthy for President buttons. They all got off at the same floor as we did, and all went into the DD&B offices. Evidently the bright young people at this agency didn't give a shit about the candidate their agency was taking money to support.

In the screening room, they showed us a commercial of a woman saying she was going to vote for Hubert Humphrey because "he takes care of the working people." Fine, except the woman was lounging on a fancy sofa with a tiara and pearls straight from Tiffany's.

Not exactly a spokesperson for "working people." Flat out stupid.

The other commercials were no better.

"What are they doing, still trying to think small?" I asked Napolitan. "Hubert isn't a goddamn Volkswagen.

"These guys have got to go."

Well he said they were highly creative people, and he'd talk to them.

I knew something about creative advertising. And these people were no Stan Freberg.

At the front desk on the way out, I told the receptionist I wanted to speak to whoever was in charge. Well, Mr. Bernbach wasn't in at the moment. Could she take a message?

"Where can he be reached?"

"Well, he's in Mexico at the moment. He won't be back until . . ."

"He must have left a phone number."

At last I got through to someone at a hotel in Acapulco who spoke enough English to pull Mr. B of DD&B out of his oceanside cabana.

I introduced myself. I told Mr. Bernbach that I was in his offices, and I'd just seen his Humphrey commercials. And they stank. And he was fired.

Did I have the authority to do that? Who in hell cared? Joe Napolitan was sort of fading into the woodwork.

After a little more conversation, Bernbach said he'd send us a bill for their work so far.

"You're welcome to send it, but you sure as hell won't get paid," I said.

We scrambled around and found another agency in Washington that did a decent job. I told Bob Short not to pay the $675,000 bill that Bernbach kept sending us. It was a moot point, anyway, because we didn't have the money.

AND YET, WE ALMOST WON. I kept pleading with Hubert to speak out against Vietnam—take a leave of absence from his office as vice president if need be. He wouldn't do it.

I suggested he demand a debate with Nixon. He was all for that, but Nixon declined.

We tried to embarrass Nixon. When he was staying at Bebe Reboso's place on Key Biscayne, off the Miami Beach coast, we bought about 200 rubber chickens and handed them out. We hired two small aircraft with trailers that flew over Reboso's house with trailers saying, "Nixon is Chicken." We bought radio spots saying, "Nixon is Chicken . . . See Closest Chicken."

But Nixon remembered his debates with Kennedy eight years earlier, when he'd come off as loser to a more attractive personality. He wasn't about to get in that same situation with Hubert. There would be no debates.

It all came down to money. Humphrey's war chest was empty. We needed at least $700,000 to pay for last-ditch advertising. Our only hope was Lyndon Johnson's home state of Texas.

A meeting was set up with about six oil bigwigs at the Petroleum Club in Houston. Bob Short and Dwayne Andreas flew down with Lee and me. Bob Strauss, the Democratic chair for Texas, met us at the airport. Bob was a great lawyer and later, a good friend of mine when he became chairman of the Democratic National Committee and ambassador to Russia. What happened at the Petroleum Club wasn't his fault.

Bob Strauss welcomed the group, then turned the meeting over to Bob Short, who explained that we needed $700,000 to $800,000 for advertising. But we weren't asking for a gift. The oil barons would get all their money back by holding dinners in Texas and other states, with Humphrey and maybe Johnson in attendance. All we wanted was an advance.

"We might could do that," one of the oilmen said. "But the candidate [he didn't even refer to him by name] is going to have to send us a letter than if he becomes president, he won't touch the depletion allowance."

I whispered to Bob Short, sitting next to me, "What the hell are they talking about?"

"The depletion allowance . . . they can write off their drilling costs. They want to be protected."

Dwayne Andreas said that was something we could talk to the vice president about.

Bob Strauss said he thought the vice president would go along with it, but he wasn't sure we could get a letter. How about a telephone call?

"We might consider that," another oil baron said, "if we could have someone else on the line to hear him give his word."

I couldn't stay quiet any longer.

They didn't know me, this peddler from the Iron Range of Minnesota. But I'd had enough.

"I'm just wondering," I said, "did President Johnson call you and ask you to cooperate?"

Not by a long shot, their expressions told me.

"Okay, let me ask you one more thing. Do you buy insurance for something that might happen? Maybe your house could burn down or you get hit by a hurricane? Wouldn't it be a good idea, even without a letter, to back Hubert Humphrey in case he gets elected . . . as insurance?

"Because if I were Hubert Humphrey, and if I were president, I'd not only take away your depletion allowance, I would also cut your balls off."

Bob Strauss and Bob Short were both kicking me under the table. I ignored both of them and walked out and downstairs to a pay phone, where I called Joe Napolitan in Washington and told him to cancel the following week's advertising, because we wouldn't have the money to pay for it.

JUST BEFORE THE ELECTION, I got through to Hubert in Salt Lake City, where he was campaigning. We were beating ourselves, I told him, and mostly because he wouldn't come out against the Vietnam War.

He'd been brooding over this, of course, during those months of indecision. And he finally made the speech that would have won him the presidency if he'd only done it earlier. He pledged to end the American involvement in Vietnam.

Immediately the polls began to shift, and so did the fund-raising.

Suddenly, when Dwayne Andreas and I arranged a meeting with a dozen Democratic contributors, we collected a little over *$3 million* inside of an hour. In fact, we had more pledges than we could spend before the election ended.

But the money, like Hubert's change of heart, had come too late.

Nixon was the winner . . . barely. He won by a margin of 0.7 percent, with just 43 percent of the popular vote, the smallest margin since Woodrow Wilson had won the presidency.

"They stole the damn election from you in Illinois," I told Hubert on the phone. "Why don't you ask for a recount?"

"I've already conceded," Hubert said. "That simply wouldn't be right."

Maybe Hubert Humphey, that great American statesman and visionary, was too damn nice to be president of the United States.

Chapter 42

Richard M. Nixon
1968–1974

*N*ixon's first term was successful. The Vietnam War dragged on, but most of his policies were sound. And this man understood global politics. His dramatic visit to China in February 1972 opened up that country and changed the balance of power around the world. Then it was time for him to run for re-election.

Hubert Humphrey made one more try for the presidency. He didn't have the fire and energy he'd once had. Even his close friends didn't know he'd been diagnosed with the bladder cancer that was taking its toll, and that took his life six years later.

Hubert didn't get the Democratic nomination. George McGovern of South Dakota did. I'm sure he was and is a nice man, but to me, he looked and sounded like a wild-eyed radical.

I went to Hubert and asked him, "What do you think? Will you feel badly if I go for Nixon?"

Secretary of the Treasury John Connally, left, led Democrats for Nixon, while Jeno led Independents for Nixon in the 1972 presidential campaign.

"No, Jeno," he said. "In fact I'll be supportive."

That was enough for me. I went to my good friend John Volpe, former governor of Massachusetts and now secretary of transportation. I'd gotten to know him when I went up to Massachusetts to receive an award from an Italian-American organization in 1967.

John was a front-runner for the vice presidential nomination, but Nixon passed him over for Spiro Agnew of Maryland. Not a good decision.

"John," I said, "I'd like to cooperate with Nixon, not because I know him or like him or am inclined to be a Republican, but because running against McGovern, I think he's the lesser of two evils. What do you suggest?"

He suggested a contribution of $25,000, to be made before April when legislation to limit contributions would kick in.

"Certainly," I said. "But I want to be involved in the campaign."

Then John and I got together at his private dining room at the Department of Transporation. He said I needed to get in touch with Chuck Colson, Nixon's right-hand man. I went to see him at the White House.

He was an energetic and outgoing man, with a sense of fun that made me like him right off.

I told him I'd like to be national chairman of the Independents for Nixon, just as I'd once been chairman of the Independents for Johnson/Humphrey in Minnesota.

"Sounds great," Colson said. "Let's see what the boss says."

Just like that he darted into the Oval Office next door and came back within minutes. "The president says welcome aboard."

He had just one thing to add. They'd already asked John Connally, the former Texas governor, now Nixon's secretary of the treasury, to be chairman of Democrats for Nixon.

"No big deal," I said. "I'll be chairman of the Independents and I'll report to Connally."

Problem solved. Chuck got on the phone to Connally and said, "Governor, we have a great friend of ours here [even though I'd just met him]. His name is Jeno Paulucci, and he'd like to get involved in the campaign to represent the Independents. How about if he came out to see you and you can work out the details?"

He listened, hung up, and said, "He says sure, come on out."

A few days later, Lee Vann and I arrived in Austin, Texas. We were met by a fellow by the name of Jacobson, who looked to me like a cigar-store Indian. Christ, he had on a starched shirt and tie and suit coat in the heat of Texas.

We got in a two-engine Cessna for the flight out to Connally's ranch. On the way, Jacobson coached us as to how to address his boss. Call him "Governor" or "Mr. Secretary," but never "Mr. Connally."

What kind of pompous idiot were we about to meet?

But he didn't seem that way at first. John Connally was tall and handsome, with a perfect wave of gray hair. He'd certainly had an illustrious career, and he'd even caught a stray bullet in that open car when Kennedy was assassinated. He'd later speculated that Oswald was shooting at him as well as the president.

He greeted us with a big smile and a firm handshake. He insisted on driving us around his ranch, every dusty and bumpy acre. Then his lovely wife Idanel (Nellie) served us tacos and enchiladas for lunch.

Finally, to business.

He made it clear that I'd be reporting to him in the campaign. I said I'd already told Chuck Colson that was fine with me.

"One other thing, Governor . . . is that what you want me to call you?"

"Oh that's fine," he said, though I was beginning to think he would prefer "Your Majesty."

"I happen to have an advertising agency called JFP & Associates. Lee Vann here is the president. We'd like to handle the creative and placement of ads for both Democrats for Nixon and Independents for Nixon, always for your final approval."

"All right," Connally agreed. "I assume you'll provide your services at cost."

I bargained for cost plus 10 percent, which worked out to about half what we'd normally charge.

We shook hands, and that was the deal.

LEE AND I SET UP OFFICES in the Madison building in Washington, next door to Connally's offices. We agreed to take turns each week commuting back to Duluth.

It should have been an ideal setup. But there was one problem. Neither one of us could ever get in to see Connally. Jacobson, the cigar-store Indian, stood guard at his door, always dressed in a dark suit complete with boutonniere. The governor was always too busy to be interrupted.

No direction, no discussion of strategy, no nothing.

Nonetheless, JFP & Associates created and placed ads for the Democrats and the Independents for Nixon. This was separate from the larger Committee to Re-Elect the President, run by Attorney General John Mitchell.

We also went out fund-raising, and one week in New York collected more than $2 million.

The situation with Connally was so frustrating that I started gulping aspirin and as a result, got a bleeding ulcer.

The worst moment came during a rare break from the campaign when Lois and I were visiting with Lee Vann and his wife Marilyn at their summer home in McGregor, Minnesota. While we were trying to relax, my secretary Gail Bukowski called from Duluth to say that Governor Connally urgently wanted to talk to me.

I called him in Texas. He was damn near berserk.

"You're making money off of us with that advertising! You're ripping us off!" he thundered.

I tried to explain that cost plus 10 percent, which we'd agreed to, wasn't exactly a gravy train.

He wasn't listening. JFP & Associates was fired.

Back in Washington, Chuck Colson wanted to see me. He said my friend, the governor, had been bad-mouthing me all the way up to the president. What was the problem?

The problem, I told him, was that Connally was a two-timing pompous ass who'd given me a bleeding ulcer.

"Chuck, my agency has produced good advertising, and we've saved the campaign about half a million in advertising costs.

"On top of that, Lee and I have raised more than five million dollars. What the hell has Connally done except comb his hair? I'm ready to pull out of this thing altogether."

He talked me out of it, said he'd look into it.

A week later, he called me and said President Nixon had laughed off Connally's criticisms as pure jealousy, and what could he offer Jeno? Secretary of transportation or commerce? I said to tell him I deeply appreciated his confidence, but I was too used to being my own boss to take a job like that.

"So you'll stay with the campaign?"

Sure. I said I'd continue with the Independents for Nixon and keep on raising funds.

JUST BEFORE THE ELECTION, when it was obvious the president was going to win, he had some of our Independent committee members into the Oval Office. We had some fine people on that committee. I especially remember William France, founder of the Daytona Speedway and a helluva guy.

Group photos were taken. I still have mine. But I noticed the president never managed a smile.

When it came time for me to give my report, I said, "Mr. President, you look kind of down in the mouth. Don't you know you're going to win in a landslide?"

He still looked morose. I had no idea that he was preoccupied with the Watergate break-in of June 17, which was going to bring down his presidency.

"In fact," I said, "we're going to deliver Minnesota to you."

He looked up. "Are you really? That's hard to believe."

"Guaranteed," I answered.

After the meeting, his honor Connally and I were walking down the street back to the Madison building.

"What the hell did you say that for?" he said. "Minnesota is always Democratic. We'll never win it."

"Sure we will," I said. "Humphrey is going to win it for us." I bit my tongue to keep from saying, "you dumb asshole."

Well, of course Nixon won not only Minnesota but every other state except Massachusetts.

However, bad things were beginning to happen. The Watergate scandal was creeping into the headlines, and Nixon made the mistake of trying to cover it up.

I continued to meet with him, quite often. Chuck Colson was always with me, as a buffer in case I seemed to be losing my Iron Range temper.

I urged him to appoint more Italian-Americans to high office, and he did, though not as many as some later presidents did.

Another favorite issue of mine was the minimum wage. I felt then, as I do now, that it wasn't fair for people to work for a wage prescribed by law, that wasn't really enough to live on. The minimum wage, I argued, should be indexed according to the cost of basic commodities like food.

This is still true today—2005—the price of cheese has gone up from an average of $1.25 a pound to nearly $3. Boned chicken costs $3 a pound. Milk is up about triple. Meat is up 20 percent. Yet the minimum wage–earner gets the same $5.15 an hour until Congress takes action (a few states, including Minnesota, have already established a higher minimum wage).

Nothing much came of these discussions, but President Nixon always listened carefully. I really liked him. And Chuck Colson hardly ever had to kick me under the table.

AS NIXON BEGAN HIS SECOND TERM, few people realized the size of the scandal that was beginning to unfold. One who did was Hubert Humphrey.

No need to go into the details that have been reported and analyzed so often. As practically everyone knows, on June 17, 1972, five burglars bungled their way into the Democratic National Committee headquarters in the Watergate complex overlooking the Potomac. They managed to get arrested by a security guard along with their walkie-talkie, unexposed film and bugging devices.

Incredibly, the break-in was apparently authorized by the White House to get information to use for Nixon's re-election—five months away but already in the bag. Even more incredibly, Nixon's assistants such as John Dean and Jeb Magruder began lying about their involvement to a grand jury, a Senate committee and a special prosecutor.

Instead of walking away, Nixon and his people were covering up, erasing White House tapes and so on. How stupid could you get?

I'd been in close touch with Hubert, but I was suprised he called me from his office on Capitol Hill and asked me to come over for a private conversation.

He didn't look well. Sitting at his familiar desk, he was not the vibrant man I'd known. When I asked him how things were going, he said he was fine. But one thing was uppermost on his mind. With his own ambitions to be President long gone, he was determined to protect the office he'd fought for so bravely but never won—the office of the presidency.

I don't remember his exact words, but they were something like this:

"Jeno, this Watergate thing could be a constitutional crisis, with grave national and even international implications. But it can be stopped. I'm not in a position to say anything to Nixon. But you're close to Nixon and his people at the moment. Could you pass on a message?"

Sure. What was it?

"Go on over to Chuck Colson and tell him my advice is this: Have the guilty parties step up, admit any improprities, and apologize. Let there be closure and an end to speculation and concern. Get it over with. Don't let this thing become a bombshell."

Next morning, I saw Chuck Colson and passed on Hubert's advice.

"Tell him thanks," Chuck said. "But we've got this thing covered. It'll blow over before long."

Well, it wasn't covered, and it didn't blow over. Those Washington Post reporters, Woodward and Bernstein and their "Deep Throat" informant, now revealed as the assistant director of the FBI, for God's sake, and a lot of others were all over Nixon like hounds on a fox.

Nixon had to resign, to avoid impeachment. A lot of people went to jail for their part in the cover-up, including his attorney General, John Mitchell, and his closest advisors, Haldeman and Erlichman (known to the press as Hans and Fritz). So did my friend Chuck Colson, which was a tragedy.

It was the sorriest chapter of Presidential corruption in history. And it all could have been avoided if the Administration had taken the advice of Hubert Humphrey, a man who always put the good of the country first . . . a statesman and an American hero to the end.

I still think Nixon did a lot for the country, and would have been one of our greatest Presidents . . . if only he'd been honest or at least had a little common sense.

ADDENDUM

This was a kind of humorous incident that took place after Nixon resigned. There was this special prosecutor named Archibald Cox who was looking into contributions to the Nixon campaign. I was on the road when my secretary called me to say the FBI wanted a meeting.

"Oh, okay, ask them what they want to meet about."

She called them and called me back. "They want to meet about financial support you gave to President Nixon."

"Fine. Set up a meeting."

Two FBI agents arrived at my office in Duluth. I had Don Wirtanen there, the president of Jeno's and a CPA, along with Lee Vann.

What could we do for them?

Well, on behalf of Special Prosecutor Cox, they were looking into financial contributions, because the legal limit was $25,000.

"I understand that," I said. "Maybe you'd like to see a copy of the cancelled check. Don, if you please . . ."

The agents mumbled to themselves for the few minutes it took Don to go and dig out the check and bring it in. They looked at it and mumbled some more.

"Well, Mr. Paulucci, this isn't the information that we got."

"Oh. Will you ask the question again?"

Clearing his throat, one of the agents said, "We want to know how much you contributed in dollars to the Nixon campaign, and whether it exceeded the $25,000 limit."

"Thanks for your question. Here's the answer," I said, handing them back the cancelled check for $25,000.

"Mr. Paulucci, that just doesn't coincide with what we've been told."

"Gentlemen, let me tell the truth . . ."

They leaned forward, expecting a confession.

"Not only did I contribute only $25,000 to the campaign, I made more than $100,000 with my advertising agency on the campaign. Now do you want those books, too?"

Ummm. They'd let me know.

It was the last I saw of them.

DESPITE ALL THE BITTERNESS of the Nixon years, I have a few happy memories. One was my opportunity to get to know Chuck Colson—that sunny, cocky, can-do man whose loyalty to Nixon wrecked his career.

I remember a time during the campaign when he and I were riding along in Miami, having a great time. Back at the hotel I got a call from my office asking me to call Mayor Ben Boo of Duluth. When I got him on the phone, he said, "Jeno, we had a hell of a rainstorm here. Some of the streets on the hill are washed out. Do you think you could get any help from the President?"

"Hell, maybe we could ask for a federal disaster area."

"Can you do that?"

"Well, let me see."

I went over to Chuck Colson's room and told him I needed a favor. I needed Duluth to be named a federal disaster area.

"Where the hell is Duluth?" he asked. "Oh, wait, that's where you live, right?"

"Yeah, it's up in northern Minnesota near the Canadian border, and they've had this terrific rainstorm, and . . ."

"Oh, what the hell's the difference. Give me the phone."

He called Washington and said, "Name Duluth a disaster area." Then he hung up and said, "Okay, it's done."

That's the kind of guy he was.

After he served his brief prison sentence, Chuck's life took a different direction. He turned to religion, became a minister, and formed an organization called the Prison Fellowship. He did a lot of good. I was one of his contributors.

I had occasion to talk to him three or four years ago, when I was working on the first draft of this book. We reminisced a bit and I asked him, "Chuck, do you remember that day when I came in to tell you what Hubert Humphrey said . . . put up a fall guy or Watergate is going to blow up in your face? And you laughed it off?"

"Jeno, I don't even want to talk about it."

I understood. That was another part of his life, and not worth remembering.

ANOTHER HAPPY MEMORY was the downfall of John Connally.

After Nixon's resignation, Connally was beginning to think that he might run for president himself. But he wasn't watching his flank.

Jacobson, his buddy the cigar-store Indian, had an argument with him and let it out that Connally had accepted a $10,000 bribe to try to fix the price of milk in Texas. The case went to trial in federal court. Connally was acquitted, but it put the kiss of death on him as a viable candidate.

I settled the score with him a few years later when President Gerald Ford, who had succeeded Nixon, was choosing a running mate. I heard he was considering Connally.

By that time, I'd got to know Gerald Ford pretty damn well. I was at the height of my influence as chairman of the National Italian American Foundation. I went to Ford and said Connally would not get him any votes, but would turn voters against him.

"Do you feel certain of that, Jeno?"

"You're damn right I do."

I hoped I'd made an impression. In any event, Ford passed over Connally and chose Bob Dole of Kansas.

Later Connally went into the real estate business in Texas, signing personal notes on about fifteen major projects. But the price of oil collapsed, and so did the economy of Texas. Connally declared bankruptcy and he and Nellie had to sell off their holdings and personal belongings in a widely publicized auction, to apply the proceeds against their debt.

What an awful position to be in. I did feel sorry for Connally . . . as I did for Dick Nixon. Here were two outstanding American leaders who were brought low when they got drunk on political power. I especially felt sorry for Nellie Connally, who I remembered as a charming and loyal wife who deserved better.

Chapter 43

Gerald R. Ford
1974–1977

*T*his is a president to whom I owe a lifetime of apology because I did the unforgivable; I broke my word to him. How and why that happened, I'll relate a little later.

I first met Ford through my dear friend and attorney, Henry Cashen.

Henry had worked at the White House during the Nixon years, and had then joined the law firm of Dickstein, Shapiro & Morin. He has been one of our attorneys for all these years since then.

Although I'm an Independent, Henry is very strong in Republican circles. It was a pleasure when he introduced me to President Ford, that decent and upright man who had become president when Nixon resigned. Ford had pardoned Nixon in an effort to get all that crap behind us, and had been vilified by the vultures in the press who weren't finished picking over the roadkill of the Nixon Administration.

President Gerald Ford appointed Jeno as his emissary in evaluating U.S. relief efforts after an earthquake in Italy.

In my judgment, Gerald Ford was doing a good job under impossible circumstances.

Shortly after that, I formed the National Italian American Foundation and appointed the ambassador to Italy, John Volpe, as president and chief operating officer. We were gaining momentum as spokesmen for some 25 million Italian-Americans. That's probably why President Ford asked me go to Italy and direct disaster relief after a terrible earthquake in the Friuli region, near the Alps.

It happened on May 6, 1976. Hundreds were killed, thousands injured, their homes destroyed.

The Italian-American congressional delegation, through the leadership of Congressmen Frank Annunzio and Peter Rodino, persuaded their colleagues to appropriate $50 million to aid the devastated citizens of the Friuli region.

President Ford asked me if I would go over as the emissary of the U.S. government to see to it that the money was properly administered. That was no idle consideration. A few years earlier there had been an earthquake in Sicily and most of the relief funds had been stolen by the Comorra, as the Italian Mafia was called down there.

Before Lee Vann and I left for Italy, we had a briefing at the State Department in Washington. A bunch of arrogant assholes lectured us on protocol, telling us exactly what to say and what not to say under all conditions.

As we left the building, I said to Lee, "We're paying our own expenses, and we'll say what we damn please."

In Rome, before going up to the earthquake area, we visited with Ambassador Volpe, who told us we'd be free to use State Department offices in Milan and also Trieste, a coastal city close to the disaster scene. Now I think John trusted me, but he couldn't come with us because of other commitments. Under pressure from State, he sent along a diplomat as a kind of Jeno-muzzler.

We flew to Trieste, then went up to the Friuli region. It was just awful. Countless homes and buildings had crumbled. Survivors searched for loved ones in the rubble while they lived in tents that had been sent in by the Russians.

And in the month of May, it was cold, damp, and miserable there at the foot of the Alps.

But this was the land of the Alpinis, mountain fighters legendary in World War II. I met with one of their leaders, a fierce old man who looked like he'd just gotten back from skiing down the mountain to attack the Germans. I also met an Italian commander named Colombo, who became the liaison between us and the local leaders.

We decided that the first thing to do was to put up a strong security structure to prevent anyone from getting their sticky fingers into the $50 million the U.S. government had provided.

Most of all, the people needed engineering help. At a meeting in the city of Uldine with mayors from surrounding towns, we were told that they needed engineers, technicians, and construction people to rebuild roads and buildings that would survive earthquakes in the future.

We decided to use some of the $50 million, which later became $100 million through the program we put together, for a brick school and a home for the aged. Those still stand as a monument to the generosity of the United States.

After we had done our work in the Friuli area, Lee Vann and I drove over to Milan, still accompanied by the State Department muzzle-man, who was still trying to keep my mouth shut, and not succeeding.

I called John Volpe in Rome and asked him to arrange for a meeting in Milan with the heads of multinational corporations doing business in Italy.

John asked what the meeting would be about.

"Oh, I just want to bring these people up to date on what's happening up here with the earthquake."

TWO DAYS LATER, John had arranged the meeting. At a hotel in Milan, he produced the local representatives of about twenty multinational companies including IBM, Coca-Cola, Pepsico, Xerox, IT&T, TWA, AT&T, you name it.

I welcomed them and thanked them for coming. None of these polished international executives looked like they were glad to be there. I said something along these lines:

"Gentlemen, multinational companies like yours have a bad name throughout Europe, deserved or not. Now you have a chance to change that perception.

"The survivors of the Friuli region need your help to rebuild. They're not asking for money, just the professional help you can provide by sending your engineers, architects, social workers, and other experts to the area for a few months.

"You'll make a great contribution to the people, and they won't forget it. They'll see your companies as friends, not exploiters. That's got to be good for your businesses."

God, you'd think I'd asked them to take the scalp off their heads. What icy looks as they filed out! I was a pariah with them and also with the State Department muzzler who said, "You shouldn't have been so direct with them. They're all top grade officials of multibillion dollar companies."

And all top-grade assholes.

I said to hell with it all. Lee and I packed up and went back to Washington to report to President Ford. I was pretty sure we'd catch hell from him because of our failure to observe protocol.

I remember it as if it were today. When I walked into the Oval Office, and was announced to the president, he looked at me and said, "Jeno, God bless you. You really did let them have it, didn't you?"

Years later, I returned to Friuli and my heart beat with pride when I saw the sturdy brick buildings provided by the generosity of the United States of America, but not the weazly corporations on the scene.

I CONTINUED TO MEET with President Ford on various matters. He was always interested and receptive.

One of the most gratifying experiences came when I presented a plan for an organization to be called the Business Responsibility Council of the United States. Lee Vann, Jim Tills, and some of my counselors at NEMO, the Northeastern Minnesota Organization of Economic Education, put together the plan modeled after a program we'd developed in Minnesota.

Some of the large companies in the Twin Cities—3M, Carlson Companies, Dayton-Hudson, and others—joined with my companies in contributing up to 5 percent of pre-tax profits for certain civic projects that would benefit the general public—everything from tearing down rat-infested buildings and replacing them to constructing playgrounds and hockey rinks. Anything to make Minnesota a better place to live.

The numbers made sense. When you took off the income tax, the 5 percent became about 3 percent. If we waited for the government to fund those projects, it would cost maybe five times more.

This had worked so well in Minnesota that I thought the same thing could be done on a national basis by setting up regional Business Responsibility Councils throughout the country.

I talked to Henry Ford II; to Irving S. Shapiro, the DuPont CEO; to Ross Perot, founder of Electronic Data Systems; to Bill Norris, founder and president of Control Data; to Curt Carlson of the Carlson Companies; to Wayne E. Thompson, head of the Dayton-Hudson Foundation; and to Lew Wasserman, one of the heavy financiers of the Democratic Party. They all liked the concept and said they'd give it support.

When I presented the idea to President Ford, I told him about the support I'd lined up and explained how each Business Council, with each company contributing up to 5 percent of pretax profits, could work with government agencies like HUD or the Department of Highways. This was going to be something entirely new in the field of business responsibility.

He was very interested. He asked me to meet with his economic advisor, Alan Greenspan (yes, *that* Alan Greenspan, later chairman of the Federal Reserve for almost 20 years). I remember talking with Greenspan at the Madison Hotel until about midnight, while he went over every detail of our large blue file called the U.S. Regional Business Responsibility Councils.

After I met with Greenspan, President Ford called me and said, "Jeno, this sounds pretty good. I want you to see Secretary Richardson at Commerce."

Eliot L. Richardson, the lanky, reserved New Englander who was secretary of commerce, was less enthusiastic. When Lee Vann and I went to see him, he spent an hour doodling on his large yellow pad.

"It seems to me," he said, "that you want to call this the Paulucci Business Responsibility Council."

"Mr. Richardson," I said, "you're being cynical and kind of sarcastic. Cut it out. I want this for the good of the people . . . and forget the Paulucci part, will you?"

"Well, President Ford has asked me to look into this. I'm not too crazy about it, but I've been asked to go to the Twin Cities to visit with some of those companies you've been working with."

As a result, Secretary Richardson did go to the Twin Cities, did talk to the companies, and did come back and recommend implementation of the program. I guess he got the facts straight on his yellow pad, and I'm grateful to him.

I got another call from President Ford. "Jeno, I'm convinced that your plan will benefit the general public, and reduce government red tape. I like it. Next year, we'll go forward . . . and Jeno, I'd like you to spearhead the whole thing.

"That is, of course, if I'm elected."

A big if.

Having inherited the presidency after Nixon's resignation, Gerald Ford was about to run on his own in 1978.

AFTER THE CONVENTIONS WERE OVER and the campaign was about to start, the president called me with an unexpected request. "Jeno," he said, "I like the way you're outspoken and say it the way it is. I would like to have you accompany me on campaign trips as a supporter. Will you do it?"

I had never done anything like that, going out on political campaigns and making talks and so forth. But I'd admired President Ford personally and professionally since he'd joined us at our first National Italian American Foundation banquet.

"Sure. I'll do that." I gave him my word.

A few days later, I packed my bags and was scheduled to go on tour with President Ford the next morning. I was to leave Duluth at four A.M., arrive at Andrews Air Force Base around seven Eastern Time, and board *Air Force One* at eight.

But that night I got a call from one of my best friends in the world, Senator Walter Mondale, who'd been chosen by Jimmy Carter, the peanut vendor, as his running mate. He was deeply upset.

"Jeno, how in the world can a personal friend like you, a guy who sat with me in a ten-foot fishing boat way the hell up in Canada, go out and campaign against me?"

I'd given my word to President Ford. But Fritz Mondale was right. How could I throw away his friendship?

At three A.M., I called Henry Cashen. "Henry, I haven't slept all night. I just can't join the president this morning. I will not support or speak for Fritz Mondale, nor will I support or speak for President Ford. I'm going to be absolutely neutral."

So I had to break my word. And that's something that lives with you forever. I'll never stop apologizing to Gerald Ford.

Among the many reasons why I'm sorry he was not elected was the disintegration of the Business Responsibility Council. He understood the need for business to take honest responsibility in society and spend some of its profits to plow back into the soil. You'd think the peanut farmer from Georgia would understand that, too. But he didn't.

In Gerald Ford, we had a very knowledgeable, humble president who had great insight, was a heartland Midwesterner, and never let all the power of the office get the best of him.

The media, malicious as usual, tried to depict him as a bumbling person. Why? Because he stumbled on the steps from an airplane or shot a golf ball in the wrong direction? Who hasn't done that? Ford had been a college football player and was probably the most athletic president in recent history. But the media was out to get him.

President Ford has never received the respect he deserves. Maybe someday he will.

Chapter 44

Jimmy Carter
1977–1981

When I think of my experiences with the unlikely thirty-ninth president of the United States . . . whew!

Hardly anybody took him seriously when he began going about the country and saying with that toothy smile, "Hi, I'm Jimmy Carter and I'm running for president." But he got the nomination and the Democrats rallied around him as the challenger to President Ford.

My contacts with him were complicated and confusing, but they sure were interesting. I hardly know where to start, but I suppose the best place would be at the beginning, during the campaign of 1976.

I'd decided I couldn't endorse either President Ford or the Carter/Mondale ticket. I'd be neutral. But Fritz Mondale, who'd persuaded me to break my word to Ford, wanted me to change my mind again.

"Jeno," he said on the phone, "I know you want to stay out of this campaign. But why don't you at least go down to Georgia and see Jimmy Carter?"

President Jimmy Carter called upon Jeno to lead the U.S. delegation to assess relief needs following an earthquake near Naples, Italy, where Jeno met Maria.

Well, why not? I didn't want to discriminate against Carter because he was only a peanut vendor from Georgia. After all, Harry Truman had been only a haberdasher from Missouri, and he'd been a great president. And I was only a pizza salesman from Minnesota who'd become . . . whatever I was.

So I agreed to meet Carter at his home in Plains, Georgia. I brought along Frank Befera, a fishing buddy of mine and Mondale's, to get his impression.

The airport at Plains, if there was one, couldn't accommodate our Falcon. So we landed in some damn cornfield-type airport nearby, and drove about fifteen minutes to Plains. We were a little late.

When we got to the modest single-story home of Jimmy and Rosalynn Carter, Secret Service people were all over the place, no doubt alerted that alien visitors were coming. Frank and I peeled our way through them, went over and knocked on the door. An older woman with a kind of snarl on her face answered the door.

I suppose this was the famous Miss Lillian Carter, Jimmy's mother, who had volunteered for the Peace Corps at age seventy and served as a nurse in India . . . but I'm not sure. We didn't know who the hell she was and she didn't know who the hell we were.

She looked us over, these two Italians in dark suits, the taller one, Frank, wearing his great big hat. We must have looked like a delegation from the Mafia.

"Who are you?" she wanted to know.

I was going to tell her, "Al Capone and company." But instead I was as formal as I'll ever get: "My name is Jeno Francesco Paulucci and this is Frank Patrick

Befera. We're here at the request of the vice presidential nominee, Walter F. Mondale."

"Well, you're late. Hey, Jimmy," she called.

Pretty soon Jimmy Carter came to the door. He had on a pair of lace boots damn near up to his knees, really down to earth, a nice-looking guy who smiled a lot, but not with much warmth.

"I've got other appointments," he said. "You're late."

"Well, in that case," I said, "we'll leave."

"Oh no, come in for a few minutes."

We sat down and exchanged a few pleasantries about our friendship with Fritz Mondale, this and that. Carter was very interested in my role in the Italian American Foundation because after all, I was carrying the flag for 25 million Italian-Americans and most of them voted. So Carter was at least halfway pleasant.

After that, Frank and I left and went back to the little airport. What were they growing there, I wondered as the Falcon took off, corn or peanuts? I couldn't tell. After we were airborne, Frank called Fritz.

"How did he like the candidate?" Fritz asked.

"I'd rather not say," Frank answered.

That's how it started. I did remain neutral, but as we all know, Carter won the election—by default, in my judgment, because Gerald Ford could never get out from under the Nixon fiasco.

IN THE NEXT FEW MONTHS, I met with Carter a number of times. I pursued my plan for the national Business Responsibilty Council, which President Ford was going to implement. But President Carter and his economic gurus always said, "Well, we'll study it." I figured I'd have to wait for the next president.

Also on my agenda was the appointment of more Italian-Americans to high offices, rather than assistant to this and assistant assistant to that. With the support of NIAF directors and officers, we'd gained some positive ground beginning with Johnson and going on to Nixon and Ford. But not enough.

I remember one meeting at the White House when President Carter said that at that point there was just no room for any appointments, even with a new administration. I took him to task. He got quite red in the face and just about asked me to leave. That was the only time I felt sort of unwelcome at the White House. I went home and wrote him a letter.

He responded by phone to point out that he'd just appointed Ben Civiletti as attorney general. I didn't cut him any slack, quoting the old saying that one swallow doesn't make a summer.

But both the Carters and the Mondales did make an effort to cultivate Italian-Americans. I'll give them that.

One evening Fritz Mondale invited all the NIAF officers and directors for dinner. He set up a tent at the vice presidential residence on the grounds of the U.S. Naval Observatory. This was a big white Victorian house that had been used by vice presidents for entertaining. Fritz was the first vice president to actually live there, and Joan had filled it with artworks borrowed from museums.

We all had a hell of a good time. Frank Befera even volunteered to work with the caterers in the kitchen.

Then Rosalynn Carter had a day at the White House for the wives. They had a little luncheon. That evening, joined by the president of Italy, we all had dinner at the White House—quite a gala affair. I was a little put off when I noticed the singer there to entertain us wasn't of Italian heritage. But he sounded almost Italian when he sang, and I guess that was close enough.

MAYBE THE MOST FUN I had during the Carter years was the coronation of Pope John Paul I at the Vatican in 1978.

President Carter didn't attend. But Fritz Mondale took a group of Catholic cardinals and bishops and the media over to Rome, on *Air Force Two.* He also invited Frank Befera and me. We sat in the back of the bus, so to speak, but had a relaxing flight . . . maybe a little too relaxing. I sipped my Fernet Branca and Frank had his wine, and we were in no pain by the time we got to Shannon, Ireland, for refueling.

"Let's go out and buy us some rosaries," Frank said.

"I've already got a rosary. What do I need with more?"

"Because we'll get them blessed by the new Pope."

So we went into the shop at the airport and bought all the rosaries they had and put them in a big shopping bag.

But Frank wasn't satisfied. He sort of sniffed at the shopping bag and said, "We need more."

So when we got to Rome, he dragged me up and down the Via Veneto buying rosaries. By then we

In Appreciation
to
Jeno Paulucci

who accompanied the
Vice President to the
Inaugural Ceremony of
Pope John Paul I

THE VATICAN

September 3-4, 1978

Vice President (Fritz) Mondale invited his fishing buddy, Jeno, to the Vatican for the coronation of Pope John Paul I.

had two industrial-size shopping bags overflowing with rosaries.

"What are we going to do with these things?" I asked.

"Get them blessed, of course, take them back to Duluth and sell them."

"Isn't that kind of sacrilegious?" I asked. He didn't answer.

Early evening. The time had come to go to Vatican City for the coronation. Walter and Joan Mondale went up ahead in a limousine, followed by a busload of people. I had arranged for a car and driver for Frank and myself.

When we got there, the celebrants were already seated in a semi-circle of about a dozen rows of chairs around the center of Saint Peter's Square. You'd never believe the scene. Royalty all over the place—kings and queens, white, black, yellow, and maybe a few who appeared to be green, all adorned in finery for this historic moment, with the dome of Saint Peter's Basilica in the background. In the front row were Walter and Joan along with Princess Grace and Prince Rainier, the president of Italy, and other dignitaries from England and elsewhere.

So we walked up front, these two Mafia characters each carrying a huge shopping bag.

"Hey Fritz," Frank yelled. "Where do we sit?"

Joan Mondale shrank into her seat, about dying of embarrassment. Fritz was embarrassed too, but he gave us a wry smile and pointed his thumb: "Way in the back."

So we sat and watched the coronation of that small, frail man who was about the 300th Pope in history. That was a majestic ceremony, historic as all hell. I wish I had paid more attention. Anyway, it didn't last as long as I'd thought it might, and I didn't fall asleep.

When the Pope was finally coronated, he went around the rows of seats saying, *"Dominus vobiscum. Et cum spiritu tuo,"* while tossing holy water with his scepter. Frank and I stood and held up our shopping bags, but we were a little too far away to catch the holy water.

The next day, Vice President Mondale had a private session with the new Pope. Being I was chairman of the Italian American Foundation, I was asked to go with him, and so was Frank. We still had our shopping bags full of rosaries.

After the vice president had his words of diplomacy with the Pope, I spoke to him in Italian: "It was nice meeting you, your Excellency. The Italian-American community of the United States sends their greetings and congratulations. And . . . would you mind blessing these two bags of rosaries?"

He laughed and said, "Oh, you're the two that were back there." He gave the bags his blessing. Frank and I took them back to the hotel and across the ocean on *Air Force Two.* A wonderful end to a wonderful trip.

Back in Duluth, Frank and I had little plastic bags made with a rosary in each bag. Must have been about 300 of them.

No, we didn't sell them. We gave them away to the faithful.

All that was a lot of fun. I shared in the mourning when John Paul I died only a few months later, to be succeeded by Karol Wojtyla, the Polish-born Pope who guided the Church as John Paul II for a remarkable twenty-six years until his death in April 2005.

AS THE CARTER YEARS WENT ON, he began talking about a national "malaise." He'd go on TV and urge us to turn our thermostats down to sixty-seven, maybe wear a cardigan like his. Be patient about 20 percent inflation and 20 percent interest rates. And trust him to find a way to free our hostages in Iran.

Every time I saw Fritz Mondale in the White House, he'd say, "Gee, Jeno, I can't do much with that little guy down the hall." That's the way he put it.

I was pretty well convinced that Jimmy Carter was a nice guy, well-intentioned, who was way over his head in that job as president.

That's when Stan Freberg and I decided to have a little fun with the president in the form of a pizza commercial.

I'd been working with Stan, that genius of advertising, dating back to the Chun King years. We decided we could sell a hell of a lot of Jeno's Frozen Pizza with a parody one-minute commercial. The scene is a Washington press conference, where "reporters were startled to hear today that frozen pizza could be the answer to the gasoline shortage." It went something like this:

The look-alike of President Carter was at the podium, with eager reporters and cameramen pressing forward.

"It seems to me," the president began in that earnest Southern voice, "that people are spending too much of their food dollars on these take-out restaurants, wasting gasoline when they could just get their frozen pizza at the supermarket . . ."

A reporter who looked like Sam Donaldson broke in, saying they'd still have to drive to the supermarket.

"Just once a week," the president answered, "and they could stock up on Jeno's Frozen Pizza, for example. Then they could just walk to the freezer . . ."

Reporters were jumping up and holding up their hands. "What about Iran?" one asked.

"If they ran to the freezer, they'd get their pizza even faster."

"What about SALT II?" another asked.

"No, you don't have to put any salt on it. Sorry I don't have any actual product to show you. Oh, lookee here, my wife has one . . ."

The Rossalyn look-alike proudly held up a Jeno's package, marked down on sale.

"If we could leave pizza for a moment," another reporter said, "what about a nuclear meltdown?"

"That's the idea," the president said, "you want the cheese to melt down . . ."

Finally, the Nixon look-alike stood up, said he wanted to make one thing perfectly clear, and gave his V for victory signal with both hands.

"Oh, here's someone who wants to order four," the president announced.

We thought it was hilarious. But the networks wouldn't run the commercial. Maybe after the president was out of office, but not before.

What the hell good would it be after he was out of office? Rather than give in, I got ahold of the vice president and said, "Fritz, the president has a sense of humor, doesn't he?"

"Yeah, he likes a joke."

"Well, I'd like to send you a tape of a commercial Stan Freberg and I made, where we mention him. Would you look at it and then show it to him? If he says it's okay, the networks will run it."

After he got the tape, Fritz called back and said, "Jeno, are you crazy? Do you think I'd show that to the guy down the hall? He'd throw me out of his office."

"You mean he doesn't have a sense of humor after all?"

"Not for that commercial you sent me."

Everybody's a critic. That commercial, never to be seen, was right out of the golden age of TV advertising. I'd run it today—if I still owned Jeno's.

AT THE VERY END of the Carter Administration, I received another commission to go to Italy to oversee disaster relief.

Another huge earthquake had struck on November 23, 1980, this time in the mountains south of Naples. A string of ancient mountaintop villages had been all but wiped out.

The Carter/Mondale Administration was a lame duck, having been defeated by Ronald Reagan and George Bush. But the president asked if I would head up a delegation, as I'd done four years earlier for the earthquake in Friuli, to administer another $50 million that had been provided by Congress through the efforts of the Italian-American Congressional delegation, backed by NIAF.

We loaded a delegation onto *Air Force One* or *Two*—I could never tell the difference. My vice chairman was Mario Cuomo, the former New York governor. Among the others I remember were Nancy Pelosi of California, Democratic minority leader of the House of Representatives (who holds that post today), and Bob Georgian, head of the largest construction union. I think Geraldine Ferraro of New York, the future vice presidential candidate, was also on that delegation, but I don't remember for sure.

First we flew into Rome, and as before I wondered what we were doing there, when the earthquake was far away. But we had to go through the pomp and ceremony, paying our respects to the Italian president and visiting with the Italian legislature, where I had to give a little talk about why we were there.

I finally said to Mario Cuomo, "Let's get the hell out of here and go to Naples where we can do some good."

We left the next morning. I had with me Lee Vann and also my cousin Celso Paolucci, whom I'd asked to come down from the villa where he lived in Bellisio Solfare, where my parents had originated. I also arranged for Mr. Colombo, the capable Italian commander whom I'd met in Friuli, at the time of the last earthquake, to meet us in Naples.

After another long motorcade with flashing lights on the way to an official Italian reception, I had a chance to introduce Colombo to the delegation. We had a long meeting about how best to use the $50 milllion and not get it stolen.

I wanted to see the devastation firsthand. We took mililtary helicopters into the mountains and what we saw there was beyond belief. Each town, at the top of its own mountain, was in ruins. People were still out there trying to find survivors.

I joined a rescue team and walked among the dead and wounded, not using a mask as most of the rescuers did.

In one town, I saw a woman in black of seventy or seventy-five, digging with her hands in the ruins of what used to be a church. The earthquake had come on a Sunday, destroying the church while it was in session. Everybody inside had been killed.

I knelt down and asked her in Italian, "May I help you?"

"I have lost all my family," she said. "I want to dig down and lie down with them."

I helped her to stand up. I held her as she sobbed. I asked her name. It was Maria. I dug in my pocket and pulled out a couple of hundred dollars to hand to her, for whatever good it might do.

She handed it back, saying, "There is no money in this world that will ever fix this heart of mine." Then she got down on her knees again to resume digging.

I glanced over at Lee Vann. Crying himself, he had taken a picture of the broken-hearted Maria and me, which I enclose with this chapter. Celso and I got down with her and started going through the rubble. We could smell the bodies, but we couldn't find them.

There's no way to describe the emotion I felt at that moment. Back in Naples, I talked with Mr. Colombo and our delegation. Should we recommend building schools and a home for the aged down in the foothills, like we'd done in Friuli? No. From all we'd heard from the people, they wanted to stay on their mountaintops. So that's where the relief money went.

To my discredit, I've never found the time to go back to those devastated towns to see if Maria and all the others were able to rebuild their lives.

Back to Rome, back to Andrews Air Force Base. And back to Duluth.

When I got home, I realized I was deathly sick. I lay in bed for about ten days. They doctors couldn't figure out what was wrong, though they speculated it might have something to do with searching around in the ruins without a face mask.

But I recovered, and was left with a memory that was not bittersweet, just very, very bitter.

THE LAST TIME I SAW JIMMY CARTER was when Fritz Mondale was running for president against Reagan. Mondale was at the Duluth Auditorium for a rally, and the former president was on hand. I met him at the airport and had our driver take us down to the Auditorium.

We'd never gotten along too well. I was pretty obnoxious, I guess. Either that or he was too meek. I don't know what the hell it was.

But during the ride downtown, he looked at me and said, "Jeno, you and I had our differences, our ups and downs. But I've got to say that I don't think I ever ran into a more interesting person than yourself, or someone more loyal to your cause."

I said something complimentary to him. So I think in the end, my relationship with Jimmy Carter wasn't all bad.

ADDENDUM

I'd be remiss if I didn't recount the story of my inviting the vice president to my Wilderness Village fishing camp in Ontario. It's a fly-in 300 miles northeast of Duluth. As I've recounted in my earlier stories about fishing adventures, it's a compound with cabins for the pilot and the chef, an apartment building for guests, a cabin for Lois and me, a dining building, and a kitchen. All in a national park on Brennan Lake. And all overseen by the Belmore family, Gordon and Violet and their sons Chris and Dwayne who live across the bay.

That July, when he was the newly elected vice president, he came up to fish with his old buddy Frank Befera at Frank's camp. I called and invited him and Frank to come up to Brennan Lake, where we'd all fish together.

"Okay, Jeno," he said. "But I've got the Secret Service around me now."

"Fine, send them up."

I had no idea how complicated that was going to be.

I had a lot of equipment up there, two classic twin-engine Beech aircraft and a twin-engine Cessna 206 on floats. Plus beautiful twelve- and fourteen-foot Lund boats. But the Secret Service flew in their own boats with gear they could use to communicate anywhere in the world.

They took over the pilot's cabin plus another cabin that I had to rent from some people in Minneapolis to take care of the excess. It got really crowded. And every time you turned around there was another Secret Service agent prowling around.

We did go fishing—Fritz, Frank, and I. But every time we'd settle in, two boats of Secret Service agents would settle in and start to fish in the same spot. After a couple days of this, I decided to test the matter. When we got down to the area I'd begun to call "Mondale Straits," I said to Frank Befera, "Holler down to the Secret Service and tell them we're going around that bend up ahead."

The agents didn't pay much attention. They were more interested in their own fishing. We pulled the boat through a little sand area, got on the other side, and started the motor very quietly. Then we started the motor wide open and went back to camp. I'd called ahead to our pilot and told him to load up one of the Twin Beeches. "Let's go to Termite Lake," I said.

The vice president of the United States knew exactly where he was. He had his intercontinental telephone and communication system with him. But the Secret Service didn't know where the hell he was.

Jesus Christ, they'd just lost him.

At Termite Lake, where I had a boat waiting, the three of us started fishing again.

Pretty soon we started to see float planes circling around, along with Secret Service agents in boats looking for the vice president of the United States.

We just kept fishing. When we were finished, we went back to shore, got in the Beechcraft, and flew back to camp.

The Secret Service converged around us. Thank God, they'd found their lost vice president. But they were madder than hell. As I was walking up the trail, the chief agent—sort of a Clint Eastwood wannabe—poked me in the back and said, "Mr. Paulucci, can I speak to you?"

"Sure. Go ahead."

"I just want you to realize that when you go fishing with Mr. Mondale, he is no longer just an old friend but the vice president of the United States, who has power to push the vital button."

"Why tell me that? Tell him. He's a grownup."

His anger grew. He demanded, "Why didn't you keep us informed as to his whereabouts?"

"You guys seemed to be busy fishing. We had a good catch. You guys have any luck?"

Secret Service agents seldom look sheepish, but this one did. He walked back down the trail, muttering to himself.

Chapter 45

Ronald Reagan
1981–1989

*M*y first contact with Ronald Reagan was arranged, as so often was the case in these political matters, by my friend and attorney Henry Cashen. I was planning a trip to the West Coast in 1978 and I asked Henry, my White House insider so to speak, if he could set up a meeting with the former governor of California, who was beginning to gear up for a presidential race.

Being an Independent, I was always looking ahead to see what man or woman, regardless of party, would be the best person to occupy the office of president. My mind was open.

Henry arranged for me to meet Reagan at a small suite of offices in Los Angeles or Beverly Hills, somewhere around there. Pretty soon, Reagan sauntered in, took off his cowboy hat, and modestly introduced himself.

"I'm Ronald Reagan," he said, as if I'd never heard of him.

"Good to meet you. I'm Jeno Paulucci."

President Reagan always maintained his direct style.

"Yeah, I've heard of you from my friend Henry." He'd also heard of the National Italian American Foundation. I made it clear that I could only speak for myself, not the 25 million members. But I'd be honored to get acquainted with someone who might be running for president.

He sat down and pulled out a story from the grab bag of anecdotes in his head. Up at the ranch he'd built overlooking the ocean near Santa Barbara—he called it Rancho del Cielo—his head horse trainer happened to be from Italy. That's where Reagan learned to handle a horse in the dashing Italian style, which he loved.

The trainer was now an American citizen, he added, and was doing a great job.

With that, he got to the point and asked, "Well, now that we've met each other, what are you going to do for me if I run for president?"

I sure liked that direct question. That's the way he was then and all the years I knew him. But I hedged and said, "I can't tell you yet, until I see who your opposition will be."

That was a serious consideration. Everybody assumed Carter was going to run for re-election, but already the media was working itself into a frenzy over a Ted Kennedy challenge for the Democratic nomination.

"I'm always looking for the best person for the job," I said.

He nodded. "That's just the way it should be."

We stood up, shook hands, and I was on my way.

IN THE 1980 CAMPAIGN, there was no doubt in my mind that Reagan, with George Bush as his running mate, was the better candidate. I never openly supported him because of my friendship with Walter Mondale, who was running for re-election as vice president on the Carter ticket. But I was glad to see him elected.

You had to admire this man, with his clear vision and determination to do what nobody thought was possible—bring down the Soviet Union. Who can forget when he stood at the dividing line between the two Berlins and said, "Mr. Gorbachev, tear down this wall." And by God, that's what they did.

He was always cordial, charming, telling stories. But he was tough as they come, like the time when he was campaigning and getting some flack, and he grabbed the microphone and barked, "Sir, I'm paying for this microphone."

Our meetings were always more than pleasant. Well, except for that time, early in his first term, when he and Nancy came to Minneapolis for some function and Lois and I were there along with about fifty others.

During cocktails, the president made a few remarks about his progress up until that point, calling attention to the legislation he'd gotten passed that lowered taxes. After he took a few questions, I spoke up loudly as usual: "Mr. President, do you think it's right to cut taxes so much for all us rich people, and then also cut benefits to poor people?"

A frigid silence settled on the room. Lois gave me a kick in the shin. The president gave me a cold stare as he and Nancy walked away to visit with some other people.

What the hell. I was an Independent, and I still think I was right and he was wrong to cut taxes so deeply and risk a rising deficit.

After that, the president and I got along just fine. I met with him at the White House and elsewhere. Once, over in Italy, the NIAF was helping to fund a special project, having to do with rescuing the sinking city of Venice from the tides of the Adriatic Sea.

Giovanni Angelli, the chairman of Fiat, hosted a dinner in his beautiful palace right on the canal. It was a very enjoyable social occasion with the Reagans that I'll never forget. Sorry I don't remember the details of that project. To this day, they're still trying to rescue Venice.

Frankly, I don't recall how often President Reagan attended our annual NIAF banquets that we held each October. It must have been seven or eight times during his candidacy and tenure. I'd always be seated next to the podium, as chairman, the president to my right, Nancy next to him. We usually sat there for two or three hours, getting reacquainted at the head table with 3,000 Italian-Americans at the other tables, along with delegations from Italy and other parts of Europe, South America, and Canada.

It was always very jovial, very friendly: "Jeno and Mr. President." He'd warm up and start telling me stories. His favorite was the one about the Italian horse trainer. I always listened intently as if I'd never heard it before.

When I had the chance, I'd bring up the subject of the Business Responsibility Council program I'd worked out with President Ford. That didn't go over too good. Once or twice I shared with him my thoughts that I'd once voiced to President Nixon, about modernizing ground transportation so we wouldn't have to rely on airplanes. That didn't go over too good, either.

But at least we had those kinds of conversations and each time it was just a great experience for me.

Sometimes the dinners could get a little hectic. One October, Nancy Reagan made it clear through Fred Rotondaro, our executive director, that she didn't want Ron to have to spend four or five hours at the banquet. We always started at seven P.M. and tried to finish by ten. But with so many politicians afflicted with diarrhea of the mouth, we often ran overtime.

This time I gave my word we'd be out by ten.

I kept looking at my watch while the politicians droned on. When it was close to the witching hour, I started pulling at the pants of whoever it was at the podium. I kept at it until I damn near pulled his pants off his hind end. He got the hint and shut up. We closed the banquet and I kept my word.

THE MOST MEMORABLE BANQUET of the Reagan years was in 1984, when he was running for re-election against the Democratic challenger, my friend Walter Mondale. Both would be present, and a lot of conflicting emotions were running through that glittering black-tie gathering of international dignitaries.

Before I describe it, we need a little background—including a confession that I have never told anyone, until now.

I was still Independent and still neutral. I wouldn't endorse either Reagan or Mondale. But I was in touch with Fritz, of course, and even consulted with him about who his running mate should be. One name that came up was Lee Iacocca, the auto magnate who had turned around Chrysler, mostly by borrowing money from the government.

Could I do him a favor, Fritz asked. Could I visit with Iacocca and see if he'd support him? I called our NIAF president, Frank Stella, who lived in Detroit, and asked him to set up a meeting.

In his sumptuous Detroit office, the lordly Iacocca offered cigars to Frank and me, which we declined, and asked, "What can I do for you?"

I didn't mince words. I told him that Fritz Mondale was seeking his support. It would mean a lot to his campaign. I also hinted that this kind of high-profile involvement could lay the groundwork for some future Iacocca run for the presidency.

He paced around the room, puffing on his foot-long cigar.

"I agree, Jeno, that my support would be very important for Mondale. It could make all the difference. But there's a price for that."

I asked him what he meant. Did he want a cabinet post? He brushed that off . . . beneath his dignity.

"No, what I want," he said, pausing for effect, "is complete veto power against any kind of expenditure. Nothing is to be allocated, no dollars appropriated, without my stamp of approval. In that way, I can save billions of dollars for the taxpayers."

He sat down and awaited approval of his magnificent idea.

"Excuse me, Lee, but what you really want is to be the unofficial president of the United States. Correct?"

"I wouldn't put it that way. What I want to be is . . . call it the czar of finance. Just tell Fritz Mondale that I am willing to support him if we can come to an agreement."

Frank and I couldn't believe what we were hearing. Lee Iacocca was fairly well-known, with all the favorable press he was getting. But the czar of . . . Good God. I thanked him for his time, and said I'd convey his thoughts to the candidate.

Frank and I left that den of egomania, just shaking our heads at one another.

When I called Fritz, he was hopeful. "What did he say, Jeno? Is Lee Iacocca going to get in our corner?"

"You don't want him in your corner. He wants your job." Then I told him about Iacocca's lofty dream—and demand—to be czar of finance.

Fritz listened and said, "He can drop dead."

About a month later, there was a teleconference between Frank Befera and me, in Minnesota, and Fritz in Washington. Three old fishing buddies, talking things over.

"Guys, I still need a running mate," Fritz said. "Any ideas?"

And here's where the confession comes in.

"Why not a woman?" I said. That was sort of flippant, but I thought it wasn't a bad idea.

"What woman?"

"Well . . . er . . . umm."

A name came to mind: Geraldine Ferraro of New York. She'd been effective in Congress, I'd heard. She was an NIAF director. I seemed to remember her as a member of our disaster relief delegation in Naples, but I wasn't sure about that.

Well, he thought it over and damned if Geraldine Ferraro didn't become the first woman vice presidential candidate in history.

She was a weight around his neck throughout the campaign, starting with allegations about her husband's involvement in the mob, and ending with her performance as a self-important prig when she debated George Bush on national TV.

Fritz probably would have lost anyway because he came out with that damn fool statement that if elected, he'd raise taxes on everybody—something I warned him against. But whenever I see Ferraro on TV, as a Fox correspondent, running on and on about nothing, I cringe and say to myself, "That's the ditzhead you loaded on Fritz Mondale . . . Sorry, Fritz."

Until now, nobody's ever known about my part in this fiasco except Fritz, Frank Befera, and me. Nominating a woman was a good idea, but choosing this one was pure horseshit.

End of confession.

So Walter Mondale became another of my almost-presidents, along with Hubert Humphrey. He remained a great friend to me and to the NIAF, and he still is.

NOW LET'S GET BACK to the unforgettable NIAF banquet of 1984.

In this election year, what was supposed to happen was for the affable Jack Valenti, head of the Motion Picture Association and again our master of ceremonies, to announce the honored guests, one by one. First would be the contenders, Walter Mondale and Geraldine Ferraro. They'd be seated, then Jack would introduce me as chairman, and I'd escort the president and Nancy in while the band played *Hail to the Chief.*

Once again, Nancy had sent word that she wanted Ron out of there by ten P.M., and once again I pledged to put this on a tight schedule.

But by seven-thirty, nothing was happening. I was in the reception room with the president and Nancy and James Baker, his chief of staff, waiting for the signal to start the proceedings. But Mondale and Ferraro were nowhere in sight.

I peeked out and gestured to Fred Rotondaro. "What's the holdup, Fred?"

"Jeno, we don't know what to do. Geraldine Ferraro is still up in her room, waiting for her suitcase. They're bringing it in from the airport."

I could see our distinguished guests pulling at their black ties and wondering what was going on. The room was getting restless. Even Jack Valenti was looking a little nervous, as if some movie he'd approved had suddenly received an X-rating.

"Bullshit," I said. "Let's get the program started. Geraldine can come in when she's ready."

Fred wondered if that would be proper protocol. So I went back in the reception room, cornered Jim Baker, and told him the problem. Jim was soon to be secretary of the treasury, and later George Bush's secretary of state and a key strategist in the Persian Gulf War—one of the most influential men of the time. But he was also worried about protocol.

I told him I'd promised Nancy to get the president out by ten o'clock.

"Hey, this isn't Geraldine Ferraro's banquet. If her pantyhose aren't here, the hell with her. Fuck her pantyhose." These were my exact words.

Baker smiled and went over to talk with the president and Nancy. Nancy gave me a nod of approval and we all marched into the banquet hall.

Geraldine Ferraro did show up, about twenty minutes later, and got probably the last round of applause of her political career.

ADDENDUM

Four years later, when Reagan was leaving office after two exceptional terms as president, the honored guests at the banquet were to be candidates George Bush, with Dan Quayle of Indiana as his running mate, and Democrats Michael Dukakis of Massachusetts and Lloyd Bentsen of Texas.

Bush would be there. But we were told Dukakis would not.

I got ahold of his aide, a Minnesotan named Mike Berman, the son of a fellow in the laundry business whom I'd known in Duluth. How come no Dukakis?

"Well, he's going to be busy that evening. He's Greek, you know, and he's meeting with a Greek organization in Washington that evening."

"Okay, when I get up to welcome everybody I'll have to say that Dukakis won't be here tonight because he's having dinner with some of his non-Italian friends."

"You wouldn't do that, would you Jeno?"

"I will, if I have to. Mike, there's something else going on here, isn't there?"

"Well, if you want the truth, what we're really worried about is that you might treat Mike Dukakis like you did Geraldine Ferraro."

"Mike, let me assure you that is not going to happen."

So Mike Dukakis did show up and as the banquet drew to a close, I asked if we'd treated him right.

"You sure did, Jeno," he said. So that turned out all right.

Dukakis didn't have a prayer in the election. The Reagan era was over, but the start-and-stop-and-start-again Bush dynasty was just beginning.

Chapter 46
George H. W. Bush
1989–1993

*T*he forty-first president of the United States—
Bush 41, as they call him now, father of Bush 43—
was just about the most personable, amiable,
intelligent, honest, and courageous president I've
ever met or read about.

In his earlier years, the media dismissed him as
a "preppy" because of his comfortable upbringing in
Connecticut and his elite education, and because he's
the son of Senator Prescott Bush.

This was the preppy who moved to Texas with his
young wife Barbara, made a fortune in the oil business, and later served two terms as a U.S. Congressman from Texas, although he lost two bids for the
Senate.

This was the preppy who served as delegate to
the United Nations, chairman of the Republican National Committee, head of the U.S. liason office in
Beijing, and director of Central Intelligence.

President George H. W. Bush (Bush 41) is "personable, amiable, intelligent, honest, and courageous."

He made a run for the presidency in 1980, lost the nomination to Reagan, and agreed to run as vice president. When he became president, after two terms as vice president under Reagan, the media couldn't find enough excuses to call him a "wimp."

This is the wimp who joined the Navy right after Pearl Harbor and at age eighteen, became the Navy's youngest commissioned pilot . . . who flew fifty-eight combat missions against the Japanese and had to be fished out of the ocean when his plane was shot down. And who never, ever tried to cash in on his wartime experiences, unlike a recent presidential candidate whose name I won't bother to mention.

This is the wimp who had the guts to marshal international support for Desert Storm, saving Kuwait and probably Saudi Arabia from Iraqi domination. This is the wimp who, at the age of seventy-five decided to relive his youth by parachuting from an airplane . . . did it again at age eighty, and hasn't ruled out another jump at age eighty-five.

I FIRST CAME IN CONTACT with this man in 1988.

With Reagan's second term expiring, Bush called me at my Florida offices to ask if I would support him in his bid for the presidency.

Like a damn fool, I said, "Sure, as long as you have Elizabeth Dole for your vice president."

That was totally presumptuous on my part. But Bush didn't take offense, he merely signed off courteously. He came to the NIAF banquet that year, and again the next year after he'd defeated Dukakis and been elected president.

I hadn't campaigned for him, and for an hour or so the atmosphere at the head table was kind of cool. But little by little we warmed up, the president and Barbara, Lois and me, and from that night we've remained damn good friends to this day.

Lois and I were often invited to White House dinners, as we had been before with some of the other presidents. But with the Bushes, it was more like family. I got to know his sons George W., who was to be elected governor of Texas in 1995, and Jeb Bush, elected governor of Florida in 1998.

During these years of social meetings, I always took the opportunity to press for my agenda.

As a recession seemed to be taking hold, I said, "Mr. President, I think what you ought to do is announce a program to reinforce our rail beds across the country. It will put tens of thousands of people to work." That was the same thing I had been preaching to John Volpe, secretary of transportation in the Nixon years.

"Jeno, we don't want to run trains," Bush said.

"Of course not. You don't want to run trains. What you do is strengthen the rail beds for fast, fast traffic, and then you lease them to operators—Japanese, German, Canadian, or American. They can supply fast rail transportation so we don't have to depend on airlines to get people across the country."

George was interested, but not convinced. Today air transportation gets worse and worse, and nobody does a damn thing about it.

I also pitched an idea I couldn't forget—the National Business Responsibility Council. Maybe it was an obsession. If so, it still is. Companies should dedicate 5 percent of pretax profits, by themselves or collectively with other companies, to meet social and civic needs, without relying on the government. With a tax rate of 40 percent, the cost would be only 3 percent of net earnings, and the results would be enormous for the economy.

I can't fault President Bush for not understanding the numbers, clear as they were. Nobody had since Gerald Ford and Alan Greenspan.

But during his four years in office, Bush 41 was a strong leader of our country and the Free World, and my respect for him grew by the day.

HE DIDN'T GET RE-ELECTED, and that's a damn shame. One reason was the words some way-too-clever speechwriter put into his mouth . . . I guess it was Peggy Noonan . . . "Read my lips, no new taxes." But he had to raise taxes in the face of a recession not of his making, and then Clinton was able to campaign on the slogan: "It's the economy, stupid."

I had a conversation with Barbara Bush, that magnificent lady, in October of 1992. "Jeno, we're going to get beat," she said. "And confidentially, it's because of his staff, his campaign people. They've let him down . . ."

She was so right.

After George Bush was no longer president, I had some further business negotiations with Barbara at their apartment in Houston. I stopped there on my way to Austin, where I was going to present a business program to the Texas governor, their son George W. A word or two about that comes later.

"Barbara," I asked, "have you ever thought about endorsing a product?"

No, she hadn't.

"Well, what if you endorsed these Michelina's frozen entrees of mine? Then I would dedicate a certain amount per case to a program dear to your heart—literacy for children. Everybody wins. Think about it."

To say that Barbara and her husband were astonished would be putting it mildly. But they laughed and both of them were all for it. But some damn legal person working for Barbara said no, and that was the end of that.

We continued to correspond. Not being close to Bush 43, I sent Bush 41 a number of suggestions about his son's campaigns, to be passed along as he chose. Some he agreed with, some he didn't. But he always welcomed my ideas and asked for more.

George H. W. Bush was the seventh and last president I advised on a personal basis. I didn't have much to do with his successor, William Jefferson Clinton. Just couldn't warm up to him.

Our current President, George W. Bush, is a good man. I was a heavy contributor to his campaigns and felt a sense of satisfaction and relief when he was re-elected in 2004. But he has his own way of doing things.

He may not be listening to me, but that doesn't stop me from speaking out . . . as will be seen.

Chapter 47
William J. Clinton
1993–2001

*N*ot much for me to say about our forty-second president. I only met him twice, and that was before he was elected. I respected him, but there was no chemistry between us.

Clinton first solicited my support when he was running for the Democratic nomination in 1992. I was asked by Fritz Mondale and Mario Cuomo to get on the bandwagon. Clinton was a moderate, they said, who wanted to move the Democratic Party to the center. Would I, as a successful entrepreneur, an Independent, and a leader of the Italian-American community, be willing to go out and campaign with Clinton?

Would I at least meet with the candidate? I agreed.

This time I didn't have to go to Georgia, as with Carter. Just to Minneapolis, where the Democrats were staging a pep rally in the street for Bill and Hillary Clinton and their running mates, Al and Tipper Gore. The speeches were rousing and the crowd was enthusiastic.

*President Clinton earned respect, "but there was
no chemistry between us."*

As the handshaking drew to a close, I was asked to get in the bus with the candidates, who were going out to the airport to board the plane for their next stop.

I sat down next to Clinton and Fritz. Pretty soon, Hillary moved in to join the conversation. Clinton started to tell me, in that homey Arkansas accent, that he'd heard a lot of good things about me and he'd be grateful to have me on his side.

I had a few questions.

"What are you going to do about taxes?"

"Oh, we're not going to touch taxes whatsoever," he said. But he sort of looked away. Something told me that I couldn't quite believe what he was saying.

I espoused a couple of ideas about being fair to all segments of our economy and also raising the minimum wage. If you have a federal limit, employers would be damn fools to pay more. But if everybody has to pay a higher minimum, everybody benefits. And who in hell cares if your hamburger costs another nickel or dime. Let's give people a living wage.

Would he take a stand in favor of an increase in the minimum wage?

He talked around it, saying something about the political implications.

I just couldn't warm up to this guy. No chemistry.

When I got off the bus, I started to say "Ciao," but changed it to "Sayonara."

A LITTLE LATER, after he'd been nominated and was running against the incumbent George Bush, Clinton came to our annual NIAF banquet. Sitting next to Barbara Bush (the president was out campaigning), I listened carefully to Clinton's speech. He covered all the bases, but I just didn't think he was a person that I could look in the eye and believe.

Clinton got elected and elected again. As far as I could tell, his domestic and foreign policies were sound enough. I had zero interest in the alleged sexual scandals and all that. And I doubt if anyone else has any interest in them at this point. Whatever happened in that room off the Oval Office is ancient history and boring beyond belief.

But when I first met Bill Clinton at that political rally in Minneapolis, something about him just didn't add up.

And that's my impression of this president who, like all the others, just wanted to be re-elected.

Good luck to him, and sayonara.

Chapter 48

George W. Bush

2001–present

*A*s a resident of Florida, with my executive head-quarters in Sanford, I was proud that my state put George W. Bush over the top in the squeaker election of 2000. And yes, godammit, the votes *were* counted.

I first met the future Bush 43 when he was governor of Texas and his father had just left office as president.

As I've related, I visited with George and Barbara in Houston. They showed me around their new apartment and told me about the new home they were building. It was a nice social visit.

Then it was on to Austin to talk with a fellow in some state corporate development agency about the feasibility of our building a food processing plant for Luigino's in the state.

While we were going over the details, not making much progress, in comes the governor, wearing cowboy boots and walking in that upright, head-up, arms-swinging way he has—sort of a strut.

I'm a strong supporter , but not an advisor, to President George W. Bush.

He shook hands and was very, very friendly.

"I understand you visited with my mom and dad yesterday," he said.

"Yep."

We chatted for a couple of minutes and then he asked, "Well, Jeno, what are your plans for expansion in Texas?"

It was true, I told him, that we were looking for a site to build a plant as an expansion of our present facilities in Duluth and Jackson, Ohio. And Texas was under consideration.

"Wonderful," he said. "We've got great sites." He went on to tell me about them. That took a few minutes, as Texas is a large state.

"Very interesting," I said. "But I've got to tell you something, Governor. I have a policy that we've practiced over the years. I'd like to get your reaction."

I explained that in my opinion, jobs are the most valuable commodity on earth because they bring security to people, help build families, and allow parents to put their children through universities.

"Therefore," I said, "jobs are a commodity that I do not give freely. If I bring in jobs, I don't bring in all the money for plants or equipment. I expect contributions and tax support from the state, as I've had in Ohio. And that's why I'm here . . . to see if Texas is interested in that kind of arrangement."

He made no commitment, said it was nice to see me. We shook hands again and he made a fast exit. That told me that Texas had nowhere near the kind of programs offered by Ohio.

I ran into him again at the Ritz Hotel in Houston, before he announced for the presidency. He invited me upstairs to a party, where he introduced me to some of his friends, and I left early.

The last time I saw him was when he flew into Duluth during his 2000 campaign. I, along with Lois, was one of the so-called VIPs there to greet him. As he got off the plane, he turned to his wife and said, "Laura, these are great friends of Mom and Dad."

It wasn't a put-down, just an indication that he viewed me as an old-time friend of his parents and probably a nice guy, but not someone whose advice he needed. That was okay by me. I was getting tired of politics anyway. But I remained a substantial contributor to the Republican Party, not for any personal political favors, but because I was pressing for a new cause that was much on my mind—elimination of the federal estate tax, or reduction to a maximum of 20 percent.

If that could be done, it would be worth millions to my family, eventually. So why in hell shouldn't I contribute a few hundred thousand a year?

The estate tax was a big issue for me, and still is.

AS GEORGE W'S RE-ELECTION campaign began to develop in 2004, I couldn't resist throwing out some unsolicited advice about debate strategy, attacking John Kerry's record and so on, through the conduit of the candidate's dad. Bush 41 always replied cordially, but told me frankly that it wasn't his role to interfere in his son's decisions.

He was right, of course. So I sat on the sidelines and provided financial support. When I reached my limit for direct donations, I contributed to those 527 organizations, named for their tax ID number, that allow additional legal contributions. I also passed along some donations to the Swift Boat Veterans, whose ads critical of Kerry made an impact in several states.

It was my fondest hope to swing Minnesota into the Republican column. That was going to be a long shot. The state is traditionally liberal and had gone Democratic in every presidential election since the Nixon landslide of 1972.

We did have a Republican senator, Norman Coleman. Our Democratic senator, Mark Dayton, had weakened himself when he got so afraid of terrorist attacks in Washington that he packed up his bags and brought his family and his entire staff back to Minneapolis to sit out the election in a bunker, so to speak. Not exactly the image of a strong leader (he has since announced he won't be running for re-election next time around).

So maybe we had a chance. Our Senator Coleman seemed to be working for the Bush campaign, but not very effectively. I urged him to come up to northeastern Minnesota, the Iron Range, where we had a chance to change the thinking of some of those deep-dyed semi-socialist Democrats, enough to tip the balance.

Even better, if Bush could spend a few minutes on TV with my friend Denny Anderson, whose station covers northeastern Minnesota, northwestern

Wisconsin, and upper Michigan, he'd gain an advantage in all three states.

Apparently these suggestions never got beyond Norm Coleman's staff. I do believe that Coleman could have made a difference if his staff hadn't ignored my telephone calls and faxes. At any rate, the upper Midwest went Democratic again, but the country didn't.

As the election drew near, Bush wasn't looking good in the national polls and I thought it would be an Act of God for him to be re-elected. On election day, exit polls told the Kerry people they had won. Too bad they had to cancel their victory celebration.

This time, the key state was not Florida, but Ohio.

In another squeaker, Bush came out on top thanks in large part to the efforts of my friend, Ohio Republican Senator George Voinovich, whom I'd come to know because of our extensive plant complex in his state. I'd been after him: Don't just be present for functions, but really get out and push for President Bush. In the last few weeks, Senator Voinovich led a determined campaign, and Ohio came out "red"—Republican territory on the televised election map. If Ohio had gone "blue," Bush would have lost the election despite his majority in the popular vote.

After the returns were in, I wrote to Senator Voinovich: "I want to thank you personally, George, on behalf of not only the Paulucci family but the American public. Without your help we would have Kerry for President. No two ways about that. The President should be eternally grateful to you."

I wrote George and Barbara: "Well, a three million plus popular vote plurality, plus four more years. What more could we ask for? I'm glad to have done my part. God bless you."

George wrote back: "Barbara and I were at the White House last night and just returned to Houston. Your nice note was waiting for me when I got to the office. There is no way I can describe to you the joy that we felt when the returns became final. Your message was icing on the cake, and I am grateful for all you did to help get the President re-elected. Warmest regards from this very happy, very proud Dad."

IN MY OPINION, GEORGE W. BUSH is a strong, forceful leader. He's made tough decisions, including the Iraq war. However, a number of urgent issues require his closer attention. I've tried to reach him through some of his staff, without much effect. I certainly tried through his father. But his father absolutely refuses to get involved.

Okay. I'll use another avenue of communication—this book. With respect, Mr. President, for your consideration, here are the Top Ten . . .

SUGGESTIONS FROM THE PEDDLER

I. Increase the minimum wage and index it to the cost of living. We can't expect people to work for $5.15 an hour and survive in today's very expensive society and economy.

II.   Pay for the war. Whether we like it or not, we have a war and we must finish the war. Pass a surtax of 1 or 2 percent or more if need be on all income taxes paid on incomes over $100,000. Those of us in that category can afford it. And that way, this country's deficit won't increase and mortgage the future of our children and our children's children.

III.   Retain your tax cut, but reduce the estate tax and the gift tax to a maximum the same as capital gains, now 15 percent, and let it stay at that, but no more than 20 percent. The "death tax," as it's called, whether estate or gift, is really double taxation and unfair to those who were able through intelligence and hard work to end up with some money. For the government to take 55 percent of it again beginning in 2011 is absolutely a disgrace, if not unconstitutional.

IV.   Review the Business Responsibility Council plan that I've been advocating for many years. I still have my "Blue Book," first presented to Alan Greenspan during the Ford Administration. It's a way for businesses all over the country to get organized and start plowing some of their profits toward growth, prosperity, and the needs of our communities, and not just wait for the government to do it all.

V. Overhaul our infrastructure of rail transportation coast to coast. Lease those railroad beds to fast train operators so that
we do not have to rely on air traffic alone,
which is becoming not only congested
and inconvenient but very dangerous to
the American traveler . . . and the world
traveler, for that matter.

VI. Be sure your policies and appointments
aren't skewed to the overly conservative
side. You're a born-again Christian, and
that's okay in your personal life. But not
in the policies of this country. Be more of
a populist president for *all* the people, not
just the right of center or extreme right.

VII. Stop cutting budget from social and community programs such as the Economic Development Administration with its block grants
and other funds that are needed for cities
and communities throughout the nation.

VIII. Head off the threat of a recession by doing
something about the cost of energy to
the American consumer, the American
worker, and the freight system—which
now hauls most of our goods from coast to
coast. We need ways and means of cutting
the cost of oil and our dependency on it.
Social Security overhaul is tomorrow's crisis. Energy is *today's* crisis and it needs

the all-out attention of your administration and Congress— or else we'll have one hell of a recession.

IX.   You simply have to do something about double-digit unemployment, especially in depressed areas, where the poor are getting poorer and the rich are getting richer. That causes social and political unrest. By passing a surtax to cover the cost of the war, you'll be able to get the support of Congress for billions of dollars in work projects to improve our infrastructure in highways, bridges, railbeds, and so forth—and create *jobs,* the most valuable commodity on earth.

X.   Most important of all, Mr. President, get off the path of isolationism. Take off your cowboy hat, put on the hat of the diplomat, and take leadership of a worldwide coalition to stamp out the global plague of terrorism.

We went into Iraq, right or wrong, and we've been trying to deliver freedom to people who've never known it. They may never be truly unified because of their tribal differences, and the struggle over who gets control of the oil, but ours has been a noble effort.

We've had only one real ally, the British. All we got from the rest of the world was condemnation and insults . . . as our casualties mounted up. Brave soldiers and tons of money going down the rathole, so to speak.

But now, as this is written, the Iraqis do seem to be moving toward a constitutional government. Let's pray it works. Therefore . . .

Isn't it time for an honorable withdrawal of most of our troops, so that we can re-deploy them worldwide to fight terrorism?

Isn't it time to take some of our troops out of NATO—what are we doing in Germany at this point?—and also re-deploy them where they're needed?

Isn't it time to join hands with other countries throughout the world who have been reluctant until now, but with our withdrawal from Iraq might be ready to join a coalition for the common good, to search out the Bin Ladens and destroy them?

Isn't it time to approach the Muslim nations and urge them to act in their own best interests—identify the terrorists, maybe form cells contra to the terrorist cells, and root out these vermin under every rock?

Isn't it time to re-engage the United Nations? Sure they have a bad record—oil for food and all that. But they can help. They're the only international body we have, and we can't allow them to sit on the East River in New York while the world goes to hell.

I offer this advice to you as a friend of your father and mother. I hope we'll still be friends in future, but I've got to speak my piece: There is no strength in isolationism. Get off that road, or your legacy may go down the drain.

Thank you, Mr. President. And thanks to all you readers who might want to make your own voices heard.

AS I SAID AT THE BEGINNING of this section of the book, Presidents Are Just People Who Want to Be Re-Elected. They're human, and they do the best they can with the hand they're dealt.

They're also moving targets. Conditions change. There's no guarantee that the political situation I've just outlined won't be out-of-date by the time this book is published. If so, believe it, I'll have more proposals on the table.

Part Seven

A Few Free Samples

As a lifelong peddler, I'd be remiss if I closed this book without leaving samples. That's one of the things peddlers do.

So here, in the remaining pages, are a few free samples, beginning with some thoughts I've jotted down from time to time about how to run a business and live a life. I call them Jeno's Credos. I don't know how profound they are, but they worked for me.

Put the samples on your shelf . . . use as required.

Chapter 49

Jeno's Credos

According to the dictionary, a credo is "a formula of belief" with religious origins. Mine are a little different— sure as hell not religious, just some thoughts from Jeno the Peddler that have occurred to me over the years as guidelines for myself and those who work with me.

Once in a while, I'd post one of them on the bulletin board at the office as a sort of philosophical pep talk. And once in a while somebody would say, "Jeno, that makes sense."

Maybe for you as well.

Jeno's Credos . . . About the Workplace

- It pays to be ignorant . . . for when you're smart, you already know it can't be done without even trying.

- The moron's code: Keep it simple. If I can understand it, you can too.

- He who gets the credit for right also gets the hell for wrong.

- To hell with committee meetings. Think, act, expedite, and push it through yourself.

- The meek have to inherit the world. They sure as hell don't know how to market it.

- Exercise your authority . . . and you fulfill your responsibility.

- Act! And you won't have to react.

- You're busy. So am I. Let's make it short.

- Only those who believe can win.

- Communication and control: key words of good management.

- Always look for what's wrong, not what's right.

- Don't abdicate your brain to a computer.

- Pick your own red flag. Please don't wait for me to wave it.

- Do what you think best, not what you think I'll think.

- The Value Credo: Each product has its own value concept. Violate it and you fail.

- Make time your ally, not your enemy.

- Try to do today what you should do tomorrow.

- Sweat is no substitute for brains.

- Be sure your aim is right, or you may piss in your own boot.

- Never underestimate your opponent.

- Quality first, cost second.

- Don't forget to ask for the order.

- Today, unfortunately, the shortest distance between two points . . . is money.

- Being an entrepreneur is not just a question of long hours and hard work. It's guts. You have to go at it with sheer determination. Otherwise, the pitfalls will put you off. That's why big companies have to go out and acquire smaller ones. There is a quality in starting a business that only an entrepreneur can provide.

- There are enough problems being honest . . . without the added danger of being crooked.

- I'm not suited to be involved in big companies . . . even when I own 'em.

- I cannot give you the formula for success. But I can give you the formula for failure . . . Try to please everybody.

- Question my tactics, yes. But never my ethics.

- What problems I don't have, I make . . . that's business.

- Don't be an expert too soon.

- When in doubt, don't. When doubt is gone, do!

- Lest you forget . . . We're here for only one reason, and that is to make money. But let's have fun doing it!

Jeno's Credos . . . About Society

- Industry must work . . . constantly, tirelessly, stubbornly . . . to make its area a better place to live and earn a living. Making a profit is not its only responsibility.

- What we need is strong leadership . . . not weak-kneed politicians always worried about re-election.

- The antithesis of welfare: Give a man work for his hands . . . and he will supply his own needs.

- Bicentennial progress? Today politicians have become a true pain in America's ass.

- Who in hell cares if I make enemies, as long as I continue to serve the common cause.

- The hands that help are greater by far than lips that just pray.

- Man benefits in many ways by his actions . . . not only for profit, but for good.

- Man cannot live by pizza alone. He's got to do some good too.

- It isn't easy to change a sick society. You meet selfishness and stupidity and hypocrisy. You feel frustration and disgust, and you want to say the hell with it. But if we speak out, if we become involved, believe me . . . we will find no greater joy or satisfaction than knowing that we are working to make a contribution to our fellow man.

Jeno's Credos . . . About Life

- If you want to be a successful entrepreneur, marry a mate who's going to let you do your own thing.

- Be wary of your enemies . . . and your backside with your friends.

- The evil done by some is never undone by good deeds later.

- The stupidity of brilliant people never ceases to amaze me.

- Timing is everything . . . and not just related to sex.

- A crooked brook follows the path of least resistance. Some people are like that.

- There's a little ego in every man. But the more the ego, the smaller the man.

- No one learns by talking . . . only by listening.

- If you have to raise your voice to make a point, you may not have a point.

- Every tub should stand on its own bottom.

- Blood is thicker than water . . . but money is thicker yet.

- Love your family . . . but keep them the hell out of the business.

- Female Formula for Success: The female of the species is not only more deadly . . . she is more determined.

- Look beyond the horizon. Today's is already old. The only new is tomorrow's.

- I never did learn to walk slow . . . thank God!

- Remember, young one, whatever route you're on . . . I've already traveled it.

- Unfortunately, in this world there are more horse's asses than horses.

- I'm so tense that when I relax, it makes me nervous.

- "Time will rust the sharpest sword"—Sir Walter Scott. "So will alcohol"—Jeno.

- What do you mean, the common man? Is there an uncommon man? I've yet to see a man born with a crest on his chest.

- There is nothing wrong with our young people . . . it's us.

- Absence makes the heart grow fonder . . . of somebody else.

- Yes, I took time once to smell the flowers, but they turned out to be plastic. It's a sign of our times.

- Memories of the past are more precious than hopes of the future.

- Enjoy life for what it is, knowing there is more unhappiness to life than happiness.

- Great Spirit: Help me never to judge another . . . until I have walked in his moccasins for two weeks.

- I speak for no one else. And no one else speaks for me. When I speak for myself, I am Jeno F. Paulucci, and I say what I damn please.

Chapter 50
In Search Of An Epilogue

*A*s promised at the outset, this book is not a true autobiography. It's more of a collection of stories—you might call them adventures in life—that I hope will prove entertaining and thought-provoking to those who read them.

Now, I suppose it's time for an epilogue.

THROUGHOUT THIS BOOK, I've passed along some suggestions that I called Pointers from the Peddler. I'd never presume to tell you how to live your life, just wanted to share a few ideas that helped me live mine. Here are a couple more for your consideration.

First, don't be afraid to ask the good Lord for help.

I'm not what you'd call a practicing Catholic. Early in life, I went to Hibbing Catholic Church and listened to Monsignor Limmer preach that all non-Catholics were going to hell. I stopped going but continued to believe in the Golden Rule: Do unto others as you would have them do unto you.

I believe in God, and I believe in the power of prayer.

Some twenty years ago, my wife Lois was stricken with cancer. She had surgery, but the specialists at Mayo Clinic said she had only a couple of years to live.

I prayed. In fact, I made a deal with God. "If Lois is cured," I told Him, "I pledge at least thirty Our Father and thirty Hail Mary prayers every day." The marvelous doctors at Sloan Kettering Cancer Center in New York and above all, Dr. Taylor Wharton, the world famous gynecologist at M. D. Anderson Cancer Center in Houston, pulled her through. With the help of God.

Prayer works.

Second, never forget that your family is all that matters.

In my early years, I wanted my father to have a better life than the iron mines. But his health was ruined and he died at sixty-one from a heart attack. How I wish to God I could have helped him.

I wanted my mother not to take in boarders or do laundry or cook and cater food. I'm so thankful she lived long enough to enjoy the comforts her rambunctious son was able to provide. She lived a serene life in Bal Harbour, Florida, up to the day she passed away at age eighty-nine.

I wanted my sister Elizabeth to get a good education at the University of Minnesota and become a teacher as well as a fine violinist. Which she did. Liz now lives in Sanford with her husband, Dr. Norman Helfrich.

From my earliest days, I was blessed with a wonderful family, impoverished as we were. Then, when it came time to start my own family, I was even more blessed.

As I've said several times, and will never stop saying, my wife Lois was my salvation.

When we were first married, I brought Lois home to a four-room apartment on Fifth Street in Duluth. I went to bed at eight o'clock and got up at four A.M. to get to my plant in Grand Rapids, eighty miles away. I'd come home at seven or eight, dead tired, and go right to bed.

What a wonderful life for a new bride.

When I would get depressed and say maybe I ought to give up the damn Chun King business and get a regular job, she'd say, "Jeno, stick it out. Don't give up. We'll sacrifice together, and if in the end you don't make it, we'll open a hamburger stand together."

When she first learned she was pregnant in 1948, she was so thrilled that she walked the mile or so from Dr. Henry Fisketti's office in the Medical Arts Building in Duluth to my little clapboard office on Lake Avenue to give me the great news.

She was just beaming all over, and I was overjoyed.

"Shouldn't we have something to eat to celebrate?" she asked.

"Absolutely," I said. "I'll have it sent over. What would you like, ham on rye or bacon lettuce and tomato?"

She laughed and chose the BLT.

ALL THESE YEARS LATER . . .

. . . we're blessed with success we never dreamed of and more important, a wonderful family—our son, our two daughters, our four grandchildren, and our three great-grandchildren.

Our health is pretty good, considering. Lois seems to get younger every day.

The last time I went in for a checkup, the doctor said I had hypertension. Was I under stress, he asked.

"Shit, I've been under stress for eighty-seven years."

He looked at his records and said, "But you're only eighty-six."

"Yeah, but I started early, before my mother let me out."

We rely so much on the family we raised.

On Mick, who stepped out from the lengthening shadow of his dad, founded his own chain of successful restaurants, and became a highly successful investor, in between travels all over the world.

On our daughter, Gina, who lives in the rolling hills of Wayzata, Minnesota, with deer and wild turkey all around.

And on our daughter Cindy, whom I used to call "Biondina," Italian for "Blondie." She's not only beautiful, but possibly the smartest blonde who ever lived.

Cindy and her husband Bob Selton sent me this letter on a recent Father's Day:

> *Dear Dad,*
> *You know that I love you and think you're a wonderful father. You have always put your family first and done whatever you could to give us comfort and security. But maybe you don't know how I see you as a person.*

I see you as a man of principle who stands up for whatever he believes in. I see you as someone who is liked and respected by many people, not only because you are fun to be with but because you go out of your way to do things for others. I see you as a man I admire more than words can say. If you weren't my father, I'd wish you were.
        With lots of love,
        Cindy and Bob

WORDS LIKE THAT FROM MY FAMILY are all the honors I'll ever need. However, it's true that over the years I've been singled out for recognition by my peers, by industry groups, governments, and others, some thirty-five or forty times. I've lost count. There is a list of them in the appendix of this book if you are interested.

At the end of the list are the awards presented for entrepreneurship by Ernst & Young, because an entrepreneur—or peddler—is what I am.

For twenty years now, Ernst & Young, the highly prestigious accounting and consulting firm, has been searching around its global operations for entrepreneurs that they think deserve recognition.

When I was nominated for the Ernst & Young Entrepreneur of the Year for Florida award in 2002, I reluctantly attended the meeting, and was surprised as hell to get the award. I was then told that there was going to be a November gathering of entrepreneurs from the various states and master entrepreneurs. I paid no attention.

On a Friday night, I got a call from an Ernst & Young representative saying, "Jeno, where are you?"

"Where the hell do you think I am? You just called me at my home in Sanford."

"Yes, but you should be out here in Palm Springs."

"What for? I don't play golf."

He was kind of hesitant, but said, "Well, it's going to be kind of embarrassing for us if you don't come out."

"Why?"

"I shouldn't tell you this, but you have been named Entrepreneur of the Year for the United States of America."

"Great," I said. "Mail me the award."

"We can't do that," he said. "We need you here. We'll even charter an aircraft to pick you up."

"No need. I'll use my own jet."

So I did go out there on Saturday morning and received the award on Saturday night, with extreme gratitude.

The following year, 2003, I was told I might be up for an award again, this time number one entrepreneur of the whole world. The ceremonies were going to be in Monte Carlo. Again, I didn't take it too seriously. But I decided to attend. Lois and I had been looking for an excuse to visit Italy anyway, and Monte Carlo was just down the French coast from there. So Lois and I, my granddaughter Tiffany, and my nephew Kelly Cardiff flew over.

The ceremonies and the galas were entertaining and a lot of fun. The award went to an entrepreneur from India. Fine and dandy. I thought he deserved it.

So we packed up the next morning and went to Rome for a few days before returning to Sanford.

I thought that was the end of it. But lo and behold, I was called a year later and told to be in Palm Springs in November because I was going to be the inaugural winner of Ernst & Young's International Lifetime Achievement Award for Activism, Entrepreneurship and Leadership, as well as the World's Number One Overall Entrepreneur for the past twenty years.

WHEN I FIRST STARTED WORKING at a grocery store at ten years of age, I never thought or dreamed of getting any distinction like this.

About 2,500 people were sitting at tables in a grand ballroom. On the walls were pictures of entrepreneurs who'd won previous awards on all levels over the past twenty years—dozens of them. The program began with some audience warm up remarks by Jay Leno. Then he turned it over to the Ernst & Young executives who would open the envelopes and ask the winners to come onstage.

My award was first on the program.

I waited backstage while John Ferraro, the Ernst & Young vice chairman, made his flattering introduction and showed a video of my products, scenes in my plants of the packaging line and me testing products, and a glimpse of the golden-age Stan Freberg commercials.

When I was shown on the screen sitting in my office in shirtsleeves and vest and saying, "As long as I believe in something that's done for the general good . . . okay . . . I'm gonna do it," I knew about what I would say in my acceptance.

The audience got a special treat. Because of this vision impairment that I developed over the past few years, it was arranged for me to be escorted to the podium by my beautiful granddaughters Brittany and Tiffany.

I began by thanking John Ferraro and Ernst & Young for bringing to the forefront the very important role we entrepreneurs have as activists and leaders in our communities, our states, and our nation.

"I accept this recognition also," I said, "in the name of a lady over there at Table 37 . . . my wife Lois Mae Trepanier Paulucci. She's not only been my supporter and fellow activist, she also helped me raise a wonderful family. She always cuts me down to size when I have those delusions of grandeur. And she still trims my hair about every two or three weeks in order to keep it the right size."

The camera then focused (I have a tape of the proceedings) on Table 37, and there was Lois laughing and looking like springtime. That was the highlight of the ceremony as far as I'm concerned.

Then I went on to say as follows (I'm going to quote myself here because this is the message I've tried to convey to my fellow entrepreneurs in this book):

"I want to take this opportunity to congratulate each and every one of you entrepreneurs for your individual success. And each of you deserves an award because if you weren't such a success in your own profession throughout the United States and other parts of the world, you wouldn't be here tonight.

"And my advance congratulations to those who will receive those very prestigious awards this evening.

"Now, I'd like to leave you with a message, and that is, we as entrepreneurs face today one of the greatest challenges there is. We have the privilege and gift of creating the most valuable commodity on earth, and that is jobs. Jobs. Because when a person has a job, he or she has self-security, esteem, self-respect, and they don't have to mix their prayers with ammunition because they don't have a job.

"And I say to all of us as entrepreneurs, we have been gifted by the Good Lord . . . excuse me [I had to grab a handerchief and wipe my eyes] . . . in being able to employ people that help us in our success, and with that comes power . . . and with that comes leadership ability within our community, our state, and our nation.

"And if ever there was a time in this world that leadership was needed from the 10,000 entrepreneurs that Ernst & Young has recognized, and the millions of others . . . that time is now.

"We must become the public's advocate. We must take on projects that others wouldn't take on. We must speak up, no matter what your partisan politics are, for the good of the people so we can maintain our way of life . . . so that we can have peace and prosperity throughout this world in our troubled times today.

"And that's where all of you come in, and others around the world. Through my years as an activist, as well as making a few bucks, raising a family with my wife of going on fifty-eight years, I can tell you that there is no greater satisfaction in life than knowing when it's all through you have done your work as an entrepreneur, that you have done something for the betterment of mankind.

"I beseech you to do the same thing, and I know you will. Thank you and God bless you."

Then I was escorted off the stage by my daughter Gina and my grandson Jeno Michael. We got an ovation I'll never forget.

Back home, I received congratulatory messages from all over. All very kind, and much appreciated. One I especially cherish came from George H. W. Bush, who wrote: "Well done; well deserved." Then he penciled in: "Jeno: You da man!"

For one brief moment, I thought, after something like this, isn't it time to finally relax, get out of the public spotlight, sell off some businesses, and just see about doing some fishing?

No, it isn't.

It's true that I was declared "legally blind" in May of 2004 due to a condition called ischemic optic neuropathy. Not completely blind. I guess that's the legal term for not letting me drive except maybe if I was drunk (but I don't drink anymore). I can't read the fine print, but I do get around quite well.

I'm still deeply involved, every day, in business, civic projects, politics . . . you name it. Keeping on top of it all is no problem, thanks to dictation machines and the great support of my assistants who read my correspondence to me with understanding and insight that help me make swift decisions.

Thanks, ladies. Hell, I should have thought of this years ago.

Thinking it over, I've come to realize that this book really doesn't have an end.

Sorry, no epilogue.

And so goodbye . . . for now.

Chapter 51

Shame on America

As this book was all but ready to go to press, something happened that jolted my thinking back to a certain deep flaw in our society. I've touched on this issue several times, but I can't finish the book without a brief final chapter—an open letter to the citizens of America.

In the early morning of August 29, 2005, Hurricane Katrina made landfall just east of New Orleans and roared inland, devastating and flooding that city and nearby Gulf states. In many ways, the aftermath of this disaster brought shame on our country. But it was a broader and deeper shame than the politicians and pundits understood.

Unfortunately, but not unexpectedly, the experts on all sides kept telling us, over and over, that Katrina was a racial matter. Almost all the refugees in the Superdome cesspool, as we could see on television, were black. Throughout the Gulf states, the majority of victims were black—67 percent black and 33 percent white, by one estimate. But that missed the point.

The shameful statistic is that the victims were *almost 100 percent poor.*

Never mind how poor the preparation, how late the relief arrived, or who was to blame. Katrina was a disaster sent by God that was a symptom of a disaster made by man—the malaise of poverty in our country.

I call poverty a malaise because it's just something we take for granted. We ignore it, like so many other diseases. People get AIDS? Well, maybe somebody will find a cure before they die. People are living in their attics as the waters rise because they don't have a car and can't get to a bus? Well, we probably should do something about that when we find time.

What we need to do—starting yesterday—is take specific measures to attack the malaise of poverty.

First, the federal government should kick out the lobbyists and raise the minimum wage. What single mother wants to make $5.15 an hour or about $10,300 a year, while paying for fuel, household expenses, and day care? Better to stay home and take welfare. The minimum wage should be raised at least 50 percent and then pegged to the cost of living.

But most important, we must create jobs . . . jobs of any and all kinds. *Jobs are the cure for poverty.*

We can begin by rebuilding our infrastructure. For instance, we need to lay out new railroad beds and bring in entrepreneurs to manage our rail system; massive programs like those of the Works Project Administration of the 1930s—the WPA—that put thousands to work for decent wages.

Those are just a couple of things the government can do. Now we come to the responsibility of the business community. As I've said in previous chapters, businesses large and small should dedicate up to 5 percent of pretax profits for projects that would benefit the general public. Among other things, bulldoze abandoned buildings in the inner cities and replace them with low-cost housing and day care centers—without waiting for the government to do it, at higher cost. We have a program like that in Minnesota, and it could serve as a model for the entire country.

In doing so, we would not only improve our communities, but even more important, *provide jobs*, which are the most valuable commodity on earth.

Beyond that, businessmen need to reach out to the disadvantaged—the so-called unemployables. Hire them and train them, turn them into loyal workers and contributors to the economy.

I've been doing that for more than 40 years and believe me, it works.

Katrina was a wake-up call. It exposed not only the toxicity of the floodwaters, but the unseen and odorless toxicity of our refusal to recognize and do something about the deep problem of poverty in the United States. Let's not let the downtrodden drown in their own water. Let's not let the malaise of poverty infect the lymph nodes of our country.

As the storm recedes into the past and the re-building continues over a period of years, let's not forget the lesson it taught us. Let's turn this Shame on America into a Claim on America—a sacred obligation to build a better life for all our citizens.

Thank you.

A Representative List of Honors and Recognition Accorded to Jeno Paulucci

Elected to Duluth Hall of Fame   1962

National Horatio Alger Award   1965
American Schools and Colleges Association

Gold Medal, Outstanding Italian
    American of the Year   1965
Italian American Society

Duluth Arena-Auditorium Exhibition Hall
    named "Paulucci Hall"   1967

Rizzuto Gold Medal for Most Outstanding
    Italian American in the United States   1968
UNICO National Italian American Society

Elected to Florida Council of 100   1968
a group formed by the governor to promote
    economic development

Outstanding Minnesota Citizen of the Year   1969
Minnesota Department Veterans of Foreign Wars

Doctor of Humanities Honorary Degree   1970
Franklin Pierce College, New Hampshire

Doctor of Business Administration
        Honorary Degree   1970
Missouri Valley College, Marshall, Missouri

Histradut Testimonial Award   1970
Minnesota Trade Union Council

Minnesota Governor's Proclamation:
        Jeno F. Paulucci Day   1971

Employer of the Year   1971
*City of Duluth and Minnesota Governor's Commission on
        Employment of the Handicapped*

United States Employer of the Year   1972
*President's Committee on Employment of the Handicapped
        and the National Association of Manufacturers*

Honorary Swede of the Year   1973
Svenkarnas Dag, Inc. (Swedish American Society)

Doctor of Laws Honorary Degree   1974
College of St. Scholastica, Minnesota

Named Among 10 Best United States
        Corporate Executives   1975
Gallagher President's Report

Minnesota Business Hall of Fame   1976
Charter Member

Chairman, Presidential Mission to Italy   1976
*Appointed by President Gerald Ford to evaluate
    disaster relief needs*

Executive of the Year   1977
Corporate Report magazine

"I Numeri Uno"   1978
*Premio Nazionale, Florence, Italy—Recognizing foremost
    achievement reflecting upon Italian heritage*

"Cavalieri del Umanita"   1979
International Register of Chivalry, Rome

National Italian American of the Year   1979
Italian Cultural Society, New Orleans

Doctor of Laws Honorary Degree   1979
—Potomac School of Law, Washington, D.C.

Wisconsin Employer of the Year   1979
—Wisconsin Rehabilitation Association

Honorary DeMolay Legion of Honor Degree   1979
—International Supreme Council, Order of DeMolay

Order of Merit, Republic of Italy   1980
—Highest civilian award conferred by the Republic of Italy

National Citation for Exemplary
Employment Practices   1980
—*National Rehabilitation Association, Louisville, Kentucky*

Chairman, Presidential Mission to Italy   1980
—*Appointed by President Jimmy Carter to evaluate
    disaster relief needs*

Advisory Board   1981
*International Language Institute—Pine Manor
    College, Boston*

Governor of Ohio for the Day   1982
—*September 24, proclaimed by Governor James A. Rhodes*

Ellis Island Congressional Medal of Honor   1990

America's Free Enterprise Legend   1992
—*Students in Free Enterprise*

Outstanding Marketing Executive   1993
—*Minnesota Association Distributive Education
    Clubs of America*

Guglielmo Marconi Award   1995
—*National Order Sons of Italy in America*

Frozen Food Hall of Fame   1997
—*National Frozen Food Association*

First "Leadership Legend" Award   2000
—*Leadership Seminole program, Florida*

Entrepreneur of the Year for the United States   2002
—Ernst & Young global business consultants

Inducted into World Entrepreneur Of
   the Year Academy   2003
Monte Carlo, Monaco—Ernst & Young

Number One Overall Entrepreneur in
   the World, and first recipient of the
   International Lifetime Achievement
   Award for Activism, Entrepreneurship
   and Leadership   2004
Ernst & Young